INVASION,
1940

INVASION,
1940

THE TRUTH ABOUT THE BATTLE OF BRITAIN AND WHAT STOPPED HITLER

DEREK ROBINSON

CARROLL & GRAF PUBLISHERS
New York

Carroll & Graf Publishers
An imprint of Avalon Publishing Group, Inc.
245 W. 17th Street
New York
NY 10011-5300
www.carrollandgraf.com

AVALON
publishing group incorporated

First published in the UK by Constable,
an imprint of Constable & Robinson Ltd, 2005

First Carroll & Graf edition, 2005

ISBN-13: 978-0-78671-618-0
ISBN-10: 0-7867-1618-5

Printed and bound in the EU

For Blue and Jane

Contents

THINGS THAT GO BUMP IN THE NIGHT

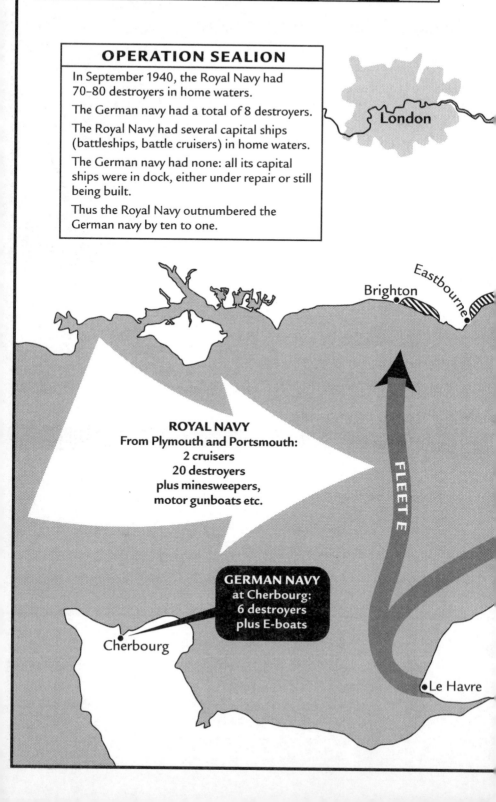

0   50   100 miles

OPERATION SEALION

In September 1940, the Royal Navy had 70–80 destroyers in home waters.

The German navy had a total of 8 destroyers.

The Royal Navy had several capital ships (battleships, battle cruisers) in home waters.

The German navy had none: all its capital ships were in dock, either under repair or still being built.

Thus the Royal Navy outnumbered the German navy by ten to one.

London

Eastbourne

Brighton

ROYAL NAVY
From Plymouth and Portsmouth:
2 cruisers
20 destroyers
plus minesweepers,
motor gunboats etc.

FLEET E

GERMAN NAVY
at Cherbourg:
6 destroyers
plus E-boats

Cherbourg

Le Havre

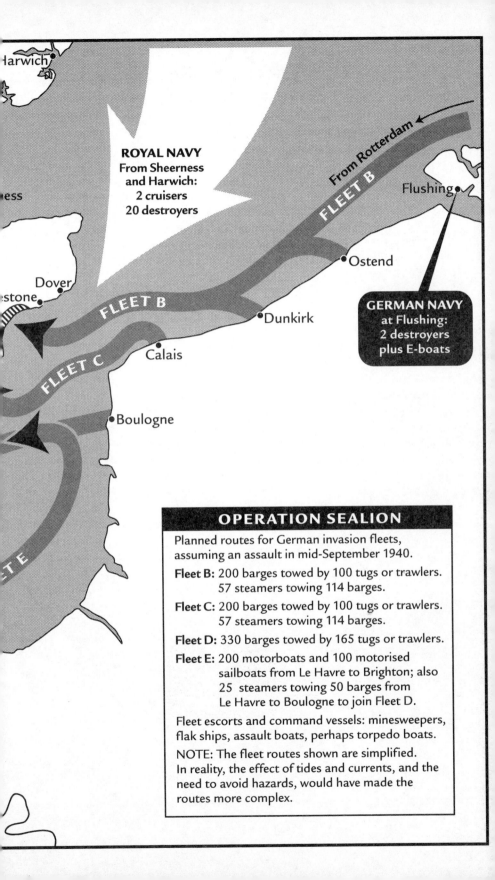

Harwich

ROYAL NAVY
From Sheerness
and Harwich:
2 cruisers
20 destroyers

From Rotterdam

FLEET B

Flushing

ess

Ostend

Dover

FLEET B

stone

Dunkirk

GERMAN NAVY
at Flushing:
2 destroyers
plus E-boats

FLEET C

Calais

Boulogne

FLEET E

OPERATION SEALION

Planned routes for German invasion fleets,
assuming an assault in mid-September 1940.

Fleet B: 200 barges towed by 100 tugs or trawlers.
57 steamers towing 114 barges.

Fleet C: 200 barges towed by 100 tugs or trawlers.
57 steamers towing 114 barges.

Fleet D: 330 barges towed by 165 tugs or trawlers.

Fleet E: 200 motorboats and 100 motorised
sailboats from Le Havre to Brighton; also
25 steamers towing 50 barges from
Le Havre to Boulogne to join Fleet D.

Fleet escorts and command vessels: minesweepers,
flak ships, assault boats, perhaps torpedo boats.

NOTE: The fleet routes shown are simplified.
In reality, the effect of tides and currents, and the
need to avoid hazards, would have made the
routes more complex.

Illustrations

German destroyers sunk in Narvik harbour.
© Cody Images

Royal Navy J Class destroyers at speed.
© Cody Images

Adolf Hitler and Admiral Raeder afloat.
Photo: akg-images, London

Fuhrer Conference at map table: Raeder and Hitler review the war.
© Imperial War Museum

German paratrooper braced for jump.
© Robert Hunt Library

Radar towers at Dover being shelled from France, as photographed by a long-range camera.
© Imperial War Museum

View, probably from a crane, of invasion barges four-deep tied up at quayside.
© Robert Hunt Library

Operation Sealion – building a ramp inside an invasion barge.
© Robert Hunt Library

Two airmen on wing of RAF fighter, reloading the machine guns.
© Imperial War Museum

Tank suspended above sea during submersible tests.
© Imperial War Museum

German troops unloading horses down a ramp from an invasion barge.
© Robert Hunt Library

Operation Sealion – extracting an anti-tank gun from inflatable boat.
© Robert Hunt Library

German tank being loaded onto steamer in French port.
© Imperial War Museum

Rare photograph of an invasion fleet taking part in an exercise for Operation Sealion shows tugs towing two barges in tandem.
© Cody Images

QUESTIONS

CHAPTER ONE

Two Powerful Myths

So many historians. So distinguished, so unanimous. And yet when it comes to the Battle of Britain, and Hitler's failure to invade Britain in 1940, is it possible they are all looking the wrong way?

Here is Sir John Keegan:

'. . . some 2,500 young pilots had alone been responsible for preserving Britain from invasion . . .'

(*The Second World War*)

Here is A.J.P. Taylor:

'. . . 15 September [1940] was the day of decision. Great Britain was safe from invasion . . .'

(*The Second World War*)

Here is Winston Churchill in *Their Finest Hour*:

'At the summit the stamina and valour of our fighter pilots remained unconquerable and supreme. Thus Britain was saved.'

That theme has continued for sixty years. Sir Roy Strong, in *The Story of Britain*, says the invasion barges 'could only sail if the victory of the skies was won'. J.M. Roberts, in *The Penguin History of the Twentieth Century*, puts it more bluntly: 'Victory in the Battle of Britain made a German seaborne invasion impossible . . .' Denis Richards, in the *Official History of the RAF 1939–45*, writes that 'in the summer of 1940 civilization was saved by a thousand British boys'.

These confident and unambiguous statements, taken from accounts of the 1940 invasion threat, are written as if the Channel and the Royal Navy did not exist.

John Terraine is an exception. His *The Right of the Line* – probably the best history of the RAF in the war of 1939–45 – does not claim that Fighter Command prevented Operation Sealion (codename for the planned German invasion). Instead he quotes the view of a German, Herr von Plehwe. In 1940, Plehwe was Assistant to the Head of the German army's liaison staff at Naval Headquarters, and therefore well placed to see the broader picture. After the war he wrote:

> 'I would like to lay great emphasis on the fact that the decisive deterrent to the operation was the expected large-scale intervention by the British fleet.'

To which Terraine adds: 'The achievement of Fighter Command was in keeping alive the possibility of that intervention.'

Which is a strange thing to say. It suggests that the ability of the Royal Navy to intervene depended on the success of Fighter Command. Nobody doubts that the Navy would have benefited from RAF protection, but it is beyond belief that, if invasion came, the Navy would stay in port because it had no fighter cover. Naval action was a stone-cold certainty, no matter what happened in the air.

Perhaps an explanation for Terraine's words lies in the persistent power of the legend of the Battle of Britain. He cannot deny the Navy's presence, yet he gives it second place to Fighter Command – despite the fact that, by the very nature of Sealion, the RAF could not have stopped the invasion fleet, and the Luftwaffe could not have guaranteed its safety.

This is not a conventional history. I am not a conventional historian.

This book is about both the myths and the facts of 1940: that is, about what people believe happened then in Britain and Germany, compared with what actually happened. Because Churchill and Hitler spoke for their countries, this book is also about the parts they played in creating those myths. And, because many historians have repeated the leaders' claims uncritically, it is also about historians' contribution to myth-making.

By definition, myths are not to be found in the archives, no matter how intense the search. The myths of 1940 exist in the national consciousness, which is a massive resource that can never be catalogued. It is clear to me that what a people *believes* has happened is just as worth studying as what *did* happen.

Historians themselves have perpetuated one mistaken belief about what happened in 1940: the myth that 'The Few' alone saved Britain from invasion. A parallel myth is that, if Sealion had been launched, the German army would have steamrollered the British defence, just as its Blitzkrieg had knocked over Poland, Norway, Holland, Belgium and France.

The fact that these claims have been so widely accepted, and for so long, is itself evidence of the durability of myths. The contrast with reality is worth examining. Fortunately, much good work has been done in the archives. We know a lot about Operation Sealion, how it was assembled, when and where it was meant to sail, and which areas it was meant to invade. The German archives are thick with this information.

Exactly how Sealion's invasion fleets were to fight their way across the Channel is less thoroughly explained. There is evidence in Fuhrer Conferences of Grand Admiral Raeder's doubts, but he spoke mainly in terms of the weather, the readiness of barges, the extent of the landing areas, and always of the necessity for the Luftwaffe to achieve air command. There is no record of Hitler and Raeder ever taking a long, hard look at the German and the British navies, comparing the numbers, contrasting the strengths, and asking each other: How do we defend our invasion fleets?

It was a question the other services largely ignored. The records show that the German army assumed that the crossing was a purely naval matter, while the Luftwaffe paid Sealion no attention at all. As early as 9 July 1940, the German naval war operations diary had this revealing definition of the invasion: 'Undertaking essentially to be regarded as a transport problem' – in other words, the crossing was expected to be unopposed. Three days later, General Jodl, in a Wehrmacht High Command planning paper, wrote of a landing in the form of 'a mighty river-crossing' in which 'bridge building will be replaced by the creation of a sea transport road, completely secure against attack from sea, in the Dover Narrows'.

That sort of language soon vanished. But on 30 August 1940, when the German Army produced its *Instructions for Preparation of Operation Sealion*, a Channel crossing still sounded remarkably straightforward:

> Luftwaffe knocks out the English Air Force . . . Navy clears minefree routes and Army gains local bridgeheads . . . These are expanded to form a connected landing zone . . .

And so on, to London and beyond.

Senior German naval officers were not fooled. One of the more candid and perceptive was Admiral Ruge. He had watched Sealion grow, and he knew its potential for huge confusion; he suggested that the word of command be: 'Formation Pigpile! Go to England.' Ruge was no defeatist; he believed a German mine barrier could have been laid. 'We could have done it,' he said, 'but it could not have stopped all British ships . . .'

And mine barriers alone would never save Sealion. The naval war operations diary for 10 September says this:

> Preparation for *Sealion* requires at this point that Luftwaffe concentrate on Portsmouth and Dover and the British fleet forces rather than on London. However, it is deemed improper to press such demands . . .

That word 'improper' tells all. The Fuhrer knew best. Goering was convinced of it, and at a Luftwaffe conference on 16 September 1940 he ordered: 'Sealion must not disturb nor burden the Luftwaffe operations.'

In Hitler's words (not when Raeder was present) the German navy was a 'poor little shallop' – a shallop was a light rowing boat used in shallow water. It was weak because Hitler had waited until January 1939 before he approved a plan to create a battle fleet big enough to challenge the Royal Navy. He assured his admirals that there would be no war with Britain before 1944 at the earliest. Eight months later, Britain and Germany were at war, and Raeder saw that 'all the grandiose plans were dissolving about him'. Then the Norwegian campaign of spring 1940 cost him half his destroyer fleet and put his big ships in dock for repair. Neither Raeder nor Hitler could do anything to make the Royal Navy smaller or the German navy bigger in the time available; and for Sealion's survival, that was crucial. The best answer to the British Navy was simply to put it out of your mind. German naval records are of little help to any researcher seeking to discover how the service hoped to protect Sealion. With few weapons, there was little hope.

The reverse face of the myth has Fighter Command as Britain's last defence against Sealion. Its C-in-C, Air Chief Marshal Dowding, rarely commented on the threat of invasion by sea. During the Battle of Britain, American journalists questioned RAF claims of the totals of enemy aircraft shot down. Dowding retorted, 'If the German figures [of aircraft destroyed] were correct, they would be in London in a week.' Yet in June 1940 he had stressed his desire to assist and protect the Navy 'because I realize that, invasion or no invasion, we lose the war if we lose command of the sea'. Both statements cannot be true. If Britain had command of the sea, the German army could not march into London.

Archives can tell only so much. When they fail, there is another resource for the historian to use. It is common sense. This book applies common sense to known facts. The first casualty of common sense is the myth.

Britain's vulnerability in the summer of 1940 is a familiar story: the troops – still stunned by evacuation from Dunkirk – drilling without rifles; Home Guards armed with pikes; while twenty-odd miles away were battle-hardened Panzers, deadly Stukas, regiments of paratroops ready to drop on England, at any time.

Books have been written to demonstrate how Germany could have successfully invaded Britain in 1940 – provided the invasion happened in July, a month or six weeks after Dunkirk. Britain was weak; nobody disputes that. But to say that Britain could not repel an invasion in July 1940 does not prove that Germany could mount one.

Two powerful myths. The first is that RAF Fighter Command alone prevented an invasion. The second is that an invasion force would inevitably have conquered Britain. Both untrue.

THE WAY WE WERE

CHAPTER TWO

Sugar Umbrellas

W̱AR, and the origin of war, generates myths, because it is
usually a lengthy business and always complicated, and most
people prefer simplicities.

Take Munich. The name has become the label of appeasement
that greased the slide into the Second World War. It has come to
symbolize failure and almost criminal stupidity. Yet that is not how
it was seen at the time; far from it.

Munich has become shorthand for the black days of 1937 and
especially 1938 when appeasement meant being considerate to
Hitler in order to satisfy his demands. Its aim was to pacify the
man: pacify in its literal sense: make peaceful. This was what the
vast majority of people in Britain and western Europe (and many
in Germany) fervently desired. For anyone who was not alive and
anxious in 1938, it must be almost impossible to comprehend the
intensity of the fear of *another* world war. More than fear: revul-
sion. Another world war would make nonsense of what everyone
knew, that the first had been a war to end all wars; and if that
turned out to be a lie, then all those men had died for nothing. This
was unbelievable, unacceptable. It was only twenty years since the
end of the Great War. Europe had not recovered from the slaughter: 1,000,000 dead from Britain and her Empire; 1,300,000
French dead; 1,700,000 German dead; 1,200,000 Austrians; over
500,000 Italians; and God alone knew how many Russians: entire
armies had vanished on the Eastern Front; in 1915 alone Russia
lost 2,000,000 men, killed, wounded, captured or missing. By the
end of the war that figure was over 9,000,000. The United States
came late to the conflict but the fighting in 1918 was fierce, and
126,000 Americans died. Civilians died too, from starvation, from

sickness, a very few from bombing. The exact total number of casualties, military and civilian, is anybody's guess. Perhaps 25,000,000. Some say 37,000,000. We shall never know. What is undeniable is that every third British serviceman in the war became a casualty. In Britain, in 1938, that knowledge was not history, it was heartache and suffering and grief. Which goes a long way towards explaining why Neville Chamberlain was a hero.

Nobody wanted war. After the lesson of 1914–18 you would have to be a maniac to want war. And it looked as if the Prime Minister was the best man to keep Europe at peace. When Germany began demanding that Czechoslovakia hand over the Sudetenland – Czech territory where the population was mainly German – this had the makings of the worst crisis in Europe since 1918. Czechoslovakia had alliances with France and Russia. If German troops marched into the Sudetenland, four countries might suddenly be at war. Five, if you count Austria, which was part of the Reich and bordered on Czechoslovakia. Six, if Britain stood by France. Eight, if Italy and Poland decided to get involved.

Chamberlain did a remarkable thing. On 14 September he flew to Germany. In 1938, statesmen did not fly; they travelled by boat or train. Chamberlain had been up in an aeroplane before, but this was the first time he had made a journey by air. Hindsight tells us that when he met Hitler he was taking a ride on the tiger, but that is not how the world saw it then. *The Times*, for instance, was consistently pro-German and it recommended that Czechoslovakia give Germany what she wanted. (*The Times* was not alone in its attitude to Fascism: earlier in the thirties the *Daily Mirror* and the *Sunday Pictorial* thoroughly approved of Oswald Mosley's British Union of Fascists. The *Mirror* ran a headline: 'Hurrah for Blackshirts'. Later the editors realized that sport, sex and crime sold more papers than politics did.)

Chamberlain flew back to London for discussions with the French premier and foreign minister. They agreed on a fig leaf which could disguise Germany's annexation: a plebiscite whereby the German-speaking parts would decide whether to stay in Czechoslovakia or to leave. Chamberlain flew back to Germany on 22 September. Hitler agreed, with one amendment: instead of a plebiscite to be followed (or not) by occupation, he insisted on occupying the areas first, *before* the plebiscite. Now the tiger was taking Chamberlain for a ride. The threat of war remained.

This is not the place to follow the whole sad story of Czech humiliation and dismemberment. The Czechs were not allowed to take part in discussions; they were simply informed what had been decided. Perhaps they could have fought and won. A Luftwaffe pilot who was based near the Czech border has been sceptical of historians who record that the Wehrmacht forces which entered Czechoslovakia were well equipped and that resistance would have been pointless. 'Certainly from my perspective and that of very many others,' he wrote, 'we were just a hotch-potch of personnel of very varied experience and training, in aircraft which either belonged in a museum or weren't armed anyway. Another gigantic bluff had come off.'

Chamberlain flew home. On 27 September he told his story to the nation on BBC radio. He said something which has been much-quoted for its alleged naiveté: 'How horrible, fantastic, incredible it is that we should be digging trenches and trying on gas masks here, because of a quarrel in a faraway country between people of whom we know nothing.' It sounds to us, today, as if he were talking about a border dispute in Outer Mongolia. But in 1938, for nearly all his listeners, Czechoslovakia *was* remote and meaningless. They agreed with Chamberlain. They knew nothing of Czechoslovakia but they knew that trenches were being dug in city parks. The ARP (Air Raid Precautions) organization was mobilized. Barrage balloons flew over London. Air-raid warning sirens were tested. Thirty-eight million gas masks were distributed, and loudspeaker trucks drove around, urging people to be fitted. I can testify to the clammy grip and rubbery smell of the masks. They were not liked but they were welcomed: there was a widespread fear of gas attack by German bombers. Both sides had used poison gas in the first war. In 1936 Italy had used mustard gas during its conquest of Abyssinia.

In his broadcast Chamberlain said, 'Armed conflict between nations is a nightmare to me . . .' For a few days, it was a nightmare shared by the nation. Germany had issued an ultimatum. If Hitler didn't get what he wanted by 2 p.m. next day, the German armed forces would mobilize. The next day was 28 September. Chamberlain spoke to a grimly silent House of Commons which had been recalled from its summer break and now expected to hear the worst. A note was passed to Chamberlain. Mussolini, acting as mediator, had persuaded Hitler to postpone mobilization for 24 hours. Instead, there was to be a four-power conference. 'I have now been informed by Herr Hitler,' Chamberlain told the House, 'that he invites me to Munich tomorrow morning.'

So London wasn't to be bombed. 'Members rose to their feet, cheering and sobbing,' A.J.P. Taylor wrote. The joyous uproar came mainly from the Government benches. The Opposition was less excited. But there was a huge and instant sense of relief throughout the country.

Chamberlain flew to Germany for the third time in a fortnight: surely the earliest example of shuttle diplomacy. France, Britain, Italy and Germany reached an agreement which Czechoslovakia was told to accept. The transfer of the Sudetenland was sewn up and the Czechs were stitched up. The four powers guaranteed the new Czech borders. There was a moment of anticlimax when Hitler, eager to sign the document, plunged his pen into the inkwell only to discover that it was dry. But ink was found and the formalities were completed.

There was still time for Hitler and Chamberlain to have a private talk in his Munich flat. Chamberlain took with him a draft declaration. It said that the Fuhrer and the Prime Minister regarded the Sudetenland Agreement 'as symbolic of the desire of our two peoples never to go to war with one another again'. It ended with a pledge 'to assure the peace of Europe'. Not a word of the draft was changed. Hitler signed on the spot. This was the piece of paper which Chamberlain waved to the welcoming party as he emerged from his aeroplane in London. 'I've got it!' he cried.

Crowds cheered him all the way from the airport to Downing Street, 'shouting themselves hoarse, leaping on the running-board, banging on the windows, and thrusting their hands into the car to be shaken'. The mob demanded that he come to an open window of 10 Downing Street, and he waved the paper again. 'I believe it is peace for our time,' he said. They sang 'For He's A Jolly Good Fellow'. He had been handed a letter from the king, inviting him to Buckingham Palace, 'so that I can express to you personally my most heartfelt congratulations on the success of your visit to Munich'. The crowds cheered more loudly when he stood on the balcony of the palace with the king and queen.

Commenting on these cheers, he is reported to have said: 'All this will be over in three months.' Chamberlain was an optimist but he was no fool. He knew that Britain, with a small army, few anti-aircraft guns and an obsolescent air force (fighters and bombers were biplanes with open cockpits) was, in Churchill's words, 'hideously unprepared for war'. Peace wasn't the best policy, it was the *only* policy.

To the eyes of the twenty-first century, Chamberlain looks antique: wing collar, Chaplinesque umbrella, unhappy moustache. But in 1938 television was scarcely invented and few citizens ever saw their leaders in the flesh. They got their information from newspapers. Every British newspaper bar one applauded the Munich agreement. 'No conqueror returning from a victory on the battlefield has come home adorned with nobler laurels,' said *The Times*. The *Daily Mail* was equally pleased. The exception was *Reynolds News*, which did not circulate widely. The *Daily Express* had the biggest circulation of any daily in the world, and on the day after Munich its front page promised: 'Great Britain will not be involved in a European war this year or next year either.'

That was good enough for most readers. They had had their bellyful of European conflicts; now they just wanted to be left alone. 'Peace was the important thing,' wrote Virginia Cowles, an American journalist who watched Munich happen. 'Chamberlain was the hero of the day. Business firms advertised their gratitude in the newspapers; shops displayed Chamberlain dolls and sugar umbrellas; and in Scandinavia there was a movement to present the British leader with a trout stream.' The ex-Kaiser wrote to Queen Mary that the Prime Minister 'was inspired by heaven and guided by God'. He was an emblem of peace to the whole world. *Punch* ran a cartoon of John Bull settling into a chair while the words

'WAR SCARE' flew out of the window; the caption read: 'Thank God, that's gone.' Chamberlain felt pleased with his achievement and he knew that most people were pleased with him.

After his first flight to Munich, the Poet Laureate, John Masefield, composed these lines in his honour:

> As Priam to Achilles for his son,
> So you, into the night, divinely led,
> To ask that young men's bodies, not yet dead,
> Be given from battle not begun.

Chamberlain's Christmas cards for 1938 showed a picture of an aeroplane with one word: *Munich*.

CHAPTER THREE

Serial Liar

Nᴏᴛ everyone cheered.

Winston Churchill denounced appeasement, but he was in the political wilderness and although they listened to his speeches, many MPs were leery of him; just a year ago he had horribly misjudged the national mood in the Abdication Crisis. (Blind to the popular rejection of Mrs Simpson, who was a double divorcée, Churchill backed Edward VIII. In the country at large, the king was labelled as 'third mate on an American tramp'.) Anthony Eden made it clear that he thought Munich was a shameful blunder, but Eden had already quit the Cabinet. He too was powerless. One man did demand, and deserve, his country's attention: Duff Cooper, First Lord of the Admiralty. In the Commons' debate on Munich, he made a resignation speech of such clarity and strength that it silenced the Government supporters. Here is a small part:

> The Prime Minister has confidence in the goodwill and in the word of Herr Hitler, although when Herr Hitler broke the Treaty of Versailles he undertook to keep the Treaty of Locarno, and when he broke the Treaty of Locarno he undertook not to interfere further, or to have further territorial claims in Europe. When he entered Austria by force he authorized his henchmen to give an authoritative assurance that he would not interfere with Czechoslovakia. That was less than six months ago. Still the Prime Minister believes that he can rely upon the good faith of Hitler.

Six months later, on 15 March 1939, Czechoslovakia collapsed. With the Sudetenland gone, under German pressure the provinces of Slovakia and Ruthenia began to break away. The Czech president resigned. Hitler nominated Emil Hácha to replace him.

Hácha was only 66 but he had a weak heart, no political skills and a mind enfeebled by premature senility. As it became clear that

Hitler intended to dominate all of Czechoslovakia, by force if necessary, Hácha requested an audience. At 10.40 p.m. he and his Foreign Minister, Chvalkovsky, were met at Berlin railway station with flowers, chocolates, and an SS honour guard which Hácha had to inspect in driving snow. They drove to the Adlon Hotel. It was after 1 a.m. when they were taken to the Reich Chancellery; another SS honour guard was waiting. Hitler received them in his study, with Goering, Keitel, a few others. The door was closed.

Hácha knew he had no cards to play. He was so desperate that he tried to appeal to Hitler's better nature. Hitler heard him out and said the order had already been given to invade Czechoslovakia at 6 a.m. and to incorporate her into the Third Reich. He 'felt almost ashamed to say that for every Czech battalion a German division would come. The military operation had been planned on the most generous scale.'

Hácha and Chvalkovsky went into another room, to continue discussions with Goering and Ribbentrop. It was here that Goering said, 'I should be sorry to bomb beautiful Prague.' (At the Nuremberg Trials, Goering said he hadn't intended doing it, but a point like that might 'accelerate the whole matter'.)

Hácha fainted. Briefly, there was panic as the Germans foresaw headlines around the world: *Czechoslovak President Murdered in German Chancellery*. But Hitler's personal physician, Dr Morell, revived him with a vitamin injection. Meanwhile a document of surrender had been prepared. Hácha asked for another injection, and was given it, and recovered so much strength that he refused to sign. Ribbentrop and Goering showed no mercy. 'They literally hunted Dr Hácha and Mr Chvalkovsky round the table on which the documents were lying, thrusting them continually before them, pushing pens into their hands, incessantly repeating that if they continued in their refusal, half of Prague would lie in ruins from bombing within two hours, and this would only be the beginning.'

By 4 a.m., Hácha was on the verge of another collapse. He had just enough strength to sign the document that handed over his country to Germany. Two hours later, German troops crossed the border that the four powers had guaranteed in Munich. From

Berlin, Hitler declared that Czechoslovakia had ceased to exist. That night he slept in Prague, in Hradčany Castle, the ancient home of the kings of Bohemia.

Duff Cooper had been right. Hitler had lied again. By a mixture of bluff and bluster and lies, he had taken back the Rhineland in 1936, he had taken over Austria in 1938, and he had seized Czechoslovakia in 1938 and 1939. In Britain, sugar umbrellas disappeared from the shops, and compulsory military service was introduced. Neville Chamberlain abandoned appeasement. This was the moment when everyone knew that Hitler's word was worthless. All politicians are selective with the truth. Hitler was much more than that. He was a serial liar. He would sooner lie than speak the truth.

As it happened, his Luftwaffe could not have bombed Prague that day: thick fog grounded all German aircraft. Not that it mattered. Hácha surrendered because he thought he knew that the Luftwaffe could totally destroy Prague. Everyone knew it. Air power wins wars. Nobody had actually done it, but everyone knew it.

CHAPTER FOUR

The Knock-out Myth

ON 1 September 1939, Hitler invaded Poland. On 3 September, as Chamberlain finished his melancholy broadcast announcing that Britain was at war with Germany, the air raid sirens in London began their roller-coaster wail. This was shocking but not surprising. War meant a massive aerial attack; everyone knew that. In fact the warning turned out to be a false alarm, a cock-up triggered by the flight of a single civilian aircraft. The knock-out blow was not thrown. In the opening months of the war, it wasn't the unstoppable bomber that damaged Britain; it was the blackout. The number of deaths from road accidents doubled. But the general dread of bombing was understandable.

The population as a whole – especially the town-dwellers – didn't need to be reminded of the horrors of air attack. In the spring of 1939, the British Air Staff had reckoned that, if war broke out, a force of German long-range bombers could drop 700 tons of bombs a day on London every day for two weeks, and that wouldn't be the end of it. The Ministry of Health had calculated that the first six months of an air war would kill 600,000 people and seriously injure 1,200,000. Cardboard coffins were stockpiled. Sites for mass graves were identified. Upwards of 300,000 hospital beds were reserved for casualties: clearly not enough, but the most that could be found.

At the outbreak of war, a million and a half children, plus mothers with children under five, accepted the Government's offer of evacuation to the countryside. As well, two million people left the danger areas without official help. Thus Hitler had driven three and a half million people out of the threatened cities, and done it all without firing a shot, except at Poland. What terror would 700 tons of bombs a day inflict on those Londoners who remained?

This was the theory of the 'knock-out blow'. It was taught repeatedly in the 1930s by authors who competed with each other to paint the next air war in increasingly gruesome colours. By 1939 even Liddell Hart – normally the most sane and sober of military analysts – had joined the crowd and warned Britain to face nearly a quarter of a million casualties in week one of an air war.

The experts were wrong, and for once the usual suspects were all to blame: the newspapers, the cinema, the statisticians, the air marshals and the politicians. Let us start with the politicians.

Stanley Baldwin was Tory Prime Minister from 1923 to 1931 and again from 1935 to 1937. His premierships dominated the years between the wars, although his was not a domineering style. Despite his background (Harrow, Cambridge, the law, private wealth) he had the happy knack of seeming to be a decent English chap, a man of the people. Most politicians were bad on radio: too stiff, too distant. Baldwin was good. He had President Roosevelt's 'fireside touch'. As A.J.P. Taylor describes it, Baldwin at the microphone 'came into his own. At his first broadcast, he struck a match and lit his pipe as the green light flashed – or so it is said. Thus relaxed, he played variations on the theme: "You can trust me."'

By and large, people did. It was in the Commons that he made his most memorable speech, and the whole nation took it to heart because Baldwin spoke, not only to MPs, but to everyone when he said:

> I think it is well also for the man in the street to realize that there is no power on earth that can prevent him from getting bombed. Whatever people may tell him, the bomber will always get through. The only defence is offence, which means you have to kill more women and children more quickly than the enemy if you want to save yourselves.

That was tough talk for 1932 (reinforced in 1934 when, during RAF air exercises, over 40 per cent of attacking bomber aircraft 'got through' the defending fighters). It influenced military thinking at every level for the rest of the Thirties. Whether the street was Whitehall or the Old Kent Road or Threadneedle Street, the man in it knew one solid fact about war: the bomber will always get through. Baldwin said so.

What prompted Baldwin to speak out was the Japanese assault on Shanghai in January 1932. There were no defending fighters or anti-aircraft guns and Japanese naval bombers virtually flattened Chapei, the Chinese quarter of the city. International protests followed. Chapei was bordered by the American sector, so newsreel footage and news photographs of the bombing were plentiful. It was the beginning of the discovery by cameramen that air war made better pictures than ground attacks. In 1935 Italy invaded Abyssinia (now Ethiopia). Mussolini's 19-year-old son Vittorio was a bomber pilot; he remarked on the aesthetic satisfaction of his work: 'One group of horsemen gave me the impression of a budding rose unfolding as the bomb fell in their midst and blew them up.' Later he helped to script a film to honour this 'courageous' air campaign. In 1936 civil war broke out in Spain, between the Republican government and the Fascist Nationalists led by Franco. This conflict was covered far more thoroughly by reporters of every political stripe. German and Italian aircraft supported Franco and got valuable experience in bombing towns, usually undefended. In particular, raids on Barcelona and Guernica made news worldwide. Franco's aircraft dropped leaflets on Barcelona: 'We will bomb you every three hours until you surrender.' In fact Barcelona did not surrender for nearly a year, and it was Franco's army that took the city; nevertheless, the bomber had got through again and again, just as it did when Guernica was destroyed. Except that Guernica was not destroyed.

Picasso has a lot to answer for. His painting *Guernica* is good art but bad history. He was not in Guernica when the German Condor Legion came; was not even in Spain. He was in Paris. He read about Guernica in a newspaper. His sympathies were with the Republicans and he believed what the press said: that the Heinkels and Junkers had destroyed Guernica. The war correspondents were not there when it happened; they filed their reports from Madrid or Bilbao (or wherever) and *then* visited the scene, by which time the news editors in ten thousand newsrooms around the globe had set the fate of Guernica in type. The Condor Legion had bombed it.

Therefore, the laws of journalism said it must have been destroyed. No editor in his right mind would permit a headline that said German bombers had *half*-destroyed a small Spanish market town. Besides, the raid took place on market day; hence the grim death-toll of peasants and farmers; and Guernica was sacred to the Basque people, which explains why the Condor Legion chose to obliterate it in a demonstration of terrorist bombing. None of this was true. But once *The New York Times* ran a big piece declaring Guernica was flattened, the myth replaced the truth; and since then it has proved to be more durable. In 1981, when Picasso's painting was moved to Spain, BBC television news said Guernica had been 'demolished'. A BBC Radio 3 discussion stated confidently: 'Guernica was the first town entirely destroyed by aerial bombing.' The Guinness History of Air Warfare says: 'Guernica was bombed to destruction.' Nobody mentions Durango.

Durango was a little town, about fifteen miles south of Guernica, and much the same size. Before the Condor Legion targeted Guernica, it had bombed Durango on four days in a row. One bomb made a direct hit on a Jesuit church in the middle of Mass. Two hundred and forty-eight civilians were killed, 525 injured. That was one reason why local farmers avoided Guernica on market day. They feared the worst. They knew that Guernica was a road and rail centre, with an important arms factory, just like Durango. It occupied a valuable strategic position: three main roads leading to Bilbao converged at Guernica. Franco's Nationalist army had launched a northern offensive, and thousands of Republican troops were retreating through Guernica. By anybody's standards in that peculiarly savage war, it was an obvious military target. Plenty of other little Spanish towns had been shelled or bombed, by Republicans as well as Nationalists, and to nobody's surprise.

None of this diminishes the fact of ruthless and indiscriminate bombing. The Condor Legion either did not know or did not care that Guernica was an ancient town, the home of Basque freedom and culture, and in April 1937 it was full of refugees as well as soldiers. The bombs cut a wide swathe through the place and killed a great many civilians, probably as many as died in Durango. Yet if the Condor Legion aimed to wipe Guernica off the face of the earth, it failed. Twenty-seven bombers and ten fighter-bombers, in perfect conditions, flying relatively low and with no ground fire to distract them, failed to hit the arms factory, or a major bridge, or the Parliament Building, or the sacred oak tree in its grounds – a symbol of independence as important to Basques as the Statue of Liberty is to Americans. About half the town was destroyed. Half survived intact. When public opinion worldwide reacted so violently, the Condor Legion was startled. All they had set out to do was harass the Republican retreat. It was a routine operation, like Durango.

Nevertheless, men everywhere (and women and children) took Guernica as proof that Baldwin was right: if an air power wanted to obliterate a whole town, it could do so, in half a day, with massive casualties. The Condor Legion thought it was knocking out a communications centre. The world decided it was conducting a laboratory experiment in terror bombing. The experience coloured everyone's thinking. When Goering bullied President Hácha with threats of bombing Prague, they were both thinking of what had happened in Spain.

Germany invaded Poland on the morning of 1 September 1939 and the Luftwaffe began bombing Warsaw in the afternoon. Artillery joined the bombers. Warsaw surrendered on 27 September. Twenty-five thousand civilians had died. Hitler flew to Warsaw, and invited the travelling pack of foreign correspondents to inspect the ruins. 'This is how I can deal with any European city,' he said.

The next victim was Rotterdam. On 14 May 1940, four days after the assault on the West began, the Luftwaffe was aiming at Rhine bridges in the Dutch city when some bombs hit the city centre and killed 900 civilians. The Dutch Foreign Minister guessed at 30,000, and the figure was readily believed. On 15 May, William L. Shirer, the CBS radio correspondent in Berlin, wrote in his diary: 'It seems the reason the Dutch gave up yesterday was that the Germans bombed the hell out of Rotterdam, and threatened to do the same to Utrecht and Amsterdam. Hitler's technique of helping his armies by threatening terror or meting it out is as masterful as it is diabolical. His High Command, for instance, tonight threatened to bomb Brussels . . . "If the Belgian government," says the communiqué, "wishes to save Brussels from the horrors of war, it must immediately put a stop to troop movements in the city and the work on fortifications."' Next day Shirer wrote: 'P., always well informed on German intentions, thinks Hitler will bomb Paris and London to daylights within the next forty-eight hours.'

Shirer was right about Hitler's technique of threatening terror: it was masterful. No capital city had ever surrendered to air attack alone, but fear that it might be done had become a weapon of war. So many films and photographs had shown bombers, unchallenged, dropping high explosive on towns and cities – in China, in Spain, in Poland, Holland, Belgium, France – and always the aircraft were on the victorious side. The Luftwaffe made a feature film about the bombing of Warsaw, called *Baptism of Fire*; Goering himself introduced it. Berlin cinemas showed newsreels of the bombing of Rotterdam while the Battle for France was going on. 'It makes one shudder for Paris,' one Berliner wrote in her diary.

The cinema helped the theory of the knock-out blow to become accepted wisdom. It was a false theory, a tumbledown house of cards, but a lot of bombs had to fall before the theory got completely blown away.

Some of the miscalculations were honest mistakes. The British Air Staff exaggerated the size of the German bomber force, and inflated the percentage of the force that would be operational, and assumed that every available bomber would be sent. Using these wrong figures, experts calculated that Germany would drop 100,000 tons of bombs on London in 14 days. In the whole of World War Two, the Luftwaffe failed to drop that total on London.

Bad was made worse when the experts ignored the fact that at least two-thirds of Greater London is open space (parks, gardens, cemeteries, roads, rivers, canals, railways, tennis courts, sports grounds, race tracks, rubbish dumps, swimming pools) and they assumed that every bomb would hit a heavily populated area. They made no allowance for 'duds'. A lot fell. (Many families – mine included – kept a German incendiary bomb as a memento of the blitz.) They made no allowance for the protection of air-raid shelters, or the effects of evacuation.

Finally, and disastrously, they used a multiplier of fifty: that is, they believed that every ton of enemy bombs would kill or injure fifty people. The multiplier was based on casualties from German bombing of England in the First World War. Such information was skimpy – German bombers had dropped only 73 tons – and it was seriously skewed because a few bombs from those raiders had, by sheer luck, hit a lot people. For example, on 13 June 1917 one formation of German aeroplanes dropped four and a half tons on East End dockland, killed 162 people and injured many more. Such exceptions distorted the casualty multiplier. Twenty years later those distortions were not understood, and the British people were frightened by forecasts that 600,000 would be killed and 1,200,000 injured in the first six months of an air attack. By a cruel coincidence, Allied bombing of Germany *did* kill 600,000 civilians – but that effort lasted five years and it required the devastation of 131 cities.

The coffins remained stacked in warehouses. The emergency wards remained empty. For this, President Roosevelt deserves credit.

When Germany invaded Poland, Roosevelt made a plea for the safety of all civilians in the war zone. He asked the combatant nations not to bomb any target where there was a risk of killing or injuring civilians. Britain and France agreed. Germany, once the Luftwaffe had finished with Warsaw, agreed too. From September 1939 to April 1940 – the eight months of the Phony War – the bombers did little but drop leaflets. This was a happy escape, although many believed it simply postponed the day of destruction, perhaps of extinction. And of course on 10 May 1940, when Germany attacked the West, the Roosevelt Rules got scrapped by everyone.

FOR YOU, THE WAR
IS OVER

CHAPTER FIVE

Only Fishbait

THE worst, and the best, witness of 1940 was Adolf Hitler.

Worst, because his opinions and his intentions varied according to his audience. All three service chiefs never met at his Fuhrer Conferences; he usually briefed them separately, and often what he told the army contradicted what he had already told the navy, and he might then change his mind while talking to the air force. In that way he kept total power.

This is not to suggest that he never spoke the truth; only that it is necessary to wait and see what happened before picking the truths from the untruths. And since he was not only the Fuhrer but also the Supreme Commander of the Armed Forces, what he did was a far clearer guide to his mind than what he said. A useful sequence of events began on the afternoon of 10 May, the opening day of the assault on the West, when the fine old university city of Freiburg-im-Breslau was bombed.

Freiburg is twelve miles from the French border. No air-raid warning had sounded. Low cloud made it difficult to identify the aircraft. Fifty-seven civilians died, including 22 children and 13 women. German press and radio denounced the raid as a British atrocity, sheer murder. Goebbels turned Freiburg into a German Guernica; as late as 1943 he was calling it *'Kindermord in Freiburg'*. He was never a man to let the facts get in the way of a good story, and the facts had been rapidly established by a secret Luftwaffe inquiry.

The bomb fragments were of German origin. An air warning unit stationed on a height that overlooked Freiburg saw three Heinkel 111 bombers cross the city just as the bombs exploded. To clinch everything, the inquiry found that a squadron of Heinkels based nearby had set off to bomb Dijon, and had lost contact with a section of three aircraft as they climbed through cloud. These three Heinkels, proceeding independently, had missed Dijon by 150 miles and bombed Freiburg by mistake.

That was not so extraordinary; other air forces made similar blunders. What is noticeable is that Hitler failed to exploit what Goebbels condemned as a monstrous provocation. He could have ordered a similar raid on Oxford, or Canterbury, or Winchester. It would have been very popular with the German people. He did nothing. Two months later, in a hugely publicized speech to the Reichstag, he referred to Freiburg and said: 'Until now I have ordered hardly any reprisals . . .' He meant reprisals against Britain. Yet the Luftwaffe had shown no scruples in its bombing of Warsaw, Rotterdam, or any other European city that got in the Wehrmacht's way. On 6 June, for example, 600 German bombers and 500 fighters struck at airfields and aircraft factories in the Paris area; inevitably there were civilian casualties. Hitler gave Britain favoured treatment. The reason became obvious after Dunkirk.

This is not the place to analyze the German triumph in the West, and the way it forced a British evacuation from Dunkirk. Others have done that very thoroughly. Enough to say that Britain may have been lucky, but there was nothing miraculous about the outcome. Dunkirk succeeded because the Royal Navy, with the help of the 'little boats', was skilful, organized and resolute, and because a steely rearguard of soldiers – French as well as British – fought off attacks on the town's perimeter, from 27 May to 4 June, buying time for the army's escape, while an umbrella of British fighters fought off the Luftwaffe. The element of luck came from Goering's vanity and arrogance, and his resentment of the German army's battle honours. On 23 May he telephoned Hitler and persuaded him to leave Dunkirk to the Luftwaffe. 'We have done it!' he told General Milch, his deputy. 'The Luftwaffe is to wipe out the British on the beaches.' He sneered at the Germany army: 'They round up the British as prisoners with as little harm to them as possible. The Fuhrer wants them to be taught a lesson they won't easily forget.'

That's what Goering *said* Hitler said. Perhaps Goering lied; or perhaps Hitler said it for effect, to make his army generals try harder. What we know is that he had more on his mind than Dunkirk. He still did not know the outcome of the Battle for France.

When the drama of Dunkirk unfolded, German forces had penetrated little more than fifty miles into France. It had been a brilliant advance, but by far the greater part of the country remained to be conquered. During Dunkirk, the German panzers in France rested, repaired, and came up to strength again. In some places, French armoured units counterattacked German bridgeheads and there was fierce fighting. The war in the West didn't end with Dunkirk. Germany had 143 divisions, some of them battle-weary. France still had three Army Groups, perhaps 65 divisions, defending a line that stretched from the mouth of the Somme to Reims: 1,500,000 men covering 200 miles. Little wonder that Hitler was willing to leave Dunkirk to Goering, and concentrate his land forces on the serious business of war, the reason they were in France: to conquer.

Dunkirk should have been a massacre: long lines of weary troops snaking across the wide, exposed beaches; very few anti-aircraft guns; stationary ships taking on their slow-moving loads of men. 'Only fishbait will reach the other side,' Goering promised Hitler. But 338,226 British and Allied troops escaped to England. The Luftwaffe had some bad luck: for three days, fog shut down their air bases, and when the weather let the bombers take off, many were hacked down by Spitfires, a fighter new to them. Goering expected much from his Stukas, but often their bombs buried themselves so deeply in the sand before exploding that few casualties resulted. Nor was divebombing small vessels as easy as the Stuka pilots expected. Dunkirk was certainly a British disaster. When William Shirer visited the town he wrote, 'here, stretched along the beaches as far as the eye could see, were mountains of arms . . . I had never seen such a vast amount of military hardware in my life.' But Dunkirk was a German failure too. The enemy got away.

Hitler did not seem disturbed by this. He had told Goering (so Goering said) to teach the English a lesson. Now he told his naval adjutant that he had hoped to capture a mass of prisoners, useful in peace negotiations. Then he told his valet: 'It is always good to let a broken army return home to show the civilian population what a beating they have had.' This was getting dangerously close to humanitarianism. Hitler had a long friendship with Frau Troost, the widow of an architect he had admired. He knew that she was not afraid to disagree with him. He told her: 'The blood of every single Englishman is too valuable to shed. Our two people belong together, racially and traditionally – this is and always has been my aim even if our generals can't grasp it.' Maybe she believed him. Maybe he believed it himself at that moment. But he also told Bormann that he had demonstrated his 'sporting spirit' when he intentionally spared Britain; and that certainly was not true. In fact, the only absolute truth at the time of the Battle for France is that Hitler genuinely wanted peace with Britain. The next proof came on the day after the last British destroyer carried away the last British soldier from Dunkirk, when General Milch and a fellow-officer took a walk on the beaches.

Peace is simple; all it requires is that men stop fighting. Yet Hitler's Blitzkrieg had built up such a thunderous momentum that the fighting men did not want to stop.

Milch was a much-decorated veteran of the first war, now Inspector-General of the Luftwaffe, which made him second only to Goering. Some said he was the real operating head of the air force. He had brains and thrust; he made things happen. He went to Dunkirk – the town in ruins, the skies still stained with smoke – because he wanted to examine the sandy battlefield. There was plenty to see: abandoned tanks, trucks, artillery, mortars, rifles, even bicycles, all the broken apparatus of a defeated army; but of the army itself he saw only a few dozen corpses. The rest, over 200,000 British troops plus the others, had crossed the Channel. 'They are not buried yet,' Milch said. 'We have no time to waste.'

That same day he persuaded Goering that Britain should be invaded at once. Even three or four weeks' delay would be fatal. His plan was an airborne extension of the Blitzkrieg: a lightning strike by paratroops under cover of heavy bombing. They would seize an airfield or two, and fleets of Ju52s would fly in weapons and ammunition, while five élite infantry divisions were rapidly shipped across the Channel, with five more to follow and deliver the killer blow. Of course there would be fierce resistance: an invasion must expect constant attack from the Royal Air Force, and the Royal Navy would charge at full speed from the Atlantic and the Mediterranean into the narrow waters of the Channel. When Goering went to Hitler with what he triumphantly called 'the blueprint for victory', he converted the likely British reaction into a great opportunity. 'This will enable me to use the Luftwaffe not only to destroy the enemy's forces in the air but their mighty force of ships at sea,' he said. But the assault must happen *now* – within days, while Britain was still weak.

It was Milch's plan, and Milch was no dreamer. Everything depended first on the paratroops, still under-strength after taking a battering in Belgium and Holland; and if they captured an airfield, everything then depended on the lumbering Ju52s, easy meat for any fighter, and on the fast ships bringing reinforcements. Could it be done? Could the Luftwaffe really destroy both the RAF and the Royal Navy in one go? Hitler didn't even ask. 'Do nothing,' he said. The operation was risky, yet he had taken bigger risks against stronger opponents, and the British were in a hopeless mess; but *that*, he told Goering, was exactly why he would not invade now. There was no need. The British would settle for peace. Inflicting yet another ignominious defeat on them would make the process more difficult, not less. Milch was furious, and told his diary so. There was no arguing. Hitler was Supreme Commander. When he said peace, then peace it must be.

CHAPTER SIX

Small War in Europe,
Not Many Dead

IT was a small war in June 1940, and when the last of the British
Expeditionary Force escaped from France the war became much
smaller.

This point may seem too obvious to need stating, but the obvious is sometimes overlooked. It is customary to date the start of
World War Two as 1 September 1939, when Germany invaded
Poland, or 3 September, when the French and British ultimatum
to Germany (to get out of Poland) expired; but this label is misleading. It was not a world war in September 1939, when sixteen
European nations were neutral; nor in June 1940. Hitler had no
territorial ambitions outside Europe in 1940 (1941 was different)
and, apart from the British Empire, nobody had a wish to fight
him.

Japan's war was in China, as it had been since 1931. Russia and
the USA were at war with nobody. There was only one global
aspect to Hitler's war: the Dominions and Colonies of the British
Empire were his enemies; but what aid they could send to Britain
would not be decisive; nor would it arrive in time. Britain continued an air and sea war against Germany and Italy, and in Egypt
a small British army faced Italian forces in Libya. But all the
shooting in Europe had stopped, and nobody expected it to restart
soon. Possibly it would never restart. Hitler said the Third Reich
would last for a thousand years, and in June 1940 there was
certainly nothing to suggest that Germany would take her boot off
Europe's neck in anybody's lifetime. In 1939 Hitler had bought
Stalin's silence by giving Russia half of Poland. Thus he had

sedated the East and left himself free to overwhelm the West. Now he was more powerful than any other nation on earth. There was nobody left to attack him.

For Britain it was different: she faced conquest or survival. Naturally, the war was all the world to Britain. But to nearly everyone else, the war was over and Germany had won it with astonishing speed and ease. Britain's rôle was to be mopped-up, as and when the victor decided.

Too many English-speaking historians see 1940 only through British eyes. They identify Britain's fate then as the fate of Europe thereafter, even the fate of the whole civilized world. But that is to impose later knowledge on to earlier events. When Hitler invaded the West, he did not hope or expect to capture Britain (or even all France). Fuhrer Directive No. 6, titled 'for the Conduct of the War', stated that its purpose was to defeat large parts of the French and Allied armies, and to 'gain as much ground as possible in Holland, Belgium and northern France as a base for successful air and sea warfare against England' – in other words, for a blockade. Far from planning to invade Britain, Hitler had in mind a siege. It was one reason why he agreed to the German navy's proposal for an invasion of Norway: those Norwegian ports would be invaluable as extra bases from which to operate a naval blockade.

And then, unexpectedly, France fell. It had all happened so fast. Less than a year ago, Germany possessed two states: Austria and Czechoslovakia. Now she owned a European empire, reaching from the Arctic Circle to the Pyrenees. The Wehrmacht was irresistible. The Fuhrer was infallible. As General Keitel said to him, when news arrived of France's surrender: 'My Fuhrer, you are the greatest Field Commander of all time!'

And what of Britain, an island so small that, thanks to the conquest of the West, the Luftwaffe's bombers could reach almost every corner of it? After Dunkirk, General Kleist was bold enough to voice some dissatisfaction with the way the B.E.F. had been able to escape. Not important, Hitler told him: 'The British won't come back in this war.' Britain was now irrelevant.

While Britain was daily expecting doom and disaster, and while the figure of Hitler dominated British thought, Hitler relaxed. He enjoyed his triumph and he revelled in the joys of peace. He still had problems to solve; Britain was not one of them. Unless these two very different priorities are understood – Britain at crisis-point, Germany relaxed, almost casual, almost indifferent – it is impossible to make sense of Hitler's apparently bizarre behaviour and Britain's apparently lucky survival.

CHAPTER SEVEN

Die At Our Posts

O N 18 June – the day after France gave up and asked for peace – Churchill made a speech which was to become famous. He urged the British people to so bear themselves that, if the British Empire and Commonwealth were to last for a thousand years, men would still say, 'This was their finest hour.' For many Americans, that sounded like a gallant suicide note.

In May 1940, a Gallup poll had found that only seven per cent of Americans were in favour of going to war alongside the Allies. This briefly surged to 19 per cent after the attack on the West, but when France fell, so did the percentage. Another Gallup poll asked Americans which side they expected to win. In September 1939, when war broke out, 82 per cent had said Britain, seven per cent said Germany. Nine months later, when France fell, 32 per cent said Britain, 35 per cent said Germany. The rest didn't know.

One man who thought he knew was the American ambassador, Joseph Kennedy, father to the future president and a self-made millionaire who schooled his large family to believe that nothing mattered but winning. Joe Kennedy was sure that Britain would lose.

His courage failed him on the first day of the German invasion of Holland. Ivan Maisky, the Russian ambassador to London, found Kennedy 'in a state of panic. Britain was absolutely power-less before Germany, he considered. The war was hopelessly lost and the sooner she made peace with Hitler the better.' When other Americans in London, made of sterner stuff, formed the 1st American Squadron of Home Guard, Kennedy reacted badly. 'It might lead to all United States citizens being shot as *francs-tireurs* when the Germans occupied London,' he warned them.

41

Kennedy was all for appeasement. As France crumbled and the likelihood of a French armistice increased, Churchill's Foreign Minister, Halifax, asked Churchill what might happen if Germany were to offer Britain similar terms – say, paying an indemnity and losing the colonies but retaining British freedom and independence. Churchill turned the idea down flat. When Kennedy heard this, he could not believe in such an attitude – then or later. 'My own impression,' he said, was 'that should anything like that be offered it would be snapped up.' Coming from a man who made his millions as a bootlegger on an industrial scale during Prohibition, this was an extraordinary declaration of faith in one's fellow-man. Joseph Kennedy believed that Hitler's word could be trusted. Hitler was a professional liar. If Kennedy didn't know that, he was alone in Britain.

At least Kennedy was consistent in his pessimism. Five days after the invasion of France, Churchill sent a plea to Roosevelt for immediate military aid. Simultaneously, Kennedy's advice to Secretary of State Cordell Hull was to send none. Kennedy thought the royal children (and the gold reserves) should go to Canada, a suggestion briskly snubbed by the queen: the family, she said, wasn't leaving. Kennedy definitely wanted to leave. As the air raids got worse, he nagged the State Department to bring him home. He hated bombs, and his predictions of doom and disaster had left him with few British friends. There was general contempt for his habit of spending the nights in a country mansion he had rented, just beyond Windsor, twenty-five miles from London, while the embassy staff had to stay in the city. His excuse was that he 'was avoiding formal dinners'.

The truth was that Kennedy never understood the British. He disliked many of the upper classes because he thought they despised him as jumped-up Boston Irish. He was primarily a businessman (after Dunkirk, he sold his shares in British companies) and he thought it was only good business practice for Churchill to do a deal with Hitler. His policy was to avoid war at all costs. A saying went around government circles in the summer of 1940: 'I thought my daffodils were yellow until I met Joe Kennedy.'

Viewed as a simple business proposition, Britain's trading position was hopeless and her prospects were virtually nil. The two sides were utterly mismatched. The British army had only two complete and fully-armed divisions – after Dunkirk they had been sent to fight in Brittany and were lucky to return. The rest were either Territorials or the battered remnants of the French campaign, some wounded, some without uniform, all dirty and weary and bewildered by the speed with which they had been beaten. More than 100,000 French troops had been rescued too; nearly all of them went straight to Southampton or Weymouth and sailed back to western France, to rejoin the struggle. A few stayed in England. Later that summer, with France out of the war, General de Gaulle assembled 2,000 of them and offered a choice: go home to Occupied France, or stay and fight with his Free French Army. Only 200 stayed. It is hard to blame the others. After all, nearly 250,000 British soldiers had chosen to leave France and return home. If the British would not stay and fight for France, why should the French stay and fight for Britain?

One answer might be that, in the battle against the brutality and slavery of Nazism and Fascism, there was no choice: Britain was now the only game in town. This sudden simplification of the war had a healthy effect on British morale. No more continental allies of dubious reliability. Now everybody knew where they stood. The ground might be unsafe, but at least it was the homeland; it was worth fighting for. The future was plain. Germany would invade. Why not? Her armed forces had taken Poland in 23 days, Norway and Denmark in 61 days, and Holland, Belgium and France in 45 days. London could not be sure of the exact size of the German army across the Channel but it was known to be at least 130 divisions, ten of them armoured. Britain had 29 divisions, most of them incomplete and none of them armoured anywhere near as well as the panzers. Judging by the air combat over France, the Luftwaffe was believed to outnumber the RAF by about three to one. Nobody needed to guess at German fighting qualities; they were all too familiar. *Blitzkrieg* had introduced a high-speed, high-explosive form of warfare to which the rest of Europe had no answer. General Rommel was a brilliant exponent; his 7th Panzer

Division had captured the Highland Division *and* the French 9th Corps, almost intact, at St Valéry. In July he wrote to his wife: '. . . by my estimate the war will be won in a fortnight.' Long before that, on 15 May – when fighting was still going on in Belgium – Churchill told the American ambassador that Hitler would probably attack Britain within a month. Maybe it was said in the hope of prompting aid from Roosevelt; maybe not. Three days later item one on the agenda of the Chiefs of Staff was 'urgent measures to meet invasion'. By now the enemy controlled the coasts of Denmark, Holland and Belgium. Halifax wrote in his diary that 9 July was thought to be invasion day.

The danger was huge, but it was simple. After the initial shock of Dunkirk, morale recovered quickly. Dunkirk (despite Churchill's warning that wars are not won by evacuations) was widely regarded as a Deliverance, rather like the Angels of Mons in the other war, but on a bigger scale and with the added benefit of newsreel coverage. (At the landing ports, General Brian Horrocks noticed that 'the letters B.E.F. began to appear in chalk on the front of steel helmets. I couldn't help smiling.' As Horrocks observed, the British soldier always has an eye on the main chance; and 'B.E.F.' or 'Dunkirk' was good for a free drink. The same trick was worked with the flash 'S.A.S.' in Cairo, later in the war. General Bernard Montgomery was less impressed: 'I remember the disgust of many like myself when we saw British soldiers walking about in London and elsewhere with a coloured embroidered flash on their sleeve with the title "Dunkirk".')

There were minor domestic distractions. A brief but hectic attempt to hunt down Fifth Columnists excited the country. In the middle of his superb handling of the Dunkirk evacuation, Vice-Admiral Sir Bertram Ramsay found time to report signs of 'numerous acts of sabotage and 5th Column activity' in Dover. They included communication leaks and – a curious piece of sabotage – 'second-hand cars purchased at fantastic prices and left at various parking places'. The *New Statesman* magazine detected a Fifth Column nest in the British Union of Fascists which, it pointed out, had 'moved into smaller headquarters'. Fifth Columnists are usually clandestine operators, so they would be unlikely to go about their business from a published address. As many thousands of Poles, Czechs, Norwegians, Austrians, French, Dutch, Belgians and Germans had taken refuge in Britain, the behaviour of some was bound to raise suspicions. When General Ironside was made C-in-C Home Forces, these rumours caused him a lot of bother: 'It is extraordinary,' he complained, 'how we get circumstantial reports of a Fifth Column and yet we have never been able to get anything worth having. One is persuaded that it hardly exists. And yet there is signalling going on all over the place and we cannot get any evidence.' He was right first time: it did hardly exist.

The hunt for German spies brought slim pickings too, and for the same reason. The German department of military intelligence responsible for training and infiltrating spies was the Abwehr. It seems not to have had a network in Britain before the Blitzkrieg, and not to be ready to assist an invasion afterwards. Nobody can ever claim with absolute certainty that no spies escaped capture, but what can be said is that those who were caught had been trained in a hasty and slapdash fashion and given only modest sums of money by their handlers, which suggests that the Abwehr did not value them highly.

In the summer of 1940, six agents were sent to Eire, as the Irish Republic was then known. The most successful, and the most memorable, was Dr Herman Goertz, aged 50, who parachuted into County Meath on the night of 5/6 May 1940. Germany had a vague plan to invade Ireland – North, South, both, nobody knew – and Goertz was to report on the Irish defence forces. He was a lieutenant in the Luftwaffe reserve, and he entered Ireland in uniform. Things went wrong from the start. The aircraft dropped him in the wrong place, and he couldn't find the container (parachuted separately) with his wireless set in it. He walked seventy miles to his IRA rendezvous in County Wicklow. This involved swimming the River Boyne which, he said, 'exhausted me. This swim also cost me the loss of my invisible ink.' He abandoned his uniform but kept his 1914–18 medals 'for sentimental reasons' and trudged on in 'high boots, breeches and jumper, with a little black beret on my head . . .' Amazingly, he made his rendezvous, found a radio, and sent messages to the Abwehr; unamazingly, they were of little military value. The Irish police arrested him in November 1941. But at least Goertz was gung-ho, which can't be said of the five Irishmen sent by U-boat on 8 August 1940. Two were IRA leaders, Sean Russell and Frank Ryan. They were at sea when Ryan died of a heart attack. The others lost interest and returned to Germany.

So much for Ireland. In the autumn of 1940, the Abwehr sent a small flood of spies to England: 25 or more. All were captured within a few hours of landing; most were tried under the Treason Act and hanged in Pentonville Prison. A few were 'turned' by a department of MI5 which perfected the Double-Cross System of running double-agents; this made it even easier to catch incoming spies whose first act was to contact a double-agent. Abwehr standards of operation were sloppy. The spies were poorly briefed: one agent knew so little about English licensing laws that he tried to order cider for breakfast; forged identity cards contained obvious, clumsy errors; some radio sets were of such poor quality that transmissions could not reach the Abwehr until MI5 technicians had rebuilt the set. And some spies were deeply hungover when they stumbled ashore. It's little wonder that Hitler said, 'We are divided from England by a ditch thirty-seven kilometres wide and we are not even able to get to know what is happening there!' The only wonder is that he waited until October 1941 to say it.

However . . .

German ignorance of the British order of battle would never stop an invasion; and Britain might be just as ignorant of German arms. Churchill's memoirs reveal how deep his anxieties were in June 1940. Germany had triumphed by surprise as much as by fire-power. 'Would they suddenly pounce out of the blue with new weapons, perfect planning, and overwhelming force upon our almost totally unequipped and disarmed Island at any one of a dozen or score of possible landing-places? He would have been a very foolish man who allowed his reasoning . . . to blot out any possibility against which provision could be made.' One possibility was the worst. On 24 June, with France out of the war, Churchill told the Canadian premier, Mackenzie King, that he himself wouldn't negotiate peace with Hitler but he could not bind a future government which, 'if we were deserted by the United States and beaten down here, might very easily be a kind of Quisling affair ready to accept German overlordship and protection.'

But that was not for publication. Churchill was a warrior, at his best when he was urging his countrymen to do battle against awful odds. In a broadcast on 14 July, he did not spare them: 'Should the invader come, there will be no placid lying down of the people in submission before him as we have seen – alas! – in other countries. We shall defend every village, every town, and every city.' What he said next gave the German generals something to think about. 'The vast mass of London itself, fought street by street, could easily devour an entire hostile army, and we would rather see London laid in ruins and ashes than that it should be tamely and abjectly enslaved.' No Briton could argue with that, although many wondered when they would get the weapons to do the fighting.

In person, Churchill could be even more pugnacious. Shortly after he became Prime Minister he interviewed a junior minister about the man's future at this moment of peril. Lawrence Thompson described the scene:

> With what appeared to be considerable relish, the Prime Minister fought graphically and dramatically beside his junior colleague until finally, their last rounds expended, they mingled their lifeblood in the gutters of a devastated Whitehall. 'Now,' said the Prime Minister, scowling ferociously. 'That is what I have to offer you if you join my government. Can you face it?'
>
> 'I don't know,' said the junior minister rather coldly. 'They are not circumstances to which I am accustomed.'

That neatly described one side of the coin. The British were not accustomed to being invaded. The last time it was done successfully was almost 900 years ago, by William, Duke of Normandy. The other side of the coin was a sturdy optimism: if the Spanish, Dutch and French couldn't do it, then Jerry wouldn't do it either. Those in Government maintained an expression of confidence which they knew was unjustified. Sir Alexander Cadogan, Permanent Under-Secretary at the Foreign Office, put his fears in his diary. 'Certainly everything is as gloomy as can be,' he wrote in June. 'Probability is that Hitler will attempt invasion in next fortnight. As far as I can

see, we are, after years of leisurely preparation, completely unprepared. We have simply got to die at our posts – a far better fate
than capitulating to Hitler as these damned Frogs have done. But
uncomfortable.'

None of this should be taken to mean that 1940 was a chequer-
board year, black and white, all plucky Britons and dubious for-
eigners. Britain had plenty to be afraid of, and anyone who felt no
fear was a rare bird. The story circulated of an elderly lady who
said, 'Oh, well, if the Germans win, at any rate I have my pension,
and they can't touch that.' It was a joke. Most people weren't
contemplating their pensions, they were thinking about German
paratroops.

Airborne attack was new. It had begun in Norway. With no
declaration of war, German paratroops dropped on to Norwegian
airfields and seized them. Airborne assaults had also speeded the
capture of Holland and Belgium. Even before reports of these
successes reached London, the Home Office had warned the public
to report descending parachutists to the nearest police station. That
was not what the British public wanted to hear; it wanted the
chance to kill the airborne invader before his boots touched
ground, before he could hurl the grenades which – so the Air
Ministry warned – he held in each hand (an impossibility, as we
shall see). The public soon had, if not the chance, at least the
armband which authorized the chance. Four days after the German
assault on the West, Anthony Eden as Secretary of State for War
broadcast an appeal for Local Defence Volunteers. He got a flood
of men; by midsummer, over a million. They were given a better
name, the Home Guard, and a uniform to replace the armband,
and (eventually) weapons. It was largely the threat of paratroops
that inspired this huge response. The menace was part of what
Churchill called the 'veil of the Unknown'; nobody could be sure
of the scale of the danger; at the start of June the Prime Minister
was warning his military adviser, General Ismay, that 'parachutists
may sweep over and take Liverpool or Ireland . . .' When Sir
Edward Grigg, an Under-Secretary at the War Office, advised the

Commons that 'imminent peril may descend on us from the skies at any moment', he was telling the nation what it already knew.

Another nightmare which the B.E.F. survivors brought back from France was the Ju87, the Stuka divebomber. It had gained a ferocious reputation when it was used as a kind of advance artillery in support of the German army. It was an extraordinary weapon. General Ernst Udet, who was Chief of Supply and Procurement for the Luftwaffe and a daring pilot, was so delighted with it that he invented special whistles, nicknamed Trumpets of Jericho, which were attached to the Stuka's bombs, 'their purpose being to put the fear of God and the Last Judgement into the victims of the attack'. In this they succeeded. One observer described – from personal experience – how the whistling scream 'worked upon the nerves so that they became wrought to the pitch of intolerable tension, whence it is a very short step to panic'. Not a few Allied units took that step.

British soldiers came back from France with frightening accounts of how they were individually targeted by screaming Stukas. This was highly unlikely – no Stuka pilot would waste a bomb on a single soldier – but the 'fury of personal hostility' did much to create the fearful image of the Ju87. Not that the horror of air attack needed any help. By 1939 everyone expected to be bombed, mercilessly, day and night, until there were more corpses than coffins to put them in.

REVENGE, WITH DYNAMITE

CHAPTER EIGHT

Hitler Hops

COUNT Galeazzo Ciano was Mussolini's son-in-law. He became Italy's Foreign Minister in 1936, at the age of thirty-three. He was intelligent, observant, sceptical: a good judge of people. Mussolini's supporters shot him in 1944, a waste of a thoughtful Fascist, who were always thin on the ground. He left a diary, and his comments on the German leaders offer shrewd insights into the way the war was fought. On 18 June 1940 he wrote: 'Hitler is now the gambler who has made a big scoop and would like to get up from the table risking nothing more.' As a one-sentence profile of the man at that stage of the war, that was good. Of course there was more to Hitler than one sentence can describe. Hitler was also a monster, and he was a complicated monster.

Goering could be just as vicious and brutal, but he had a chubby, cheerful face that the German people liked; it helped create a 'good old Hermann' image. Nobody dared think of Hitler as 'good old Adolf'. He rarely smiled in public. His official face was stern and statesmanlike; governing Germany was serious work. Only once did he beam with pleasure and perform a little dance-step in the presence of his staff, and that was on 17 June 1940. It was not because his army had won a great battle – by now battle honours were nothing new to him – it was because he had just heard that France wanted an armistice. So the war was over. Now everything would be perfect.

His staff were astonished by his outburst of emotion. They had never seen Hitler like this before; but then he had never been master of Europe before. He could not contain his joy. He slapped his thigh, and did a little hop. (Hitler's cameraman recorded the event, shooting eight frames; later, John Grierson, a documentary film-maker in the Canadian army, doctored the frames by looping them to invent a foolish-looking dance. But the truth is Hitler merely hopped.)

Next day he went, not to Paris (which was safe enough, an open city occupied by German troops), but to Munich, to meet Mussolini. On the way he collected Goering.

They had been through a lot together. Goering had marched with Hitler in the failed Munich *Putsch* of 1923, had been badly wounded, shot in the thigh and the groin; now the long struggle seemed worthwhile. The war was won. They embraced. 'I shall come to an understanding with England,' Hitler told him, and Goering was delighted. 'Now at last there will be peace,' he agreed.

More than peace: harmony. Hitler surprised, and almost certainly disappointed, Mussolini by remarking that the British Empire was 'a force for order in the world' and therefore its destruction might not be a good idea. Ciano was there, heard this, found it hard to believe, and turned to Ribbentrop for clarification.

Ribbentrop, Hitler's Foreign Minister, was a curious case. Like his Fuhrer, he won the Iron Cross for bravery in the first war; unlike him he had travelled widely (USA, Canada) and he spoke fluent English. He got a job selling champagne, married the boss's daughter and became very rich; then he got himself adopted by a rich aunt and so became *von* Ribbentrop, like her.

He was something of a fixer. He fixed up the top-level meeting that led to Hitler becoming Chancellor in 1933. He set up the Anglo-German Naval Treaty of 1935. He signed the Anti-Comintern Pact with Japan in 1936. He was endlessly flexible when it came to doing deals. He negotiated the Munich Agreement in late 1938 – the one that guaranteed Czech borders – and renegotiated it in early 1939, when the borders fell. In between, he carried through a declaration of friendship with France, and he crowned everything, one week before Germany invaded Poland, with the treaty that amazed the world: the Soviet-German Non-aggression Pact. All these pacts except the one with Japan were broken, some within months of being signed.

Hitler called Ribbentrop a diplomatic genius. As ambassador to

Britain from 1936 to 1938 he made some friends in high places. He also, fatally, made a horse's ass of himself. He had been on good terms with Edward VIII, who was thought to be sympathetic to the Nazi regime (and certainly behaved as if he might be). After the abdication, Ribbentrop attended a court reception given by George VI where he greeted the new king with a Nazi salute and announced: 'Heil Hitler.' To make his meaning clear, he repeated this, twice. Few ambassadors can have behaved with such crass pomposity. The British mocked him, and so he despised them. In 1939 he assured Hitler that, if Germany attacked Poland, Britain would not go to war. Five months earlier, Britain and France had guaranteed Polish independence. Ribbentrop knew how worthless such guarantees were – he had given several himself – and in this case he was half-right: Britain and France could not keep Poland free. But he was also half-wrong, and the long-term consequence was a Second World War.

So when, in Munich on 18 June 1940, Count Ciano turned to Ribbentrop, he knew he was speaking to a man who would be only too pleased to see Britain follow France into ruin. Ciano asked what was the preferred policy: peace or war? 'He does not hesitate a moment,' Ciano's diary records. 'Peace!'

Hitler wanted Mussolini to know that this was a time for self-restraint. Italy was not the most reliable of partners. When the Axis – the 'Pact of Steel' – was formed in 1938, Italy and Germany had vowed to aid each other immediately in time of war, but a year later Germany invaded Poland and Italy stayed neutral, pleading military weakness. Next year, when Germany was over-running France, Italy joined the war while there was still time to claim some of the spoils. 'We take the field against the plutocratic and reactionary democracies,' Mussolini announced, and his army invaded France: 32 Italian divisions against six French divisions. The attack was stopped at the border town of Menton. Mussolini blamed lack of equipment: 'Even Michelangelo had need of marble to make statues. If he had only clay, he would have become a potter.'

When France surrendered, the Italian army made better progress and occupied a slice of her territory. Mussolini had great imperial ambitions. He had Libya and Ethiopia. If his armies took Egypt he would soon have Suez and the Sudan. He had recently annexed Albania. He saw the Mediterranean as Italy's Lake. Now he wanted Corsica and the French colony of Tunisia. This was totally at odds with Hitler's plan for a magnanimous peace. Mussolini left Munich virtually empty-handed.

Hitler was not about to dismember France. He planned an armistice which would demonstrate to the British that he could make peace as skilfully as he made war. Hitler was practising moderation. He had faked it often enough in the past. Now his act had to be genuine, at least temporarily so. It did not come easily.

CHAPTER NINE

Hitler Declares Peace

IF Hitler's attitude towards Britain seemed restrained, it soon became almost apologetic.

The Luftwaffe's war on Britain in June 1940 – immediately after Dunkirk – was puzzling rather than frightening. In the first week, about fifty Heinkel bombers came over on three nights, wandered about, did a little bombing, mainly at airfields which they missed as often as not, killed a few, disrupted the sleep of many, and went home. Then nothing, until 18 June, by which time France had capitulated and the Luftwaffe returned to its regular but scattered attacks. It was all a far cry from the pounding by massed ranks of aircraft in the Blitzkrieg against France.

The purpose of the plan is still obscure; maybe the Heinkels were just probing Britain's defences. They learned that they risked being shot down if they flew low enough for searchlights to catch them; but the higher they flew, the harder it was for them to find and hit their target. In the historian Telford Taylor's words: 'A night raid was like a boxing match between two blind men . . .' Both sides needed better aids: radio and radar.

Meanwhile, RAF Bomber Command was roaming around the skies of Germany, setting off the sirens, robbing the people of their sleep, and making a liar of Goering. He had promised them that no enemy bomber would fly over the Fatherland. 'If they do,' he said jovially, 'you can call me Meyer.' It loses something in translation. *My name is mud* is closer to the spirit.

Bomber Command's night operations were as hit-and-miss as the Luftwaffe's (until 1942 its offensive killed more RAF aircrew than German civilians) but the hits were galling. On 5/6 June 1940, 92 bombers found targets in France and Germany, especially Hamburg, where ten fires were started and 16 people killed. Next night, 24 Hampden bombers visited Hamburg again: five fires, 16 dead. On 7/8 June, 24 Hampdens bombed an oil refinery at Hanover. On that and the next three nights, a total of 336 bomber sorties hit various targets in Germany and France. On 11/12 June, 18 Wellington bombers carried out incendiary raids on the Black Forest, but the trees would not burn. On 14/15 June, 16 Wellingtons went to the far south of Germany and some may have hit their targets; others went too far and bombed neutral Switzerland: Shirer's wife was living in Geneva and her house shook from the blast. Bomber Command rested for two nights, and then sent 139 aircraft to several parts of northern Germany and the industrial Ruhr. Twenty high-explosive bombs hit the centre of Cologne, sank a cargo ship and killed six people. And so it went on.

The greatest damage was to Goering's prestige. Towards the end of June he urged Hitler to respond with massive retaliation on English cities: damage enormously greater than German towns had suffered. 'Give them back ten bombs for every one of theirs,' he urged.

Hitler dismissed the idea just as briskly as he had rejected Milch's plan for an airborne invasion. Colonel Warlimont (Chief of Planning for the Wehrmacht High Command) was present. He recalled that Hitler found the British raids hard to understand. They were 'senseless bombings . . . which the RAF might be undertaking on its own'. Warlimont kept note of Hitler's opinions:

> 'He thought it quite possible that the British government was so shaken by Dunkirk that it had temporarily lost its head, alternatively that the reason for the attacks on the civilian population was that the British bombers had inaccurate bomb sights and were flown by untrained crews. In any case he thought we should wait before taking countermeasures.'

Hitler guessed right about the inaccurate bombsights and wrong about the untrained crews. But his whole attitude is oddly hesitant. What makes it even stranger is that he had already ordered exactly what Goering was now requesting.

A month earlier, on 24 May 1940, Hitler had issued Fuhrer Directive No. 13. This reversed Directive No. 9, the one that had selected siege and blockade as the way to bring down Britain. Directive No. 13 ordered a large-scale air war on England 'as soon as sufficient forces are available'. The timing was curious: on 24 May his Panzer divisions had come to a halt in Belgium, and German forces in France had been checked by a British counter-attack at Arras. The war was in Europe, not over England. What was Hitler thinking of?

The answer is that he wanted what Goering wanted, a month later: revenge. Directive No. 13 spoke of a 'crushing attack in retaliation for the British raids in the Ruhr area'. These had been few and ineffective, but they damaged German pride and they angered Hitler. He reacted impulsively and emotionally. His Directive was not a thought-out strategy to finish off Britain; it was a bad-tempered answer to a few bombs on the Ruhr. It was just words. Hitler's words might mean something or nothing. You had to wait and see.

When he turned down Goering's plea for retaliatory air strikes in June, and suggested that RAF bombing might quite possibly have happened because 'the British government was so shaken by Dunkirk that it has temporarily lost its head', Hitler looked like a man groping for something to say that will justify his position, which was: England will make peace. His position is unalterable and it must be true, because Hitler has commanded it. This is a circular argument, and therefore cannot be defeated. Reason is useless.

The truth was that Hitler's mind was elsewhere. The big Armistice signing at Compiègne, the climax of his life, was only days away. As Telford Taylor has said, a swift, cheap and exhilarating victory is not conducive to sober reflection on the consequences. 'For the British, Dunkirk and Compiègne supplied the adrenalin that stimulated a vast outpouring of energy. Among the Germans, these same events induced a rosy daze that lasted through the crucial weeks of June and July.' Nothing illustrates this better than Hitler's gossipy meeting with Admiral Raeder on 20 June at his rustic headquarters in the Belgian village of Brûly-de-Pesche.

The discussion ranged far and wide: as far as the French naval bases at Dakar in West Africa and Madagascar in East Africa; as far north as Trondheim in Norway; even further, to Iceland. The

German navy had always yearned to escape from the North Sea and exercise some real blue-water power. Now that France was defeated, Raeder liked the look of Dakar as a naval base, excellent for control of the South Atlantic. Similarly, Madagascar would make a fine base on the Indian Ocean. France could be given part of Portuguese Angola in exchange. Hitler welcomed these ideas, although he had his own plan 'to use Madagascar for settling the Jews under French supervision'.

As for Iceland: Raeder was against a proposal to occupy it. What he really needed was stronger air protection for the Trondheim naval base. He had requested this, but all he got was a crudely offensive telegram from Goering telling him to mind his own business. Raeder read it aloud. Hitler was non-committal: part of his divide-and-conquer policy. They talked about new U-boats. Raeder had been promised them but the building programme was constantly delayed. (Goering's influence again.) Raeder was assured that all his demands had been approved. (This did not guarantee that they would all be met, and in fact they never were.) Finally the two men exhausted their global aims and turned to a local chore: Britain. The admiral missed no tricks; he ran through his invasion agenda: transport ships, mine barriers, landing areas, landing craft, the French fleet neutralized, air superiority. Hitler was not enthusiastic. It was a high-risk, heavy-loss operation. He was always acutely sensitive to his popularity back home. Success had made it. Failure – or costly success – might undo it.

'How can we take on such casualties after conquering France with none to speak of?' he asked. And when Raeder urged that the Luftwaffe start bombing British naval bases to destroy ships in the yards, Hitler said he was contemplating 'taking such action soon'. That might mean anything. It turned out to mean nothing.

When Raeder revealed that the German navy had no landing craft, and that the best he could hope for was forty-five seaworthy barges in two weeks' time, Hitler was not disturbed. Yet it meant that there would be no invasion this month or next month, perhaps not even this summer. Hitler was no sailor. 'On land I am a lion,' he often said, 'but with the water, I don't know where to begin.'

*　　*　　*

People tend to see the world not as it is, but as they wish it were; and dictators suffer from this fallacy to a greater degree, since their aides and ambassadors learn to tell their leader what he would like to hear.

In June 1940, Hitler saw many signals that Britain was edging towards peace. His Foreign Ministry knew of various neutral countries – Sweden, Spain, Switzerland, the Vatican – where men allegedly of goodwill offered to act as honest brokers between London and Berlin. One of the more exotic was Prince Max of Hohenlohe-Langenberg. He met David Kelly, the British Minister in Berne, four times. The prince said he brought an offer from the German Foreign Ministry. It was always the same offer. If Britain gave Germany a free hand in Europe, then Germany would guarantee not to trouble the British Empire. Kelly showed keen interest, but nothing more. He was playing for time. As he said in his memoirs: 'It was obvious that every day gained for the production of Spitfires and the training of crews was priceless.'

Kelly and the prince talked of mutual friends in England, members of the government who (Berlin liked to think) were appeasers. Lord Halifax, the Foreign Secretary, was the most important, but Chamberlain too was in Churchill's War Cabinet, and Hitler definitely remembered *their* meetings with pleasure. An even bigger figure who might lead a campaign for peace was Lloyd George, prime minister in the first war, a pacifist in the 1930s, a man who, after Hitler's smash-and-grab of Poland, had dared to tell the Commons that Hitler's peace offering was worth considering. Nobody agreed. Lloyd George's political influence evaporated. He refused to serve in Churchill's government. ('I am not going in with this gang. There will be a change. The country does not realize the peril it is in.') As long as Hitler dreamed that the British people would rise, overthrow Churchill and demand peace, he could name the two puppet leaders he would need. Lloyd George would be installed as Prime Minister and the Duke of Windsor would be made king once more.

The Duke had escaped from France to Spain, then to Portugal. Hitler's certainty that Britain would give up can be measured by a giddy plan of Ribbentrop's that involved bribing the Duke with fifty million Swiss francs to join the German side; if that failed, to kidnap him. Both men – Lloyd George and the Duke – had burnt their boats; even as puppets they would have nothing to offer their countrymen. Hitler never understood the British or their political system. When he looked across the Channel, he saw what he wanted to see. He saw a country that had backed down or lost in Czechoslovakia, Poland, Norway, Belgium and France. She would back down now. Peace was her only option, as surrender had been the only option for France.

Even before that surrender, Hitler had told a correspondent of the *New York Journal-American* on 14 June that he earnestly desired a peaceful Anglo-German settlement as soon as it could be arranged. And after Hitler's hop of joy on 17 June, his top priority was the Armistice signing. Britain could wait.

CHAPTER TEN

That's My Meat

IN the summer of 1940, Hitler was widely regarded as a supreme master-planner. His conquests were military stepping-stones, each coldly calculated to lead to a greater triumph. We know now that this was not so.

Hitler was a brilliant improviser, usually in conflict with his generals. He had wanted to invade the West immediately after the Polish campaign, on 12 November 1939, but there were rainstorms and the attack was postponed to 19 November; postponed again to 22 November; again to 3 December; to 9 December; to 11 December; to 17 December; always because of poor flying weather. Postponed to 1 January 1940, then to the period 9–14 January. The next planned date was 17 January. A week beforehand, a German aeroplane crashed in Belgium. It carried secret orders and maps of the attack on the West. Hitler was furious, cancelled everything, and blamed Goering, who transferred the blame: heads rolled; or rather, deputy heads rolled. Goering sought the help of a clairvoyant, who told him the secret documents had been destroyed; so all was well after all. Hitler, calm again, cancelled the cancellation. Fog rolled in: another postponement, to 20 January. (There were 16 in all.) The weather failed to improve. He called the whole thing off until the spring.

Now, in mid-June 1940, this much-postponed offensive (which his generals never liked) had suddenly, unexpectedly rushed him to the peak of his career: revenge for the Treaty of Versailles which had humiliated and punished Germany in 1919.

If one emotion bound the German people to Hitler it was hatred of Versailles. He used its power from the start of his political career. In 1922 Goering was at a small meeting of the newly-formed Nazi party. Later, he recalled what Hitler said:

> 'You've got to have bayonets to back up your threats. Well, *that* was what I wanted to hear. He wanted to build up a party that would make Germany strong and smash the Treaty of Versailles. "Well," I said to myself, "*that's* the party for me! Down with the Treaty of Versailles, God damn it! That's my meat."'

Two years later, in *Mein Kampf* Hitler analyzed the art of propaganda:

> The receptivity of the great masses is very limited, their intelligence is small, but their power of forgetting is enormous . . . [Therefore] all effective propaganda must be limited to a very few points and must harp on these slogans until the last member of the public understands what you want him to understand by your slogan.

Hitler never let anyone forget that he wanted a Germany strong enough to smash Versailles. He told them what they knew: that it was a 'slave-treaty', unjustly imposed on a nation that had not been defeated: the Western Allies had never fought on German territory and the German army had been betrayed by a 'stab in the back' from a cowardly government. Germany had been blamed for everything; had been sent home, people said, 'with a dunce's cap on its head'. Versailles had stripped Germany of her colonies, her armed forces, her merchant navy; had taken away Alsace-Lorraine, Schleswig, part of Silesia; had sliced Prussia in two. She was made to pay for the damage she had done.

'Squeeze the German orange until the pips squeak,' Lloyd George had said, but that was in the last days of the war, and he soon calmed down. In the 1920s, reparations were often renegotiated and always they were scaled down, until in 1932 the whole debt was cancelled. But A.J.P. Taylor, in *The Origins of the Second World War*, got to the heart of the matter:

> Reparations hit every German, or seemed to, at each moment of his existence . . . The business-man in difficulties; the underpaid schoolteacher; the unemployed worker all blamed their troubles on reparations. The cry of a hungry child was a cry against reparations. Old men stumbled into the grave because of reparations. The great inflation of 1923 was attributed to reparations; so was the great depression of 1929.

It was not as simple as that; in fact Taylor has calculated that 'Germany was a net gainer by the financial transactions of the nineteen-twenties; she borrowed far more from private American investors (and failed to pay back) than she paid in reparations.' But the German people *thought* it was as simple as that; and Hitler exploited their loathing of Versailles from first to last.

Life in Nazi German could be bleak. In Berlin, a week *before* the outbreak of war, William Shirer noted the new scale of food rations per person per week:

meat	–1½ pounds
sugar	– 10 ounces
marmalade	– 4 ounces
coffee (or substitute)	– 2 ounces

The soap ration of four and a half ounces had to last a month. There were also ration cards for shoes, cloth and coal. Four months later, the government decreed no baths except on Saturdays and Sundays. Petrol was scarce. Toilet paper was very scarce. A Berliner recorded: '"Shopping" these days means essentially food shopping. Everything is rationed and it takes time, as most shops have long queues.'

Berliners grumbled about rationing and (like Londoners) feared bombing, but Hitler had promised the German people revenge for 1919 and that bought their loyalty. On 22 June 1940 he delivered revenge, and as he did so he made the French pay a few emotional reparations for all the pain of Versailles.

CHAPTER ELEVEN

Afire With Scorn

FRANCE was made to surrender at the exact spot where Germany had been made to surrender, 22 years before: in a pleasant clearing of the Forest of Compiègne, north of Paris.

Every detail was stage-managed to complete the French humiliation. The terms of the Armistice document seemed reasonable, but that was not important – Hitler could (and did) break them if he wished. What mattered was the style of the occasion. The 1918 ceremony had taken place in Marshal Foch's private railroad dining car, later kept in a French museum. German army engineers tore out a wall, hoisted the railroad car through the hole, and placed it back on the site.

Hitler's motorcade arrived at 3.15 p.m. He brought with him Ribbentrop, Hess, and the commanders-in-chief of his army, navy and air force. The cars stopped at the entrance to an avenue which was dominated by a statue celebrating the restoration of Alsace-Lorraine to France in 1918. Shirer, covering the occasion for CBS, knew that the statue showed the great sword of the Allies, 'its point sticking into a large, limp eagle, representing the old Empire of the Kaiser'; but now the whole monument was invisible under a mass of German flags with big swastikas. Hitler strode slowly along the avenue and into the clearing. This was a circle about two hundred yards across, ringed with tall oaks, cypresses and pines. The afternoon was sunny. He paused while his personal flag was raised in the centre.

Nearby was a granite block, standing three feet high. Hitler, followed by his party, walked over to it. The inscription, in massive letters, read:

HERE ON THE ELEVENTH OF NOVEMBER 1918 SUCCUMBED THE
CRIMINAL PRIDE OF THE GERMAN EMPIRE . . . VANQUISHED BY
THE FREE PEOPLES WHICH IT TRIED TO ENSLAVE

Shirer's binoculars gave him a perfect view of Hitler's face: 'It is
afire with scorn, anger, hate, revenge, triumph.' Then Shirer captured a special moment, Hitler playing Hitler, pure theatre:

> He swiftly snaps his hands on his hips, arches his shoulders, plants his feet
> wide apart. It is a magnificent gesture of defiance, of burning contempt for
> this place now and all that it has stood for in the twenty-two years since it
> witnessed the humbling of the German Empire.

The French delegates arrived at 3.30 p.m. Everyone went into
the dusty old railroad car. The representatives sat on opposite sides
of a wooden table, just as in 1918. Hitler took the chair which the
Allied commander, Marshal Foch, had sat in. He didn't stay long:
twelve minutes: just long enough to hear the reading of the preamble. Then he stood up, saluted, and left them to the dull,
detailed discussions. His party strode more briskly back along the
avenue, past a guard of honour, and the band struck up 'Deutschland, Deutschland über Alles'. The motorcade departed.

Goebbels' Ministry of Propaganda broadcast the full story of the
Armistice, emphasizing the generosity and magnanimity of its
terms, a message intended more for England than for France, and
somewhat spoiled when the programme ended with Goebbels'
favourite marching song, 'Wir fahren gegen Engelland', a Luftwaffe march with the pounding chorus, 'Then we strike, then we
strike, then we strike at England!'

As soon as the documents were signed and the delegates
departed, a unit of German army engineers set to work to transport
the railroad car to Berlin. Before they left, they dynamited the big
granite monument.

After the Armistice, Hitler left his Belgian village (too many gnats)
and moved his headquarters to a small town in the Black Forest,
codenamed Tannenburg. Here he rested for ten happy days, keeping his generals at arm's length, sightseeing, entertaining a few
guests with picnics and monologues on global politics. One lucky
visitor was Secretary of State Otto Meissner. The time had come,

Hitler told him, for a peace proposal to Britain on a grand and generous scale. At night, while his adjutants enjoyed the local tipple, iced punch with wild strawberries in it, he worked on the first draft of a big speech he planned to make to the Reichstag.

Between 23 June and 11 July, there were no Fuhrer Conferences with Raeder or Brauchitsch, C-in-Cs of the navy and army. (Goering rarely attended them.) The supreme commander was recharging his batteries. He could afford to: with victories in Poland, Norway, and now Holland, Belgium and France behind him, he had earned the right to consider an offer from Britain. It was just a matter of time, of recognizing what was best for both sides. Hitler told Walter Hewel, Ribbentrop's liaison officer, that he didn't want to conquer England. 'I want to come to terms with her, I want to force her to accept my friendship . . .' It was a classic case of Hitler's ability to carry contradictory ideas in his head at the same time: force and friendship.

At the end of June, General Jodl – usually a reliable megaphone for Hitler's views – wrote a six-page memorandum on 'The Continuation of the War against England'. It stated, as a given truth, that Germany's final victory was certain. Britain must offer a ceasefire; that would be the cherry on Hitler's cake. There were ways to hasten this: siege, or terror attacks, or – third and definitely last – invasion. The Luftwaffe would delete the RAF. Then it would destroy all stores of food and deliver terror attacks. Invasion would be mere occupation, because the air war would 'paralyze and finally break the will of the people to resist and thereby force their government to capitulate.' That must be what Hitler meant by forced friendship.

CHAPTER TWELVE

Neutral Gear

A T their narrowest, the Straits of Dover are 18 miles wide. From Cap Gris Nez on a clear day you can see Dover. On a very clear day you can see the town hall. German troops built a viewing platform on the hillside at Cap Gris Nez. So many admirals, generals and field marshals came here that it was nicknamed the Holy Mount. Using stereoscopic periscopes, those officers with good sight could read the clock on the town hall; or so it was said. Certainly, as the summer wore on, they could spot the fall of shells from the huge coastal guns installed nearby. And inevitably they contemplated invasion.

The itch reached Wehrmacht High Command. One of its planners, General von Lossberg, recalled the feeling that two million victorious troops could not be left idle, not with the chalk cliffs of Dover in sight. Exalted by their success, they 'came to believe themselves capable of things that no one even dared to think of before the West Offensive. Thus, more out of the mood at the front than from the sober evaluation of the Armed Forces Leadership, the thought was born to land in England.'

Decision by mood: this is not standard operating procedure in any army.

Lossberg was wrong. When it came to making strategic decisions, Hitler's mood was the only one that counted. He was the engine that drove the German war machine. For the first half of June he ignored Britain and concentrated on France. After the fall of France the engine slipped into neutral, and almost nothing new got done until July. It was a curious spell, a blend of anticlimax and self-congratulation while each of the Armed Services went its own sweet way.

The navy worked on a study of invasion possibilities, not because Admiral Raeder liked the idea but so as to be ready to pre-empt any stupid proposals from elsewhere. Wehrmacht High Command did some preliminary work, too. The army had its hands full, taking on the administration of Belgium and Occupied France while it tried to follow Hitler's orders to demobilize *and* to create fifteen new mechanized divisions. There was a severe shortage of motor transport. Demobilizing infantry would not create trucks.

It was a headache, and it left little time to solve the problem of Britain. If it *was* a problem. Hitler is said to have told General Jodl, 'The English have lost the war, but they haven't yet noticed it; one must give them time, and they will soon come around.' For Germany, this was the ideal strategic position: no need to go to any great effort; the enemy must approach the victor; Britain had no alternative. As Jodl (echoing Hitler) put it in a memorandum, the final German victory was only a matter of time, and 'Germany can therefore choose a course of action that spares her strength and avoids risks.' Everything – even the choice of weapons – was in Germany's favour. Of course Britain would sue for peace. She would be foolish not to.

THE HEIGHT OF FOLLY

CHAPTER THIRTEEN

Heil Germania!

IN his biography of Hitler, *A Study in Tyranny*, Alan Bullock writes that the Fuhrer constantly exalted force over the power of ideas, and the sole theme of the Nazi revolution was domination.

Hitler would have disputed that.

Bullock points to 'this emptiness, this lack of anything to justify the suffering he caused rather than his own monstrous and ungovernable will which makes Hitler both so repellent and so barren a figure'.

Hitler would have shrugged off *monstrous, ungovernable* and *repellent* – he had been called worse than that – but he would have taken the strongest exception to *barren*. Far from being empty (he would have argued), he was full to overflowing with plans to make Berlin – renamed Germania – the most beautiful city in Europe, followed by the renewal on a magnificent scale of Hamburg, Bremen, Leipzig, Cologne, Essen and Chemnitz, with others in due course: over forty 'Fuhrer cities' in all. There would be more, in Norway for instance, and all Europe would be joined by a superb network of *autobahnen*. In March 1941, when the Luftwaffe was still bombing Britain by night, Hitler is reported to have regretted that 'all these magnificent building ideas could not yet be executed because Churchill was robbing him of a third of his time.' From Hitler's point of view, Churchill, by not settling for peace, was the real vandal. And time was short. Hitler was 51, and he did not expect to live much longer.

After the signing of the Armistice, Hitler sent a message to the German people, congratulating their soldiers on 'an heroic battle against a brave foe. Their deeds will be entered in history as the most glorious victory of all times.' He humbly thanked the Lord for his blessing, ordered the display of flags throughout the Reich for ten days and the ringing of bells for seven days. Then he took a long holiday.

First he took a bath in nostalgia. He rounded up a couple of First War comrades – one was his old sergeant, Max Amann – and they spent a few days happily revisiting the Flanders battlefields, wandering through the trenches now kept as memorials, talking about which attack happened where. Hitler did the talking; he knew everything. Then, on 28 June, he rewarded himself with what he called 'the dream of my life' when he visited Paris, and he did all the talking there, too. Hitler was a poor conversationalist and a bad listener.

With him he took to Paris his two favourite architects, Speer and Giesler, plus the artist Arno Breker. This was no victory parade. It was a cultural tour. There was a small entourage, only a dozen generals and adjutants. Everyone was in uniform, including the artists, but Hitler wore a snow-white topcoat, with no insignia, perhaps as a gesture of artistic purity.

They saw the usual sights: the Opéra; then past the Madeleine and across the Place de La Concorde to the Champs-Élysées and the Arc de Triomphe. Too small, Hitler said. On to the Trocadero, the Palais de Chaillot, the Invalides. He stood for a long time at Napoleon's tomb. Then the Louvre, Notre Dame, the Place des Vosges: all disappointing. The Rue de Rivoli: better. Another look at the Opéra, then to Montmartre for a panoramic view, and the tour was over. Hitler had done the architectural splendours of Paris in three hours, a visit which would be of no importance to history except for what he said that evening when he received Speer alone. 'Wasn't Paris beautiful?' he exclaimed. 'But Berlin must be made far more beautiful.' And he ordered Speer to press on with his rebuilding plans more vigorously than ever.

Architecture was Hitler's great love; indeed, love is not strong enough, it was a grand passion, an obsession. Compared with Hitler's vision for Berlin, Britain's fate was a mere footnote to an old story. Great German architecture was not the reward of Hitler's war, it was the *purpose* of his war. He put it differently: raising big buildings was for the greater glory of Germania, the name he chose for the new Berlin; and Speer was the man to make it all happen. At this stage their collaboration distracted Hitler from the main job, which should have been Britain. It makes Speer a major player in the events of 1940.

Magnificent building ideas had been on Hitler's mind long before 1937, when he appointed Albert Speer Inspector-General of Building for the Reich Capital. Speer was probably the best brain in Hitler's inner circle. With most people, Hitler found it difficult to relax and share a discussion, but he enjoyed Speer's company. Some said Speer was the son Hitler never had. He was certainly the architect Hitler had dreamed of becoming.

Timing is everything. In 1933, the year Hitler came to power, Speer was a young architect, not known, not successful. By luck as much as anything, he got the chance to redesign the May Day rally of the Party at Tempelhof Field in Berlin. He met Hitler and was excited by the 'something' uplifting in him, and Hitler liked talking architecture with a man whose tastes agreed with his.

Next year Hitler gave him the entire Nuremburg Party Rally to design, and Speer showed his brilliance. He persuaded Hitler to switch the big meetings from day to night: Speer had noticed that too many Party members were fat, or couldn't march in step, or both. He surrounded the arena with a ring of 150 searchlights, aimed vertically to create domes of brilliance, miles high; there were thirty thousand banners; it was a magical experience, a National Socialist cathedral of light. It exalted Hitler, it magnified his presence and made him seem godlike (which many Germans, especially women, already believed him to be).

Suddenly, Speer was Hitler's architect. He designed the new German embassy in London and the gold-medal-winning German pavilion at the 1937 Paris World Exhibition. His masterplan for future Rallies at Nuremburg proposed a Grand Avenue one kilometre long leading to the Märzfeld (for military displays) overlooked by a goddess of victory 50 feet higher than the Statue of Liberty. It had a Congress Hall modelled on the Colosseum, and two arenas, and a Great Stadium which could hold 400,000 spectators. All was planned on a massive scale. There was to be a Reich eagle with a wingspan of 250 feet.

When Speer first met Hitler he had a few small designs to his name. 'For a commission to build a great building,' he wrote in his memoirs, 'I would have sold my soul like Faust.' In 1937 Hitler commissioned him to rebuild the heart of Berlin and create some of the biggest buildings in the world. He had unlimited powers, unlimited money, unlimited staff. The only person he answered to was Hitler. Speer was 31.

Hitler gave him an office next door to the Reich Chancellery – not so that Speer could be summoned more quickly, but so that Hitler could visit Speer more easily. According to Joachim Fest, 'In the following years, Hitler often went across to see Speer, sometimes almost daily, usually after nightfall. Bent over the drawing tables, surrounded by elevations and countless sketches on the walls, many of them by Hitler himself, they were lost for hours on end shaping the Berlin of the future.'

Language fails. When one tries to describe this new city, 'big' is not big enough, and 'huge' and 'vast' become diminished by sheer repetition. Size was everything. Berlin must exceed every other capital; a favourite phrase of Hitler's was that the new Berlin would make buildings like St Peter's in Rome 'seem like toys'.

The core of the whole project was, like Nuremberg, a grand avenue. When Hitler briefed Speer he said, 'The Champs Élysées is three hundred and thirty feet wide . . . we'll make our avenue seventy-odd feet wider.' He wanted the avenue to be two-and-a-half times the length of the Champs Élysées. This would have made it five miles long.

At one end was the Southern Railway Station. When State visitors stepped out of the station, Speer wrote, 'they would be overwhelmed, or rather stunned, by the urban scene and thus the power of the Reich. The station plaza, 3,300 feet long and 1,000 feet wide, was to be lined with captured weapons, after the fashion of the Avenue of Rams which leads from Karnak to Luxor.'

Half a mile away, at the far end of the plaza, the visitor would see a triumphal arch. Napoleon's Arc de Triomphe is 160 feet high.

Hitler's was to be 386 feet high (and 550 feet wide and 392 feet deep, making it almost fifty times the size of the Arc de Triomphe). 'Sighting through the 260-foot opening,' Speer wrote, 'the arriving traveller would see at the end of a three-mile vista the street's second great triumphal structure rearing out of the haze of the metropolis . . .'

This was to be the Great Assembly Hall, the biggest domed building in the world, 'into which St Peter's Cathedral in Rome would have fitted several times over.' The designs of the hall and the arch were based on sketches which Hitler had made in 1925. 'I never doubted that some day I would build these two edifices,' he said as he gave the drawings to Speer.

The size of the Great Assembly Hall was almost beyond imagination. At its peak it was 726 feet high. Its dome rested on a rectangle of granite whose sides were to be 1,040 feet long and 244 feet high. Berlin has sandy soil; it was estimated that 3.9 million cubic yards of concrete footings would be needed to take the colossal weight.

Inside, the domed hall would be free-standing, with no internal struts or columns to interrupt its astonishing space. The diameter was 825 feet, room for 150,000 people. It was, Speer said, 'essentially a place of worship', and it had only one sculptural feature: 'on a marble pedestal 46 feet in height, perched . . . a gilded German eagle with a swastika in its claws.' And here is where it all began to go wrong. The eagle was a 'symbol of sovereignty . . . the very fountainhead of Hitler's grand boulevard' and beneath it would be the podium from which he would address the peoples of his empire; but when Speer visualized it he saw only failure. 'Under that vast dome Hitler dwindled to an optical zero.'

Speer and Hitler planned many other giant buildings: the Soldiers' Hall above an immense, flame-lit crypt where Germany's field marshals would lie in perpetual state; the Fuhrer Palace, bang in the middle of Berlin and covering twenty-two million square feet (visitors to Hitler's personal office would have had to walk a quarter of a mile); Goering's headquarters which, with an 800-foot frontage and a similar wing for the ballrooms, would have had a volume of 754,000 cubic yards – the plans included a four-storey flight of stairs and a two-and-a-half-acre roof garden with swimming pools, tennis courts and a summer theatre; and eleven ministry buildings along the avenue, as well as a Town Hall, a War Academy, and separate headquarters for the Navy, the Armed Forces High Command, and Berlin Police; and much more. All were designed on the same mammoth scale. When Speer commissioned (for Hitler's benefit) an architectural model of the avenue and buildings, it was a hundred feet long.

Immensity defeats itself. When everything is too big, it ceases to impress and begins to depress. Years later, Speer recognized 'the fatal flaw' in his and Hitler's designs: they had 'lost all sense of proportion'. This was not architecture; it was elephantiasis; it was ideology via stone, as if Hitler believed he could create a new Germany from the drawing-board. Speer was swept along by the intoxication of power. It took a war to make him realize that he had been collaborating with a megalomaniac who called himself an 'artist-politician'.

Speer and Hitler were much more than architect and client; they were almost colleagues. Speer knew that, in his youth, Hitler 'had carefully studied the plans of Vienna and Paris, and he revealed an amazing memory for these'. He could draw the great buildings of Vienna in correct proportions. He regarded Haussmann – who had rebuilt Paris – as 'the greatest city planner in history, but hoped that I would surpass him.' Each man respected the other. 'Hitler perpetually drew sketches of his own . . . he drew outlines, cross-sections, and renderings to scale. An architect could not have done better.' Speer refused to take more credit than he believed he deserved. He signed the plans for the great domed hall: 'Developed on the basis of the Fuhrer's ideas.'

Total cost of rebuilding Berlin was anyone's guess. Long afterwards, Speer's estimate was between 16 and 24 billion Deutschmarks at 1970 values, but as Hitler had told him not to worry about cost, the final figure was literally inconceivable.

By 1945 it was all irrelevant. Most of the colossal building ideas were never begun. None was finished, either in Berlin or Nuremberg. The capital was utterly reshaped, but it was by Allied bombing. Speer had toiled for five years, ceaselessly planning and designing. When the war was over, the only evidence of all this effort to be found in Berlin was a few street lamps.

NOT IN THE SCRIPT

Chapter Fourteen

Thunder in the Mediterranean

'NEVER has a great nation been so naked before her foes,' Churchill wrote of Britain in June 1940. Dunkirk had kept the army alive, but where were its arms? Overseas, largely. Scattered about France were 7,000 tons of ammunition, 2,300 artillery pieces, 8,000 machine guns, 400 anti-tank guns, 90,000 rifles, and countless motor vehicles. The army had almost no field artillery and only 500 heavy guns, 50 infantry tanks and 100 cruiser tanks: this, to defend the whole of Britain.

The good news was that on 1 June, President Roosevelt ordered the American army and navy to report what arms they could spare; on 3 June the army Chief of Staff, General Marshall, approved the list; packing began that same day; and by 11 June the material – rifles, machine guns, field guns, ammunition – was being loaded on to British freighters. The bad news was it would take nearly a month to cross the Atlantic.

Outwardly, Britain was determined, as the Prime Minister had said, to fight on the beaches, on the landing grounds, in the fields and in the streets, and in the hills, and never to surrender. Inwardly there were many fears, especially in the case of men who had fought in France. On 2 July, General Alan Brooke spent the day with the 50th Division in Hampshire, Dorset and Somerset. Afterwards he wrote: 'The more I see the nakedness of our defences the more appalled I am! Untrained men, no arms, no transport, and no equipment. And yet there are masses of men in uniform in this country but they are mostly untrained, why I cannot think after 10 months of war. The ghastly part of it is that I feel certain that we can only have a few more weeks left before the Boche attacks!'

Alan Brooke kept this to himself. Defence Regulation 18b prohibited acts that might spread 'alarm and despondency'. You could go to jail for that. (Germany had its own 18b; between 1941 and 1945, it executed 15,000 German civilians as parasites or defeatists.) Alan Brooke put on a brave face and hid his worries in his diary. As a serving officer he was forbidden to keep one but he did. So did General Ironside. He had a different slant on the chances of invasion. Early in July he wrote: 'The weather still remains very fine, worse luck. We could do with storms.'

A storm of a different sort was boiling up on 3 July. That day, the Director of Intelligence at the War Office warned the Chiefs of Staff of 'a considerable body of evidence which pointed to an invasion of this country at an early date'. The evidence was of increased troop movements, especially parachutists, in Norway, Denmark and Holland, and a gathering of shipping in the Baltic. Also, Hitler had postponed his victory parade in Paris until after 10 July. He might mean to use the occasion to announce a great assault; it was the sort of thing he enjoyed doing.

The War Cabinet met on 3 July and discussed a request from the Chiefs of Staff to begin compulsory evacuation of 19 towns on the east coast, then considered to be the probable landing zone. But the public was jumpy, as witness the number of false alarms claiming that enemy parachutists were landing in various parts of England; and the Cabinet decided that mass evacuations would damage morale at a time when there was precious little to cheer about. The U-boat war was going badly, with shipping losses of over 250,000 tons in May and over 500,000 in June. Churchill had asked America to release 40 or 50 old (but reconditioned) destroyers for convoy duty. Roosevelt couldn't persuade Congress to agree. (It was an election year and isolationist feeling was strong.) In France, Marshal Petain had been advised by his senior generals that 'In three weeks England will have her neck wrung like a chicken'; and that was two weeks ago. There was gloom everywhere, except for the weather, which remained obstinately fine.

But on that day of 3 July, there was thunder in the Mediterranean.

All war is a tragedy. In the American Civil War, President Lincoln rebuked a general for saying that 'only' a few men had been killed in an encounter. Even one man's death, Lincoln said, is a tragedy for someone. If there can be such a thing as a greater tragedy, it happened at the Algerian port of Mers-el-Kebir on 3 July 1940, when friend killed friend, and not by accident.

The train of events went back to 28 March 1940. In the uneasy days of the Phoney War, Britain and France signed a mutual pledge that neither side would make peace without the permission of the other. Three months later, in mid-June, the B.E.F. was back in England, the French army was in full retreat, its command was falling apart, and the government had decamped from Paris to Bordeaux. The French leadership could see only one way to end their disaster – by surrender – and they asked to be released from the pledge. Britain agreed, with one condition: before any armistice discussions, the French fleet must sail direct to British ports. That message was sent from London, but who received it? And did anyone agree to it? The Bordeaux government was demonstrating the truth of the army saying: order, counter-order, disorder. Everyone argued; nobody decided. Perhaps the condition for releasing the pledge got lost in the confusion. The War Cabinet sent more telegrams, seeking confirmation. 'But,' Churchill wrote in his memoirs, 'we were talking to the void.' At the Armistice, most of the French fleet was still within the invader's reach.

The German navy was quick to see an opportunity to grow strong at no cost. Italy would like some free warships, too. It is easy to understand their appetites: the French navy was not only powerful, it was virtually undamaged. A small part of the fleet was at anchor in Portsmouth and Plymouth – two battleships, four light cruisers, eight destroyers, some submarines – and a French battleship and four cruisers were in Egyptian waters, at Alexandria. All those were safe from German hands. The real prizes were in the French colony of Algeria, at Oran and especially its military port of Mers-el-Kebir.

The German navy had two of the most dangerous battlecruisers in the world, *Scharnhorst* and *Gneisenau*. Knowing this, France had recently built two immensely powerful battlecruisers that could outsail and outshoot them: *Dunkerque* and *Strasbourg*. In a telegram to Roosevelt on 12 June, Churchill had foreseen a French collapse and said: 'It would be disastrous if the two big modern ships fell into bad hands.'

With them at Mers-el-Kebir were two French battleships, some light cruisers and several destroyers. Along the coast at Algiers lay seven French cruisers. At Casablanca, and at Dakar in West Africa, were two unfinished battleships. Other warships were at anchor in Toulon. The German navy wanted them, preferably all of them, but especially *Dunkerque* and *Strasbourg*.

Hitler thought otherwise. He ordered that the French navy must not be touched, and this was spelt out very clearly in the terms of the Armistice. He gave his guarantee that no French warship would sail under the German flag.

Admiral Darlan, the Minister of Marine, knew how much Hitler's guarantee was worth. Two days after the Armistice was signed, he sent a coded signal to all French naval commands:

(1) Demobilized ships must remain French, with French crews, in French-controlled ports;
(2) Secret preparations for scuttling must be made;
(3) If the Armistice Commission decided otherwise than paragraph 1, all warships must immediately set sail for the United States or be scuttled. Darlan hammered his message home: *no orders of any foreign admiralty will he obeyed*. And he added an interesting warning: *these orders remain valid, whatever contradictory orders you may receive hereafter, even if signed by me*.

Churchill may have known about Darlan's secret orders. It made no difference. Churchill had been First Lord of the Admiralty in World War One; he remembered the German fast cruisers *Emden*, *Leipzig*, *Dresden* and others, which had caused havoc as commerce raiders from the Atlantic to the Pacific. On 23 June, the day of Hitler's guarantee, the Chiefs of Staff in Washington recommended that, if Germany controlled the French fleet, most of the American fleet would transfer from the Pacific to the Atlantic, a huge strategic switch; and Roosevelt gave his qualified approval. But America was not at war, whilst Britain was fighting for her life. If the *Scharnhorst* and *Gneisenau* were to range the high seas in partnership with the even more powerful *Dunkerque* and *Strasbourg*, they could sink a transatlantic convoy in ten minutes, and its Royal Navy escort too.

And if Britain began losing, not just ships, but whole convoys, then American confidence would also vanish, and any British hope of winning the war would shrivel while the risk of conquest grew large: immediately the German navy absorbed the French fleet, the strength of an invasion force in the Channel could be multiplied.

On the evening of 2 July, the battlecruiser *Hood*, the battleships *Valiant* and *Resolution*, the carrier *Ark Royal*, two cruisers and eleven destroyers sailed from Gibraltar into the Mediterranean. This was Force H. It arrived off Mers-el-Kebir next morning. In command was Vice-Admiral Somerville. One of his officers was Captain Holland, a former naval attaché in Paris and a friend of France. They, and the rest of Force H, had a wretched day ahead of them. Churchill knew it, and he sent Somerville a message that is probably unique in the long history of the Royal Navy:

> You are charged with one of the most disagreeable and difficult tasks that a British admiral has ever been faced with, but we have complete confidence in you and rely on you to carry it out relentlessly.

The Admiralty's orders to Somerville were straightforward. He was to tell the French commander at Mers-el-Kebir, Admiral Gensoul, first that 'it is impossible for us, your comrades up to now, to allow your fine ships to fall into the power of the German or Italian enemy'. After various reassurances ('Should we conquer, we solemnly declare that we shall restore the greatness and territory of France.'), Somerville was to offer Gensoul three options: either sail with us and fight the enemy; or sail to a British port and hand over your ships (the French crews would be repatriated); or sail to a French port in the West Indies where the ships can be demilitarized. 'If you refuse these fair offers, I must, with profound regret, require you to sink your ships within six hours.'

Failing that, Somerville's orders were 'to use whatever force may be necessary to prevent your ships from falling into German or Italian hands'.

There could be only one kind of force.

Somerville sent Captain Holland to negotiate but Admiral Gensoul would not meet him, so Holland sent the ultimatum by messenger. Gensoul replied in writing: the French warships would never fall intact into enemy hands, and force would be met with force. The day dragged on. Gensoul was in an impossible position. Either he disobeyed his commander-in-chief ('No orders of any foreign admiralty will be obeyed') or he went down fighting; and there was no doubt he would go down. His ships were trapped in harbour. They did not have steam up. Some crews had been partly demobilized. *Dunkerque* was docked with her stern to the sea; her forward guns could not be brought to bear on Somerville's Force H. By one account, the British had mined the only usable channel between the French anti-submarine nets.

All morning and afternoon, Captain Holland persisted with a task which he and Somerville found hateful, as did many in London. Gensoul reported his dilemma to the French Admiralty, and got nowhere. At 3 p.m. the French Council of Ministers met, but they were no help either. At 4.15 p.m. Gensoul finally met Holland; their discussion was described as 'frigid'. Gensoul produced Darlan's orders of 24 June. He gave his word of honour that, in the event of any German threat, he would take his ships to Martinique in the West Indies, or to the U.S. But he would not do so *now*, not under the threat of force. It was a brave statement and some would say an acceptable offer, some not. London said not. Gensoul ordered his ships to make steam and clear for action. His crews cheered. They thought they were about to sail with the British.

Somerville had delayed and delayed, begging the Admiralty to relax its ultimatum. Instead, his orders were hardened. If Gensoul did not comply, 'you are to endeavour to destroy repetition destroy ships in Mers-el-Kebir.' At 5.54 p.m. Somerville opened fire. The bombardment lasted about ten minutes. *Dunkerque* was hit in both engine rooms by 15-inch shells, set on fire, torpedoed by aircraft and forced to beach. The battleship *Bretagne* was heavily shelled until she capsized. Her sister ship, the *Provence*, was reduced to a wreck. A destroyer had her stern blown off when a shell hit her depth charges. *Strasbourg* was damaged by a torpedo but escaped to Toulon. (Two years later her crew scuttled her there.) Twelve hundred and ninety-seven French sailors died. Somerville had seen enough. He ceased fire.

While the shells were falling on Oran, all French warships in British ports had been seized in a surprise action, with little resistance. At Alexandria, the French admiral agreed to disarm his ships; their crews went home. At Dakar, the battleship *Richelieu* was attacked and disabled. In due course, warships in the French West Indies were also immobilized. The bulk of the French fleet was now out of Hitler's reach. But what Churchill called 'the deadly stroke' was Oran, as the bombardment became known.

'We all feel thoroughly dirty and ashamed,' Somerville told his wife. Oran was 'the biggest political blunder of modern times and I imagine will rouse the whole world against us'. His disgust was understandable. His analysis was wrong. Oran amazed and impressed the whole world.

Some members of the War Cabinet were fearful of overseas reaction when Britain sank the ships and killed the sailors of the nation she had been fighting alongside only two weeks before. The French Vichy government broke off diplomatic relations; that was predictable. There was talk of declaring war on Britain, and French aircraft stationed in North Africa actually dropped a few bombs on Gibraltar. They did little damage. It was a gesture. By now, Vichy France was firmly in Germany's pocket, and everyone knew it. Churchill, in his memoirs, quotes something told him after the war by a member of the Resistance, later Defence Minister, M. Teitgen. Two families in a village near Toulon had each lost a son – sailors killed by British fire at Oran. For the funeral service, the families asked that the Union Jack should lie on the coffins side by side with the Tricolour, and their wish was granted. The French did not like Oran, but they liked being conquered even less.

Next day, Churchill reported to the Commons what had been done and why: a sombre speech which won him the longest and warmest reception since he became Prime Minister. Fine phrases were well and good; no doubt Britain *would* fight on the beaches, but here was *action*, ruthless and effective action, the best proof of policy.

Militarily, Oran was the day when Britain kept command of the sea. Psychologically, its effects were widespread. Later in 1940, Hitler tried hard to get Spain to end her neutrality and join the Axis. Franco stonewalled. He remembered Oran; perhaps Germany was not unbeatable. Turkey, too, stayed neutral, an attitude that might have been different if the German and Italian navies had ruled the Mediterranean.

There was no need for the War Cabinet to worry about what America thought. Americans discovered a fearlessness and a ferocity in Britain that dissolved all those stories of a nation on its knees, helpless before a looming invader. The Oran action 'immensely impressed Roosevelt with the grim determination as well as the ability of the Churchill government to fight on . . . At table, Roosevelt spoke of it as abundantly justifying the American policy of all-out aid to the British.' Some months later, Harry Hopkins, the President's personal emissary to Churchill, visited England and was a guest at Chequers. 'It was Oran,' he said, 'that had convinced Roosevelt that, in spite of Ambassador Kennedy's defeatist opinions, Britain would continue to fight, as Churchill had promised, if necessary for years and alone.' The 'deadly stroke' had been the most powerful form of propaganda. If Britain was prepared to do this to her ally, what might she do to her enemy?

CHAPTER FIFTEEN

Fuhrer Knows Best

IT sounds better in German: *Donnerschlag*. Thunderclap. That was how Hitler's naval adjutant remembered the explosion of dismay and disbelief when the news of Oran hit Tannenburg. It was incomprehensible, it was *wrong*. This was not what the Fuhrer had ordered. Everyone was waiting for peace feelers from Britain, and instead the French fleet got a broadside from the Royal Navy. Hitler raged. Those present got caught in the fury. Churchill was his main target. For the past month, Hitler had done the decent thing – look at Compiègne, where the Armistice terms were a model for a fair deal with Britain – and now at a stroke Churchill had ruined everything. Tannenburg was wrenched through a psychological half-circle, a painful experience which left everyone looking at a longer war, without any doubt; perhaps a very long war.

This was the moment for the supreme Commander to concede that his peace offensive had failed. Hitler was incapable of admitting that he was wrong, and given the straitjacket of military dictatorship, there was nobody to tell him.

When in doubt, go back to basics. Goebbels cranked up his propaganda machine. The Nazi press urged the British people to hang Winston Churchill in Trafalgar Square. On 6 July, all Berlin turned out to cheer the return of the conquering hero. Their love did not soothe him; he had seen and heard it all before. When he met his commanders-in-chief and their staff officers he raked them as savagely as if they were the British War Cabinet: they were the nearest dogs and so they got kicked.

Clearly it was time for a change, yet the only change Hitler made was to postpone the meeting of the Reichstag where he intended to deliver his hammerblow of a speech, the one he had been working on ever since the Armistice. Then he went to his sprawling chalet, the Berghof, high in the mountains at Obersaltzberg. It was now six weeks since Dunkirk and there was still no sense of urgency.

Hitler soon found comfort in Oran, Ciano noted in his diary. It was reassuring to think that the French and the English were now bitter, permanent enemies, all because Hitler had been wise enough *not* to seize the French fleet. Oran was an act of desperation by Churchill, probably a last act. Peace would come. Nothing had changed.

Hitler clung to that belief for a further sixteen days. It was an extraordinary act of self-deception. Sixteen wasted days made a crucial delay: exactly what Britain needed. Oran sent the loudest possible message and Hitler refused to hear it.

CHAPTER SIXTEEN

The Fuhrer is Puzzled

SPEER had probably the best view of Hitler. Others – Bormann, Goebbels, Hess, Keitel, Jodl – may have been in his presence more often, but Hitler liked and trusted Speer. He may even have been honest with him. In return, Speer worked himself to exhaustion; yet he kept a clear-eyed view of Hitler's lifestyle. His memoirs record:

> In the eyes of the people Hitler was the Leader who watched over the nation day and night. This was hardly so. But Hitler's lax scheduling could be regarded as a life-style characteristic of the artistic temperament.

Artists sleep late, keep people waiting, eat at unusual times, talk too much, watch bad movies, put off work, and stay up until the small hours, talking, talking, talking. That is a brief summary of Hitler's 'lax scheduling' when he retreated from the business of government. His inner circle was familiar with his mood swings. His life was either hectic or lethargic. When it swung into lethargy, everyone had to wait until he emerged.

Hitler encouraged this concept of the Leader, a man turning his back on petty day-to-day problems and consulting his genius in the lofty solitude of his chalet: '. . . by night at the Berghof, I often remain for hours with my eyes open, contemplating from my bed the mountains lit up by the moon. It's at such moments that brightness enters my mind . . . All my great decisions were taken at Obersalzberg.'

After the *Donnerschlag* of Mers-el-Kebir, Hitler spent the next six weeks either in Berlin or at the Berghof, and what is interesting about his decisions is how indecisive most of them were. Hitler didn't seem to be marching towards victory. He seemed to be dawdling towards compromise. The Paris victory parade was cancelled. The Reichstag victory speech was postponed. Invasion was hypothetical, to judge by a Fuhrer Directive issued on 2 July. It said that Hitler had decided a landing in England was possible, given air superiority etc. Date: uncertain. Preparation: immediate – but on the basis that it was only a plan, not a decision.

Possible. Uncertain. This was not so much a Directive as a shuffling of the feet. Hitler didn't even sign it; he left that to Keitel, who was not so much a general as an echo chamber. Meanwhile Halder, a real soldier and Chief of the Army's General Staff, was nudging Leeb, Chief of Army Ordnance, about amphibious tanks. Leeb said he'd been told to forget invasion. Be that as it may, Halder said, 'If political command demands a landing, they will want everything done at top speed.' Halder knew better than to wait for brightness to enter Hitler's mind.

Admiral Raeder came to the Berghof on 11 July. The navy was against an invasion, he said, except as a last resort and then only with air superiority; the navy was for an economic blockade, helped by large air raids on, for instance, Liverpool. Hitler nodded. That nod might mean *I understand*, or *I've heard enough*. It might even mean *I agree, do it*, although that assumption was dangerous. Sometimes Hitler just nodded, as a way of not saying anything.

But they had a cordial discussion about seizing Dakar, and perhaps getting the Canary Islands from Spain in exchange for French Morocco. Raeder came away with authority to build several new battleships. This was a meaningless gesture by Hitler, irrelevant to the war, because it would take years to build battleships. In fact, throughout World War Two, the German navy built nothing bigger than a destroyer.

On 13 July, Brauchitsch and Halder came to the Berghof with briefcases full of the Army's plans for invasion. It could be done, the Army believed, if the other services did their stuff. Hitler told them to start preparations immediately, which was not what he had told Raeder. Then he moved on to something more enjoyable: an armchair tour of the new German empire. The French Chamber and Senate had voted themselves out of existence, turning Pierre Laval into Hitler's puppet and France into Germany's colony.

Hitler wanted 'to draw Spain into the game'. Ribbentrop would offer Gibraltar to Spain as a reward. (Admiral Canaris, head of the Abwehr, was already in Spain, talking to the Spanish army, spying out the British defences, and discovering that the Rock was impregnable.) Hitler had plans for the French and Belgian Congo; Germany had earned a place in the sun. (William Shirer noted next day that 300 SS men in Berlin were learning Swahili, 'the lingua franca of the former German colony in East Africa'.) The Balkans needed some adjustment. Rumania would have to concede territory to Hungary and Bulgaria. The King of Rumania had asked for Hitler's protection: no problem there, then. Mussolini kept offering Italian divisions and squadrons to assist in the conquest of Britain. Hitler suggested that Italy attack Britain elsewhere, in Egypt for instance, 'but it does not matter in the least, Duce, where these various blows will fall'.

That was an amazingly foolish remark to come from 'the greatest Field Commander of all time'. His throwaway line suggested that the British Empire was so fragile that any random attack would succeed. Hitler enjoyed making grand statements to his junior partner in the Axis. And his remark is symptomatic of another characteristic, one that shows itself again and again in 1940. When faced with a baffling problem, Hitler, instead of admitting its seriousness, would often dismiss it as unimportant. In that way his failure disappeared and he did not lose face. In July the problem of Britain was beginning to baffle him. As Halder reported:

> The Fuhrer is greatly puzzled by Britain's persistent unwillingness to make peace. He sees the answer (as we do) in Britain's hope in Russia, and therefore counts on having to compel her by main force to agree to peace.

An alliance between Churchill and Stalin? No doubt Churchill would have done any deal if it weakened the German threat. (Shortly before Hitler attacked Russia, Churchill remarked: 'If Hitler invaded Hell, I would make at least a favourable reference to the Devil in the House of Commons.') But even if Stalin were prepared to shake hands with a descendant of the Duke of Marl-borough, Russia was unlikely to go to war in 1940. She had just *been* to war, with Finland, and the Finns had made the Soviet army look very shabby. Stalin had the Russian commander shot for failure.

With or without Russian involvement, Hitler decreed that his peace offensive must win, because:

> . . . a military defeat of Britain will bring about the disintegration of the British Empire. This would not be of any benefit to Germany. German blood would be shed to accomplish something that would benefit only Japan, the United States and others.

This is a classic example of Hitler's philosophy that what's good for Germany is good for the world. He could not see the picture from the other side of the Channel. In London, Churchill lost no sleep over the possible disintegration of the Empire. It wasn't on his agenda.

CHAPTER SEVENTEEN

Hitler Does the Decent Thing

HITLER worked for a month on his speech to the Reichstag, and when the occasion came it was both a triumph and a flop.

He was already drafting the speech when he moved his head-quarters to Tannenberg, on 29 June. He 'monologued ideas', Walter Ansel writes. 'This speech, he frankly advertised, would point towards his private plan of settlement with Britain.'

A week later, in Berlin, he discussed the current situation with Count Ciano. As often happened at their meetings, Hitler talked a good fight. Ciano recorded: 'He is rather inclined . . . to unleash a storm of wrath and steel upon the English. But the final decision has not been reached, and . . . he is delaying his speech, of which, as he himself puts it, he wants to weigh every word.'

Nothing is static in war: all things are moving at all times. In July the German Army High Command kept moving towards approval of invasion, and on 13 July Hitler, after very little discussion, accepted the Army's recommendations. He wasn't committed to an actual invasion, but the threat might come in handy as a lever for peace. Then came Churchill's speech of 14 July. Hitler should have learned from it, but he did not.

Churchill spoke to the nation, and to America. The Democratic Convention was meeting in Chicago to renominate Roosevelt for a third term. There were isolationists in Chicago who shared Joe Kennedy's belief that Britain was gone, Hitler was rampant, and America should keep all her arms instead of shipping them to Britain to be captured by Germany. Churchill's speech was not a plea for help, it was a battle-cry for freedom:

> We await undismayed the impending assault. Perhaps it will come tonight. Perhaps it will come next week. Perhaps it will never come. We must show

ourselves equally capable of meeting a sudden violent shock or – which is perhaps the harder test – a prolonged vigil.

Now came words that rankled in Berlin and won admiration in Chicago:

> But be the ordeal sharp or long, or both, we shall seek no terms, we shall tolerate no parley; we may show mercy – we shall ask for none . . . Hitler has not yet been withstood by a great nation with a willpower the equal of his own . . . in our island we are in good health and in good heart . . . Let all strive without failing in faith or in duty, and the dark curse of Hitler will be lifted from our age.

Two days later, Hitler signed Fuhrer Directive No. 16. Its preamble was less than Churchillian:

> Since England, despite her hopeless military situation, still shows no sign of readiness to come to an understanding, I have decided to prepare a landing operation against England and if necessary to carry it out.

For the first time the operation had a codename: Sealion. And a deadline: 15 August. But that applied only if the big speech didn't work. Hitler called a session of the Reichstag for 19 July.

He may have genuinely believed that Churchill's leadership was falling apart. Perhaps he had got wind of Ambassador Kennedy's message to Roosevelt, reporting that 'if the English people thought there was a chance of peace on any decent terms, an upheaval against the Government might come' and – Kennedy claimed – Churchill would be overthrown.

Berlin was well aware of Kennedy's beliefs. According to Breckinridge Long, an assistant secretary at the State Department, 'Kennedy told me Hitler had twice sent him a message asking him to go to Germany for a conference.' (Roosevelt told Kennedy to refuse.) Kennedy's doom and gloom mounted. 'He does not believe in the continuing of democracy,' Long noted later. 'He thinks that we will have to assume a Fascist form of government here . . . Furthermore, he thinks that the spirit and morale of the world is broken.' The truth was that, in Britain, the spirit and morale that was broken was Joe Kennedy's.

Ribbentrop saw an advance copy of Hitler's speech. 'A very magnanimous peace offer to England,' he told Paul Schmidt, the official interpreter. 'When Lloyd George hears of it, he will probably want to fall on our necks.' Soon, Ribbentrop predicted, everyone would be seated at a peace conference.

The Reichstag met in the Kroll Opera House. All the deputies were present, but it was not a parliamentary occasion. 'Under one roof I have never seen so many gold-braided generals before,' Shirer wrote. 'Massed together, their chests heaving with crosses and other decorations, they filled a third of the first balcony.' Diplomats, ministers, gauleiters, Party bosses, foreign journalists, packed the theatre. A 'fantastic show', Shirer called it. 'It is solemn and theatrical,' Ciano noted. Hitler strode to the rostrum, waited for the ovation to die, and began what he called his 'appeal to common sense' with a blast of blame, abuse and denunciation. The audience roared its approval.

He took the credit for all the strategic planning that had brought so many victories to 'our magnificent soldiers'. He showed his genius for milking an audience. 'Suddenly pausing in the middle of his speech,' Shirer recorded, 'Hitler became the Napoleon, creating with the flick of his hand (in this case the Nazi salute) twelve field-marshals, and since Goering already was one, creating a special honour for him – Reichsmarshal.' Shirer noticed that, when Hitler handed him the box containing the insignia, Goering 'could not deny himself a sneaking glance under the cover of the lid.'

Then back to business. The war had been forced on Germany by the 'Anglo-French warmongers', and they got a good tongue-lashing for the monstrous suffering they had caused, pain so great that they could answer for all of it 'neither in this world nor the next'. Hitler's speech had greater impact because he kept his voice level and quiet, the usual pounding rant was missing. In Shirer's opinion: 'His oratorical form was at its best.' He admired the way Hitler used his hands, face and eyes, 'and the turn of his head for irony . . . especially when he referred to Mr Churchill.'

Here was the only obstacle to peace: Winston Churchill, a megalomaniac, a criminal warmonger who was duping the British people and wrecking whole nations and states. Hitler revived memories of the 'atrocity' at Freiburg-im-Breslau six weeks before, and he promised 'a terrible retribution' which would bring 'unending suffering and misery' to Britain. Now Hitler allowed his anger to show:

> Mr Churchill ought for one to believe me when I say that a great empire will be destroyed, an empire which it was never my intention to destroy or harm. It gives me pain when I realize that I am the man who has been picked by destiny to deliver the final blow to the edifice which these miserable men have already shaken.

Throughout, his speech won a tremendous reception. Count Ciano, in the front of the diplomatic box, 'jumped up constantly like a jack-in-the-box every time Hitler paused for breath, to give the Fascist salute'. But now Hitler had reached the object of this exercise, the climax, the appeal for peace; and the cheering and the thunderous boot-stamping ceased. There was silence. Hitler spoke of his duty and conscience to appeal to British reason and common sense. He was not the vanquished, begging favours, but the victor, speaking for reason:

> I can see no reason why this war must go on. I am grieved to think of the sacrifices which it will claim . . . Possibly, Mr Churchill will again brush aside this statement of mine by saying that it is merely born of doubt in our final victory. In that case, I shall have relieved my conscience in regard to the things to come.

So there it was. Hitler was doing the decent thing; or so his German audience thought. They rose in applause. The speech was a triumph. That night, the Luftwaffe dropped leaflets over Britain giving the full text of *A Last Appeal to Reason*, by Adolf Hitler.

BBC Radio sent the first answer within an hour of the speech. Sefton Delmer was an English journalist, fluent in German, who had interviewed Hitler in the past. Without waiting for official approval, he broadcast, in German, a message for Hitler. The language was not diplomatic. It bluntly rejected the appeal. It said: '. . . we hurl it right back at you – right back into your evil-smelling teeth.'

Shirer was in the room when senior officers and Nazi officials heard this. They were amazed. One shouted at him: 'Can you understand those British fools? To turn down peace now?'

Churchill ignored the speech. It sounded stirring, in German, in an opera house. Next day, in English, in cold print, it was just boasting and bullying. Hitler's interpreter, Paul Schmidt, read it on the radio in English; afterwards, he said he couldn't understand how Hitler ever believed that 'such a meaningless, purely rhetorical observation would have any effect upon the sober English'. Yet Hitler did believe it. Two days after the Reichstag speech, a night attack on Southampton by 220 Luftwaffe bombers was cancelled 'for political reasons'. He was still hoping for an answer.

The greater significance of Hitler's Reichstag speech was that, while he had wasted all those weeks, the sober English were gratefully rearming. Now he was short of time.

Chapter Eighteen

A New Use for Cheese-cutters

HERE are two contrasting snapshots of Britain in midsummer, 1940.

On 9 July, the first convoys bringing arms from America reached port. Special trains were waiting to speed 200,000 .300 rifles and ammunition far and wide, mainly to the Home Guard. This released .303 rifles to the Regular Army. Overnight, 200,000 troops were armed. And more weapons were on the way. It was Britain's best news since Dunkirk.

On 20 July, General Alan Brooke left Southern Command HQ and replaced Ironside as C-in-C Home Forces. This made him responsible for the British army in the entire UK. He went straight to his new HQ, at St Paul's School, Hammersmith, and found it dirty, ill-equipped and – as his diary records – empty. '. . . when I arrived there Ironside had already gone! There was a note from him stating that he had arranged with the owner of the Rolls-Royce he had been using for me to take it over, and the best of wishes. That was all! Not a word concerning the defences or his policy of defence, etc., absolutely nothing!'

The War Cabinet had picked the right man in Alan Brooke, probably the most able British general of that war. However, of the two events, the delivery of the rifles – an unmistakeable token of American support – was the more important: even the greatest soldier cannot fight without weapons. Tanks, artillery and aircraft make large holes in the battlefield, but only the infantry can seize and hold the land. In 1940, on both sides, the basic weapon of the infantryman was the rifle. Now, in July, the British army had enough of them to arm every fighting man.

As well as the American weapons, 75,000 Ross rifles were coming from Canada. The Home Guard had a million Molotov cocktails: bottles filled with petrol and ignited by a cloth wick. The Finns, in their war with Soviet Russia of 1939–40, had proved these devices could be lethal against men, trucks and even tanks. Throwing a Molotov cocktail might well be a suicidal act. If invaders came in force, the Prime Minister saw the prospect of massacre on both sides. He had prepared the slogan: 'You can always take one with you.'

In July–August 1940, the invasion problem boiled down to three key questions: Where? How big? What weapons?

Britain is a small island but its ragged coastline adds up to over two thousand miles, almost any of which might be invaded. The east coast of England was nearest to Germany (and to Holland and Norway), so it looked at first to be the prime target. Then the French Channel ports fell into German hands; so did the Atlantic ports; that brought all the south coast of England within their range. And an invasion fleet from Norway could threaten Scotland.

So *where* was virtually *everywhere*. As to *how big*, the Admiralty reckoned that about 100,000 enemy troops 'might reach these shores without being intercepted by naval forces'. Here the Royal Navy seems to have been curiously modest about its abilities; but perhaps pessimism was a wise policy. The main assault by 50,000 was expected on the east coast, with 25,000 landing on the south and the rest on Scotland. The attacks might well be simultaneous.

Churchill, characteristically, was not pessimistic: 'the invading strength seemed even in July to be well within the capacity of our rapidly-improving Army'. Indeed, he told the Chiefs of Staff that 'the scale of attack might well be doubled' and the Home Army should still be able to deal with it.

Which leaves: *what weapons?* In the weeks after Dunkirk – when the British army had left behind almost all its armour, especially tanks and anti-tank guns – the main fear was that a German invasion would be headed by tanks. The Blitzkrieg was built around the speed and firepower of tanks; they had cracked France wide open; they could out-run and out-shoot any British unit. But they faced one problem. A German invasion force would need large ships. That was the only way to take heavy weapons (tanks, artillery) across the sea. And a large ship needed a harbour to unload its cargo. Every port and harbour on the east and south coasts was defended, inside and out, with gun batteries inland which would cover the sea approaches. Before the enemy could get a ship into harbour, the Royal Navy could seal the entrance with blockships or even dynamite the entire port.

'The Admiralty have over a thousand armed patrolling vessels, of which two or three hundred are always at sea . . .' Churchill noted on 10 July. The German navy would have to be very lucky to smuggle an invasion fleet through this patrol, and doubly lucky to make port with its big ships. Churchill, in a Minute called *Defence Against Invasion*, urged the Chiefs of Staff to keep highly mobile reserves always ready for strong counter-attacks: 'Such attacks should be hurled with the utmost speed and fury upon the enemy at his weakest moment, which is not, as is sometimes suggested, when actually getting out of his boats, but when sprawled upon the shore with his communications cut and his supplies running short.'

So: the enemy could probably make a landing but not with his tanks, and his supply lines would soon be cut: that was the theory. Whether or not it worked, Britain would have to wait and see.

The beaches were mined and wired. Inland, bridges were prepared for demolition. Roadblocks and tank-traps by the thousand were set up; fields were barricaded against glider landings; a cross-country line of concrete pillboxes was built. (Many survive).

The British army was short of everything except men, rifles and cold courage. If Germany came, Churchill wrote, 'They would have used Terror, and we were prepared to go all lengths.' That included incinerating the invaders with burning oil, pumped on to the sea. Experiments created an impressive inferno but only when the sea was a flat calm. The idea was dropped. Not so poison gas. Britain had 'thousands of tons of various types of deadly gas' in store, and even before war broke out, 142 Squadron of Bomber Command had tanks fitted to the bomb racks of its Fairey Battles so that it could practise Gas Spraying. After Dunkirk, the Chief of the Imperial General Staff urged that, as a last resort, poison gas should be used against German invaders, and on 30 June Churchill's Cabinet agreed.

It was a time for extreme measures. Home Guards were taught how to garrot an enemy with cheese-cutters, and how to disable a tank by thrusting a crowbar into its track wheels. The army had 26 divisions, and none was anything like fully equipped with field guns, mortars or anti-tank weapons. But Britain had bought the entire production of the Thompson Machine Gun Company of Chicago – 5,000 Tommy guns a month – and these, along with knives and coshes, seemed a better answer to the German paratrooper, who was feared as the most dangerous threat of all. We know now that he was probably the most overrated soldier of the war.

CHAPTER NINETEEN

The Jolt was Violent

GERMAN paratroops were the forlorn hopes of the Second World War.

The phrase comes from the English Civil War of the 1640s, when the quick way to capture a castle was to send a picked force of men with ladders to scale the ramparts; supposing they succeeded, musketeers would follow. If any of these 'forlorn hopes' survived, they got paid an extra twenty shillings, a lot of money in those days. Most died; so the cost was not excessive.

A German paratrooper jumped without the equivalent of a musket. When his boots touched the ground, he carried with him a rush of adrenalin and a pistol, plus a small knife to cut the parachute shrouds if he became entangled on landing. Any heavier equipment (rifle, machine gun, ammunition) was dropped separately, in a weapons container. Until this item could be found, the paratrooper was almost defenceless. Also, he was probably alone. If the enemy could get him in their sights, his immediate chances were slim. This assumes that they had not shot him already, as he floated down.

The German paratrooper carried no more than a pistol because of his parachute design.

With a conventional parachute, the user aims to be more or less upright as the canopy opens, and he hangs in a sling of straps. By contrast, the German paratrooper was linked to his canopy by one single strap which was fixed to his harness at the middle of his back. If his body was not horizontal when the canopy was opened, there was a risk of serious injury. Broken ribs were not unknown.

So a German paratrooper did not jump; he dived. He left the aircraft by a door in the side of the fuselage. He was trained to brace against the doorway with his hands and feet, then kick and shove at the same time so that his body was horizontal when his parachute automatically opened. This left him without a free hand to hold a weapon, and in any case it's doubtful if he could have kept hold of one: when the canopy opened and snatched at his body, the jolt was violent. (Many aircrew who baled out were stopped so suddenly that their flying boots came off.) The paratrooper could not reach his shrouds and so he could not control his descent. A hard landing was to be expected. For all these reasons, it had been decided not to strap another weapon to his body: it might have done more damage to him than to his enemy.

If he landed unhurt his first task was to link up. A stick of twelve paratroops was inevitably scattered. The Luftwaffe calculated that the ideal landing pattern covered a thousand square yards, but wind and terrain (and the black of night) might make a nonsense of that. Four years later, the Allies began their D-Day invasion with night-time drops throughout Normandy. Some groups of paratroops found each other quite quickly; some were hopelessly lost and found nobody; some achieved their objectives; some fell into flooded fields and drowned; some fell as far as 35 miles from their intended drop zone; and a few, having searched for hours with no success, simply fell asleep – an indication of the stress that even a highly trained soldier can feel when he is alone at night in enemy territory. If German paratroops had dropped in England at night there is every reason to suppose that they too would have been scattered, stressed and vulnerable.

But these hazards went hand-in-hand with the unique advantage of airborne troops: surprise. They could drop out of the sky, silently, almost secretly, without warning. There was no 'front line' with paratroops. They bypassed traditional barriers and carried the fight wherever they pleased. They might capture Liverpool, so the Prime Minister warned General Ismay. Or Ireland. Or anywhere. This was a new kind of warfare.

Risk was built into it. An airborne operation was most useful when it captured enemy positions deep inside enemy territory and held them until ground forces arrived. How deep was 'deep'? It was a difficult question, as the Allies were to discover in 1944 when the Arnhem operation proved to be 'a bridge too far'. And how great an advantage was surprise? The Luftwaffe got the answer to that in April 1940, when surprise was total, and then in May 1940, when it was not.

On 9 April, without declaring war, Germany invaded Denmark and Norway. The paratroop units that dropped on Denmark were small – a company here, a platoon there – but there was no resistance, and that part of the invasion was over in a day. In Norway, surprise was almost complete and one airborne battalion captured four widely separated airfields; but there were failures too. High winds and low cloud meant a drop on Oslo airfield had to be cancelled. Defensive fire at another airfield kept the paratroops away from their weapons containers for over half an hour, and the field was taken only when German infantry were flown in. Just to underline the hazards of airborne operations, on 14 April a company of paratroops was dropped to counter an attack by British infantry. The weather was foul, some aircraft flew too low for the parachutes to open completely, many paratroops were killed, the remnants got no support, fought alone, and surrendered after five days. Surprise had been no help to them.

And later, in the assault on the West, airborne attack wasn't always a trump card. The Germans used their entire airborne forces, a total of 4,500 men. When war broke out there had been only 1,500; clearly some intensive recruiting had been going on, but it was still a far cry from the divisional strength (say, 15,000) which Luftwaffe High Command had ordered in 1938. All too often in the Luftwaffe, the word was taken for the deed.

On 10 May 1940 the airborne troops were sent ahead to do two big jobs. In Belgium they had to capture the huge fortress of Eben Emael, 900 yards long and 700 yards wide, studded with gun turrets and manned by 1,220 Belgian troops. It guarded the bridges where the Albert Canal joined the Meuse River, a key defensive line which the German Sixth Army must cross. Nine Luftwaffe gliders, carrying 71 paratroops, had been towed to a height of 7,000 feet. They released their tow-ropes when they were 20 miles from the target, so their approach was silent – but not secret: Dutch anti-aircraft batteries opened fire but failed to score. In the misty twilight of early dawn, the gliders landed on the roof of the fortress.

Contrary to legend, Eban Emael was not taken by surprise, nor was it captured easily. Its garrison was ready and waiting. The paratroops used extremely powerful explosives to cut through thick armour plate and shatter the guns, but fighting in the fort went on all day and all night. It was 26 hours before the army relieved the paratroops and 32 hours before the fortress surrendered. There was plenty of action elsewhere – Belgian engineers blew three bridges over the River Maas and one over the Albert Canal, which held up the Sixth Army – but the capture of Eban Emael was crucial.

Holland was not taken by surprise either. Two regiments of paratroops were dropped and they captured three important bridges between Leyden and Rotterdam but only at the cost of heavy casualties. They captured Waalhaven airfield and then found themselves shelled by the Dutch and bombed by the RAF. When reinforcements were flown in, the transport aircraft were caught in the barrage; many were destroyed while they were unloading. When Dutch forces counter-attacked at the Hague aerodrome, they overwhelmed the paratroops and recaptured the field.

By now, two days had passed and Dutch troops were punching holes in the German perimeter around the captured bridges. Luftwaffe transports attempting to fly in reinforcements could not use their intended airfields and had to land on a motorway, where they made an easy target for Dutch artillery. It wasn't until 14 May – four days after the paratroops dropped – that the German army fought its way into Rotterdam; and the situation was still so precarious that the Germans threatened to bomb the city unless the Dutch surrendered. (They bombed it anyway; a failure of communications was blamed.) The German paratroops were either dead or exhausted. Their leader, General Student, was in hospital with a head wound.

(Student recovered. He rebuilt his force, and a year later he was given another chance when Hitler ordered his airborne troops to capture Crete. They took the island and paid a heavy price, despite the fact that the defences were bombed in advance and the Luftwaffe had air supremacy at all times. Of 22,000 airborne troops, 6,650 were killed, wounded or missing. Taking Crete cost Germany more in casualties than the conquest of Jugoslavia and Greece. The Luftwaffe lost 220 aircraft; 119 were Ju52s. A further 148 were damaged; most were Ju52s. The claim that airborne forces alone could be the spearhead that wins battles turned out to be a forlorn hope. Hitler was shocked. He never risked another major airborne operation. His paratroops became infantry.)

After Dunkirk, the German paratroop force was in no condition to lead an invasion of England; and even if Goering could find the men, he could not find the aircraft.

CHAPTER TWENTY

Hacking Down Auntie Ju

WHAT is often lost in the glare of the Blitzkrieg is the savaging of Ju52s, the standard German transport aircraft.

Everyone liked the Ju52. Its nickname was 'Tante Ju' – Auntie Ju. It was a good trainer, a roomy transport, and it was the machine that towed gliders and carried paratroops. Tante Ju was the Luftwaffe's workhorse: a sturdy tri-motor with a corrugated, slab-sided fuselage and a top speed of 172 m.p.h. Pilots liked it because it was obedient and reliable. This was especially important at the drop zone, when it had to fly straight and slow – 110 m.p.h. at 500 feet – until its stick of twelve men had gone. All these qualities, however, made the Ju52 easy meat for enemy fighters and anti-aircraft gunners. It couldn't take evasive action and it was usually unarmed. It just flew into the bullet-stream or the shell-burst. One solution might have been to protect the transports with fighter escorts, but this was not so easy. A Ju52 was so slow that its escort would have been crawling along: not the way to get the best out of a fighter.

When Germany invaded the West on 10 May 1940, the Luft-waffe had its worst single day of the war. On all fronts, it lost 304 aircraft destroyed and 51 damaged. More than half of those destroyed – 157 – were Ju52s. As Kenneth Macksey has observed, 'Some were hacked down in the air (39 in one interception at dawn), more were bombed on the ground. It was a massacre.' By the time the Battle for France was over, the Luftwaffe had lost 213 of the 475 transport aircraft it began with, and many of the survivors were in poor shape. That left, at most, 262 Ju52s available for operations in June 1940. Each transport could carry 12 paratroops. So the Luftwafte could lift a maximum of three thousand paratroops to England. Such heavy losses were inevitable, and yet the Luftwaffe had no Ju52 reserves. For their operational needs, Luftwaffe commanders simply raided the training units. The best instructors usually flew these Ju52s. Many of them were killed. Training standards suffered and never really recovered.

It seems strange that Hitler could conquer most of Europe and yet find himself short of something as basic as transport aircraft. The root cause was his plan for a quick war; if that worked, then replacement would not be a problem. Yet when he invaded Poland, the Luftwaffe was not ready; it was short of replacement aircrew and aviation fuel. After the campaign, bomb stocks and steel supplies were both so low that Hitler ordered a switch to concrete bombs, filled with shrapnel. Millions were made. The Luftwaffe found them sadly inferior to the real thing.

This was the result of bad planning and lazy supervision, or no supervision at all. The Munich crisis had prompted Britain and France to start rearming. Hitler responded by authorizing a massive increase in the Luftwaffe. His plan was to enlarge it to nearly five times its existing size. This did not happen. The German aircraft industry was sluggish, and the politics of the Nazi economy were a tangle of self-interest and jealousy. Instead of expanding the Luftwaffe fivefold, Goering ordered that all existing units be brought up to full strength: not the same thing at all. Even this did not happen. When war came, 20 per cent of the bomber units, 30 per cent of the Stuka units, and at least 50 per cent of the fighter units were seriously below strength.

If Hitler noticed the difference, there is no evidence that he took any action. He was a soldier; he did not understand aeroplanes, or at least that is what Goering claimed. Hitler 'could not think in the third dimension', he once said. And when there was a move to develop a four-engined bomber, he quashed it: 'The Fuhrer doesn't ask me how big my bombers are, only how many there are.' Goering liked to act as if he alone understood air war and the Luftwaffe was his private air force. It is hard to believe that Hitler was such a simpleton. On the other hand, he certainly left the air war almost entirely to Goering. When Goering's boast that he would destroy the British army at Dunkirk fell flat, Hitler let it pass. Perhaps he persuaded himself that the great escape didn't matter: for them, the war was over, Britain would make peace. Then Hitler dismissed the Milch/Goering plan for an immediate airborne assault, without discussing the details. He must have known how many paratroops were dead.

Even in July, the Luftwaffe had neither the paratroops nor the Ju52s to strike at England, and the German navy had no landing-craft to put infantry on the beaches. Hitler was not disturbed. His peace offensive occupied the front of his mind. Thus, the great irony of that early summer is that, just when Britain most feared an invasion, Germany was least able to attempt one, and Hitler didn't want to try.

HARDWARE

Chapter Twenty-One

No Picnic in Poland

Four months before the Second World War, an Me109 made headlines. It was in the record books for setting a new world speed record.

This feat startled Air Ministries all over Europe, indeed throughout the world. The new record was 469.22 miles an hour. Top speed of a Spitfire was 362 m.p.h., of a Hurricane, 328 m.p.h. The best Soviet fighter, the Yak 1, made 364 m.p.h. The Japanese Zeke, or Zero, reached 340 m.p.h. Italy's Macchi C.202 managed 330 m.p.h. at most. In France, the best the Dewoitine D-520 could do was 329 m.p.h. In the U.S. Army Air Corps, the P-36 Mohawk might, with luck, beat 300 m.p.h.

And now, suddenly, here was the Luftwaffe's standard fighter, over 100 miles an hour faster than the best of them. The record had been confirmed by the *Federation Aeronautique Internationale*. The reputation of the Luftwaffe leaped several notches. Its basic fighter was so advanced that it made other air forces look tired. It was all a trick. The Luftwaffe lied.

The record-breaking aircraft was not an Me109. It was not even a fighter. It was a propaganda exercise, a one-off racing special, built by Messerschmitt on orders from the Nazi government, and known in the factory as the Me209V1. The FAI had been told it was a 109, and their scrutineers cannot have looked very hard. Everything was different about the 209V1: the fuselage, the undercarriage, the cockpit position, the tail shape, the radiator, and of course the engine, which was so overboosted that it was good for only one run at the record. After that it had to be taken out and replaced.

But the FAI was conned, the world was alarmed, and so the trick worked.

Messerschmitt tried to convert his 209 into an advanced fighter and failed totally. A racing special was not a gun platform. The project was scrapped.

So the Luftwaffe went to war with Me109s that were no faster than Spitfires. During the Battle of France, several 109s got shot down by Hurricanes and by Dewoitines, which should have punctured the claim of 'invincibility'. Yet German propaganda had been so effective that men on both sides of the Channel still believed it. On 1 August 1940, Goering told his commanders that he planned to have the enemy 'down on his knees in the nearest future'. The same day, a British Air Ministry report said that morale amongst Luftwaffe prisoners of war was high: 'They almost pity us, because we do not realize to the full the terrific might of the attack when it does come. They think that the aeroplanes will come over in waves of at least 1,000 at a time and that they will pulverize all objectives.' After the war, Sergeant Pilot Philip Wareing recalled the words of his squadron commander in August 1940: 'You've got to shoot down four enemy planes before you're shot down yourself because that's what the odds are. Otherwise you're wasting your time.' It must have seemed like a reasonable summary of the situation. In the event, Wareing got one 109, which was rather more than the average score for a pilot in the Battle of Britain (and enough to help keep the balance of air power).

The truth was, nobody knew what the odds were. In August 1940, when the monthly output of new Me109s fell below 200, production experts advised Goering that, to maintain its strength, the Luftwaffe must destroy four British fighters for each one it lost. Everyone was guessing. This was unknown territory. Until the Battle of Britain, the Luftwaffe had never fought a major air campaign.

Air supremacy helped to speed the Blitzkrieg, but – in the words of one of Germany's most successful pilots, Adolf Galland, 'the fighter arm represented a *quantité négligeable*.' He explained: 'In Poland as well as in France a greater part of the enemy air force had been destroyed on the ground, a minor part only in the air.'

What Galland did not mention was the battering taken by the Luftwaffe in both campaigns.

Victory in Poland did not come cheaply. If Galland was right, and most of the Polish air force was in fact bombed on the ground, then the remainder – helped by anti-aircraft fire – did a lot of damage before it was overwhelmed, because according to the Luftwaffe Quartermaster-General, 235 German aircraft were destroyed in Poland. The losses included 78 bombers, 31 Stukas, 67 reconnaissance machines, 12 Me110s and – most surprising of all – 67 Me109s. A further 279 aircraft got knocked about badly enough to be taken off squadron strength. So, in all, 514 German aircraft were put out of the fight by the outnumbered defenders and their obsolete machines. It seems that Poland was not an easy repeat of Spain. The Luftwaffe still had something to learn.

The attack on the West was twice as expensive, although Galland was dismissive of the aircraft he shot down: 'In addition to obsolete Hurricanes the pilots flew French types: Morane, Bloch, and Potez. Our Me109E was technically superior to them all.' By the time Dunkirk fell, he believed: 'The enemy air force was heavily damaged . . . The extensive losses it had sustained began to make themselves felt . . .'

It is true that the French air force was virtually demolished and the RAF took terrible punishment, with over 900 aircraft lost, including 453 Hurricanes. What is very relevant is the manner in which those Hurricanes were lost. Terraine's analysis shows that 378 of them 'were either destroyed on the ground, or were aircraft under repair which had to be abandoned . . .' That leaves a maximum of 75 Hurricanes lost in combat. In the same campaign the Luftwaffe lost 367 fighters, mostly Me109s, and probably not destroyed on the ground.

This is not to suggest that 75 Hurricanes fell while knocking down 367 Messerschmitts; the air war was far more complex than that. But few historians of the assault on the West point out that it cost the Luftwaffe 1,389 aircraft of all types, and that 367 of these were the 'technically superior' fighters.

In Cajus Bekker's words: 'At the end of the Polish campaign the legend went around the world of an air force of irresistible strength and crushing power – a legend that wily propaganda did its best to maintain.' If anything, this legend was stronger when France fell. Yet Galland knew that the Luftwaffe played only a minor part in both campaigns, and that, despite facing less powerful defenders, the Luftwaffe lost nearly 2,000 aircraft. The Battle of Britain would be its first real test. Everything that went before was just the overture, and the evidence showed that the Luftwaffe had not performed as brilliantly as the legend liked to claim.

The greatest glory usually follows the biggest battle. Not in this case. When Hitler handed out honours during his Reichstag speech, he rewarded the Luftwaffe on a Ruritanian scale. Goering was made the *Reichmarschall des Grossdeutschen Reiches*, a unique rank, senior to every officer in the land. The three generals commanding the air fleets which faced Britain, Milch, Kesselring and Sperrle, became field marshals. All this was because Goering had guaranteed victory in advance: he had sold the skin before he shot the bear, or in this case, the lion. His Luftwaffe had been decked with honours. Now it was time to earn them.

CHAPTER TWENTY-TWO

The Warhorse and the Thoroughbred

SEVERAL myths litter the history of the Battle of Britain. One is that the fight was primarily between the Spitfire and the Me109. This is the result of a romantic bias by the British public (especially the makers of feature films) and a blinkered view by Luftwaffe pilots. They were possessed by Spitfire snobbery; eventually the more honest of them admitted it. 'Luftwaffe pilots insisted that virtually everything they shot down was a Spitfire and almost invariably claimed to have been the victim of a Spitfire.'

The Spitfire looked so good and performed so well that in any fair and proper war it would have won the Battle on its own. War is never fair and seldom proper. In 1940, most of the aircraft in Fighter Command were Hurricanes, and most of the German losses – destroyed and damaged – were inflicted by Hurricanes. One authority estimates that Hurricane pilots 'were credited with four-fifths of all enemy aircraft destroyed in the period July–October 1940.'

In Fighter Command as a whole, Hurricane squadrons outnumbered Spitfire squadrons by a ratio of 3 to 2. More to the point was their majority in 11 Group, since this was where the heaviest fighting went on. The Battle is often thought of as happening over Kent, perhaps Sussex and (towards the end) above London. But 11 Group defended an area that reached as far west as Southampton, as far north as Lowestoft: 140 miles in each direction: a vast expanse to cover. Hurricanes did most of the work. Throughout the Battle, 11 Group always had at least twice as many Hurricane squadrons as Spitfire squadrons. On 1 September the numbers were 14 to 6.

The highest-scoring RAF pilot in the Battle was a Czech, Sergeant Josef František, DFM. He flew only Hurricanes, and shot down 17 enemy aircraft, including nine Me109s. Another Hurricane pilot, Flying Officer W. Urbanowicz (from Poland) destroyed 14 bombers and fighters. Clearly, a Hurricane in the right hands was an excellent machine, and not only during the Battle. Francis K. Mason, in a remarkable piece of research, has examined the claims in every traceable report of air-to-air combat by RAF fighter pilots in the Second World War. They total 11,400. He found that Hurricane pilots made 55 per cent of all kills, Spitfire pilots 33 per cent, other fighters 12 per cent.

There is no dispute that the Spitfire was the better all-round fighter. It was fast and agile at all heights, whereas the Hurricane – bigger, heavier, less streamlined – began to labour above 18,000 feet, some say 15,000 feet. At higher levels, only the Spitfire could match the 109 in close-quarter combat, and throughout the summer they clashed again and again.

When the struggle was at its most intense, fighter pilots were scrambled four, five, six times a day, until some were too tired to get out of the cockpit, too tired to talk to the Intelligence Officer, too tired to eat. Meanwhile, the ground crews would be working through the night to make the fighters fit to fly next day, and here the Hurricane had a clear advantage.

Sopwiths, makers of the famous Camel, had been one of the best aircraft companies in World War One. After 1918 nobody wanted fighters, and in 1920 Sopwiths went under. Its chief test pilot, an Australian called Harry Hawker, picked up the pieces and formed H.G. Hawker Engineering. Within a year Harry Hawker was dead – killed practising for an air race – but with T.O.M. Sopwith as chairman, Hawkers kept going. In 1925 it got a new Chief Designer in Sydney Camm. During the inter-war years, Hawkers built a fine series of biplane fighters for the RAF, notably the Demon and the Fury. The Hawker Hurricane first flew in 1935, and it was in squadron service by late 1937.

Its design came naturally to Hawkers; it was an advanced version of the Hawker Fury, with the top wing removed, the wheels retracted and the cockpit enclosed. Later in the war, a sort of biplane version of the Hurricane was tested, called the Hillson Slip-Wing. Its upper wing increased the lift of a standard Hurricane that carried an extra fuel load to enable it to fly from the UK to the Mediterranean. The upper wing was 'slipped', or jettisoned, when no longer needed.

Camm and his team never forgot that the RAF was short of money. Their fighters grew faster, sleeker, stronger, with a better rate of climb, but they were always easy to repair. Inside the fuselage was a metal framework, and inside the wing was a metal spar, but the *shape* of the aeroplane was all ribs and stringers and fabric; remove the fabric and it looked very like a First World War fighter. Nothing fancy. In the early years of Hawkers, one of Camm's colleagues, Fred Sigrist, had said, 'Find me a chippy with a spanner and we'll mend the aeroplane.'

That remained the philosophy at Hawkers: simplicity was more than a virtue, it was a necessity. Hawkers made a fighter that could be put right by its ground crew, ready to fly and fight tomorrow.

There was a further virtue in fabric: it let the bullet pass through. The fuselage of Sydney Camm's Hurricane contained more space than framework. Many an enemy gunner hit a Hurricane with a bullet that left only an entry hole and an exit hole in the fabric, quickly repaired with a patch and a splash of dope. The Hurricane was the most rugged and resilient fighter in the Battle. There were combats in which Hurricanes took enormous damage and still carried their pilots back to base. Pilot Officer Ken Mackenzie was in a Hurricane when he attacked an Me109. He used up all his ammunition but the enemy flew on. He got alongside it and whacked its tailplane with his wing. The tailplane collapsed and the 109 crashed. Mackenzie lost three feet of wing, and did not crash.

It is hard to imagine a Spitfire being manhandled in that way, or being mended by a chippy with a spanner. All too often a Spitfire with combat damage had to be dismantled and trucked to the nearest airfield that had specialist repair facilities. This was the inevitable knock-on effect of its designer's goal: Mitchell aimed to make a fighter that was as near to perfection as the materials and methods of his time allowed.

His Spitfire was the ultimate endorsement of the aviation saying: *If it looks right, it flies right.* Even today, a low-flying Spitfire can stop the traffic in the streets. But there was nothing sentimental about Mitchell. For him, the beauty of the fighter lay in its supreme efficiency. It delivered what every fighter pilot wants: speed, height and punch. Given enough warning of a raid, he could climb to more than 30,000 feet, get an overview of the enemy, and pick his moment to attack. In a chase, he could catch the enemy. In a fight, he could fling the Spitfire about the sky. It was astonishingly strong. Mitchell's monocoque ('single shell') design meant that almost all of the load was taken, not by an internal frame, but by the metal skin. The Spitfire was not the first all-metal aeroplane but it was the first to use metal so creatively that the pilot could change direction with a sudden violence which would rip the wings or the tail unit off many other modern fighters. Mitchell had succeeded in giving his fighter wings that reconciled the irreconcilable. They were thin, for speed, yet thick enough to carry eight machine guns. They were lightweight, yet large enough to provide great lift. They were strong, yet flexible. When it was steeply banked, a Spitfire stretched the skin of one wing until it was smooth as glass while it slightly wrinkled the skin of the other. No wonder so many pilots spoke of it as if it were alive: they called it 'a thoroughbred'. The Spitfire's controls were so light, it almost flew itself. And a three-second burst of the eight Brownings could disintegrate an enemy machine. A New Zealander, Desmond Scott – at 25 the youngest Group Captain in the RAF – said, 'For the sheer joy of flying, no aircraft could compare with the Spitfire . . . It flew as if it were truly born to the heavens. Snug in its narrow cockpit you felt part of it, and while rolling, looping and stall-turning, its smooth Rolls-Royce Merlin engine would accept every challenge without a note of complaint.'

Every challenge except one: a sudden dive. When a Spitfire pilot had to shove the nose down hard, negative-g put the float carburettor briefly out of action and the Merlin, starved of fuel, coughed. (Hurricanes, with the same engine, did likewise.) The Me109's engine had fuel injection; it lost no power in a dive.

In fact negative-g made the Merlin cough twice. The first power loss was a 'weak cut', little more than a hesitation, quickly followed by what engineers called a 'rich cut', lasting about one and a half seconds. What pilots called it can easily be imagined. In combat, one and a half seconds without power is ample time to be killed.

The RAF knew about the Merlin's behaviour (or misbehaviour) before the war, and did not think it mattered. Fighter Command was expected to attack unescorted bomber formations, so dogfighting was not on the cards. That scenario changed violently, but the Merlin stayed the same, partly because Rolls-Royce couldn't solve the negative-g problem in 1940 (it had better luck later) and partly because it had experience of direct injection and knew that its benefits came with drawbacks. One was heat. The operation of the Merlin's carburettor delivered considerable cooling, and this played an important part in the engine's performance. There were other technical factors, outside the scope of this book.

All engine design is a compromise. Rolls-Royce decided that the Merlin's virtues outweighed its vice. But if you were in the cockpit, that vice might be lethal. A week before Germany attacked the West, the RAF had captured an Me109E intact. Comparative trials showed that the Merlin's float carburettor put the Spitfire 'at a distinct disadvantage' because the 109 'could always elude the Spitfire in a dive'. In the Battle, pilots had to find their own answer to negative-g power loss. Roland Beamont flew Hurricanes with 87 Squadron. His solution:

> . . . consisted of putting everything into the left-hand front corner of the cockpit. If you saw a 109 on your tail, and it hadn't shot you down at that point, you put on full throttle, fine pitch, full left rudder, full left stick and full forward stick. This resulted in a horrible manoeuvre, which was in fact a negative-g spiral dive. But you would come out of the bottom of it with no Me109 on your tail and your aeroplane still intact.

It worked for Beamont, who finished the war a double DSO and double DFC and then had a brilliant career as a test pilot, no doubt helped by his experience with horrible manoeuvres. But there can be no doubt that the average RAF pilot would have been happier without moments of negative-g fuel starvation, however brief.

Given height, speed and agility, the acid test of a fighter is how it performs as a gun platform. The Hurricane was more solid, more stable. Its thick wings allowed the machine guns to be fitted in two clusters of four, each about seven feet from the wing root, so the bullets made a compact stream. The thin wings of the Spitfire compelled the designers to spread the guns. The nearest was about six feet, and the furthest about eleven feet, from the wing root, making the bullet-stream more widespread. Both machines shuddered, sometimes violently, from the sudden jolt of eight machine guns, but the Hurricane, being heavier, took the shock more comfortably.

One discomfort which they shared was cold. There was no cockpit heating. Pilots flew at heights higher than the Himalayas, at speeds equivalent to several gales, and the freezing air found cracks in the cockpits. Al Deere, after leading 54 Squadron's Spitfires at 33,000 feet over Kent, recorded that 'my feet were like lumps of ice and tiny prickles of cold stabbed at my legs just above the knees', while Tom Neil, with 249 Squadron at 25,000 feet over the Thames Estuary, found the Hurricane 'wretchedly cold'. Even with three pairs of gloves 'my hands invariably turned to stone, as did my feet'. But Neil had neglected to put on his fleece-lined flying jacket. The Hurricane cockpit was roomy; it let the pilot wear many layers. The Spitfire cockpit was more cramped. It made a difference: prolonged, intense cold could sap a pilot's attention. Cold could be a killer.

Dowding made the best of each fighter in the Battle. He sent his Spitfire squadrons high, against the top escorts of Me109s, and used the Hurricanes to disrupt and chew on the lower bomber formations. The German bomber crews felt neglected, and they complained. Goering then tied many of his fighters to the bombers, thus handicapping their performance. Even so, the Me109 was – as the RAF pilots who tested it said – 'a formidable opponent to be treated with respect'.

CHAPTER TWENTY-THREE

Hitler's Merlin

ENOUGH has been written about the Rolls-Royce Merlin, a splendid aero-engine. Not enough has been written about the Daimler Benz DB-601A and 601E, arguably even better aero-engines in 1940, when they powered the Me109E. Daimler Benz got 1,150 horsepower out of each of them; the Merlin III produced a maximum of 1,030 horsepower. One result was that the Me109E had an initial rate of climb of 3,000 feet a minute – better than the Spitfire MkI (2,530 ft/min.) *and* the Spitfire MkII with the Merlin XII (2,600 ft/min.)

Speed was something else. Each side claimed to have the faster machine, and since there are so many conditions that affect performance – the altitude, the temperature at that altitude, the age of the aeroplane, its level of servicing, even how clean or dirty its skin is – each side was probably right: sometimes a 109 outpaced a Spitfire, sometimes it lost the race. Beyond doubt, in combat the 109 had a better angle of climb. When an RAF pilot tested a 109 in a mock dogfight with a Spitfire, he let the Spitfire get close and then: 'I pulled back the stick, and laughed to see the Spit shoot underneath as the little Messerschmitt stood on its tail and climbed steeply away.' The Spitfire pilot tried to follow, and 'I jammed the nose down so hard that a Spitfire or Hurricane doing the same manoeuvre would have choked its engine, but the direct-injection system did not even falter.' Daimler Benz scored again.

Messerschmitt's design concept has been neatly summarized by Martin Caidin: 'Mate the most powerful engine available to the lightest and smallest airframe that could be designed around that engine . . .' The result was a fighter that was small on the outside and big on the inside. The Me109E, fully loaded, weighed only

5,523 pounds – about 700 pounds lighter than the Spitfire I or the Hurricane I. Yet it had a metal fuselage and wings, carried twin machine guns mounted on the engine and two 20mm cannon in the wings, back armour for the pilot, all his equipment (including an inflatable dinghy, which RAF fighter pilots did not have), and an 88-gallon fuel tank, bigger than the Spitfire's or the Hurricane's tank.

With an engine more powerful than a Merlin, lifting 700 pounds less than a Spitfire, the 109 was impressively agile, and thanks to fuel injection the response was immediate: no matter how fast the pilot opened the throttle, the engine delivered at once. If he was attacked he could 'slam' the 109 into a vertical dive with an instant acceleration that might well save his life. Then, however, the trouble began.

In 1940, power steering for aircraft was a thing of the future. The control surfaces were moved by muscle. At low speeds the Me109 was a delight to fly: it behaved beautifully. Above 350 m.p.h. – which means in a dive – the controls became increasingly stiff. Above 400 m.p.h. – in a power dive – the pilot needed all his strength to move the control column. Unless he was a very power-ful man, all his strength might not be enough. In Roland Beamont's words, a 109 had 'positively frightful lateral control in the dive', and sometimes no lateral control at all; to roll the aeroplane was virtually impossible.

Cinema and fiction have invented an image of the fighter pilot as ice-cold and rapier-like in action. The reality was that the g-forces felt in combat drained the strength of even fit young men. Some-times RAF and Luftwaffe pilots landed with aching muscles and soaked in sweat. Me109 pilots who got involved in high-speed manoeuvring were soon very weary. The controls could become so heavy that at times they seemed to have locked.

Most fighting did not happen at 400-plus m.p.h., and much close-quarter fighting involved two aircraft tail-chasing, each man trying to tighten the turn and get a shot at the enemy. Calculations on the drawing board have proved that the Me109E was best at this: it could out-turn the Spitfire, narrowly, and the Hurricane, easily. But the chase did not take place on the drawing board. To a great extent it took place between the pilot's ears. He could turn as tightly as he *believed* he could turn; and there is some evidence that Luftwaffe pilots did not have total faith in the ability of the 109 to be flown to its alleged limits. A combat report by Heinz Knoke, the veteran fighter pilot, made no bones about the Spitfire's superiority: he said the 'bastards can make such infernally tight turns; there seems to be no way of nailing them.'

Every prototype has bugs to be ironed out. Messerschmitts acquired a reputation for structural weakness. With the twin-engined Me110 it was the tail unit: so many broke off that it was nicknamed the Flutterschmitt. The 109's designers had similar trouble and they braced the tailplane with struts on each side: not a perfect solution. Perhaps they should have made the fighter a little heavier and a lot stronger. Doubts like this should not be passing through a pilot's mind as he reefs his machine into a tighter turn, knowing that the strains on the airframe are mounting because he can feel them on his body: '. . . the G-force draining the blood from my head and a dark haze beginning to encroach on my peripheral vision – greying out, the precursor to a complete black-out'. When that happened, it took a very good pilot indeed to cling on to the turn, let alone to tighten it even more.

Yet in order to aim *ahead* of the enemy aircraft – an essential deflection shot, otherwise his bullets would pass behind it – he *must* tighten the turn. If he relaxed, he risked sliding through his enemy's gunsight. A couple of seconds was a matter of life and death. Film-makers are fond of showing a pilot glancing in his rear-view mirror to see an enemy fighter close behind him. This is the leisurely pace at which the cinema can tell a story. It is not the reality of the Battle. Sudden death could be very sudden indeed.

In most respects the 109 was admirable. It had its quirks: on take-off and touchdown, the port wing tended to drop, and the splayed-out landing gear which gave it such a knock-kneed look was never really strong enough. But in the crucial areas of stall and spin the recovery was quick and easy. RAF test pilots commented admiringly on its fine aerodynamic finish: everything fitted per-fectly, with no draughts in the cockpit. Fighter Command might have benefited by stealing a few details. The radio transmission button was on the control column, far more convenient than the RAF's switch on the oxygen mask, and 109 pilots had throat microphones, thus avoiding the saliva that fouled the inside of an RAF mask (and caused some pilots to grow a handlebar moustache to absorb the moisture). The seat in a 109 had been intelligently designed too: it was angled back to raise the feet, lower the head, and cut down the effect of g-force.

Given all of the above, there was not much to choose between the opposing fighters. When they met, the outcome largely depended on the skill and the determination of the pilots. However, there was one further difference. The men of Fighter Command were either Britons, fighting for their homeland, with nowhere else to go, or Czech, Polish, French and Belgian pilots who had lost their homelands and were ferocious in their search for revenge. The Luftwaffe, by contrast, could always go back to Germany, and eventually it did.

CHAPTER TWENTY-FOUR

Radar: A Muddled Picture

THE first radar-assisted interception of enemy bombers by fighters happened in bright daylight on 18 December 1939. The radar unit was German. Its operator detected incoming aircraft at a range of 80 miles. They were Wellington bombers, heading for Wilhelmshaven. The fighters were Messerschmitt 109s and 110s. They needed 20 minutes to get airborne; nevertheless they shot down 12 of 22 Wellingtons.

There is a notion that the RAF won the Battle of Britain because it had radar, in much the same way that Victoria's army had the Maxim Gun, which – as Hilaire Belloc put it – we have got and they have not. This is a myth. Germany had radar. What is beyond understanding is Germany's failure to exploit it fully, and her failure to realize how valuable it was to the RAF. But of course the full story was not as simple as that.

Although radar was already at the heart of the RAF's defence of Britain, nobody at the higher levels of Bomber Command seems to have drawn the obvious conclusion from the sudden appearance of 50 Messerschmitts steering straight for 22 Wellingtons off the coast of Germany. Instead of suspecting the worst, and conceding that radar guidance might be available to German fighters, 'Bomber' Harris (then Air Vice-Marshal, commanding 5 Group, to which the Wellingtons belonged) looked on the bright side. Twelve Wellingtons had been lost, which was a disaster, but ten had not, which was a tribute to their close-formation flying and the accurate crossfire of their gunners; and this, Bomber Command believed, was the key to beating off fighter attacks. Soon the Command would have to admit that daylight raids by bombers without fighter escort could be horribly expensive. Later, the Luftwaffe had to admit it, too. Perhaps the moral of 18 December is that, in war, each side is reluctant to learn from the other.

The RAF should have known that Germany had radar, because the Royal Navy knew. On 14 December 1939, the pocket battle-ship *Admiral Graf Spee* had been forced to take neutral sanctuary in Montevideo harbour. For three days, any British intelligence agent with a pair of binoculars could scrutinize the ship. On 17 December *Graf Spee* went back to sea and her crew scuttled her in waters so shallow that she just sat on the seabed and they had to set her on fire instead. Clearly visible despite the smoke was an unusual aerial above the bridge. It was shaped like a large window frame. A British radar expert went aboard and identified it.

Graf Spee had gun-ranging radar. She could find an enemy ship in rain, fog or smokescreen and range her guns on it with consider-able accuracy. This was bad news for the Royal Navy, which did not have equivalent gun-ranging radar in 1939. (Some warships had conventional radar for detecting aircraft.) It would have been bad news for the RAF too, but the Navy failed to tell anyone until 1941, and by then the RAF had begun to discover just how lethal German flak could be.

Flak was part of Goering's empire. His Luftwaffe manned all anti-aircraft batteries, and in August 1939 he was so impressed by the demonstration of a battery using gunlaying radar that he made his rash guarantee: no enemy aircraft would fly over the Reich. He confused the word with the deed. Gunlaying radar used Würzburg dish aerials to track aircraft. A year later, most flak batteries still had no Würzburg, and most gunners were still aiming by eye and by ear and by guesswork, planting the shell where they hoped the aeroplane would arrive.

The story of German radar in 1939 and 1940 says much about Hitler's military machine and its mindset. The navy treated radar as an aid to its big guns, and as an early-warning system to help protect the North Sea coastline, with its major naval bases. The Luftwaffe used it as an aid to flak. German radars were of high quality (a British mobile radar captured in France was thought to be primitive) but nobody in the Wehrmacht High Command seems to have realized that this was a revolutionary new weapon of war, except General Martini, head of the Luftwaffe's Signals Service, and he had too little clout to make a difference. When Germany's leaders underused her own radar, it was a lapse of judgement. When they failed to take seriously Britain's chain of radar stations, stretching from Southampton to the Orkneys, that was a major blunder.

Those radars were Britain's eyes. The Luftwaffe had all summer of 1940 to blind them. They were not hard to find. Most were placed near the sea, often on raised ground, with no hills nearby. A typical radar station had a cluster of three or four transmitter masts, each 350 feet high, and a separate group of four receiver masts, each 250 feet high. The function of the masts was simply to hold the stacks of aerials strung between them. On the ground were a transmitter block and a receiver room where operators used cathode-ray tubes to convert radar signals into the basic facts of a raid: its range, bearing, strength and altitude. Information on the first two was usually reliable; on the last two, less so.

Adjacent radar stations might pick up the same raid, so a Filter Room at Fighter Command HQ converted all the duplicated information into one plot with its own serial number, and positioned the aircraft on a table map with a grid drawn on it. A teller passed the four-figure grid reference of this plot to Ops Rooms at Fighter Command, Group, and Sector Stations. All got the information simultaneously and showed it on their own table maps. (Each Group had five or six Sectors. The biggest air base in each Sector was the Sector Station; it controlled interceptions allocated to it by Group HQ.)

The system may sound complex; in fact it was simple and very speedy. The Filter Room eliminated clutter, and the tellers passed new plots as fast as they appeared. Having spent my National Service doing the job, I can confirm that an experienced plotter could handle five or six plots a minute, using a kind of croupier's rod with a magnetic tip to slap the coloured arrows in place – the colour changed every five minutes to show how fresh or stale the plot was. I can also reveal that the cathedral hush of the ops room, so beloved of feature-film makers, is garbage: when business was brisk, the air was loud with the bang of rods and the shouts of plotters telling their assistants to make up plaques to go with new raids – 'Hostile 230, 50 plus at Angels 15', for instance. There might also be a certain amount of effing and blinding if the assistant got it wrong. This was rare. The work was noisy but slick. From Fighter Command HQ down to Sector Station, every Ops Room showed the same up-to-date picture on its General Situation Map – provided the enemy had not bombed the radar masts.

There were 18 British radar stations in 1939. General Martini suspected that an investment in giant radio masts on this scale must have some military meaning, possibly radar. So, in May 1939, he and a team of signals experts were on board the airship *Graf Zeppelin* (776 feet long) as it cruised off the east coast of England, out of sight of land but not undetected by RAF radar.

The British stations' maximum range was 120 miles. By contrast, German radar stations were short-range. They used dish aerials, not 350-foot masts, and they operated on short wavelengths – gunlaying radar had a wavelength of 53 centimetres; for coastal radar it was 240 centimetres. Martini's men switched on their equipment and searched for signals in that range. They hunted around on the ultra-high-frequency band, and found nothing but static on the headphones and blizzards on the tubes. The British had no shortwave radar, Martini observed; therefore they had no radar. The *Graf Zeppelin* flew home. He should have looked harder. British radar used a wavelength of ten metres. While he had been convincing himself that it didn't exist, it had been tracking every move he made.

That was May 1939. In August the *Graf Zeppelin* came back, looked again and found the same nothing. By February 1940 the British radar chain had grown to 30 stations. It wasn't until the Battle of Britain began that Martini recognized that the RAF had a very good system of detection that was robbing the Luftwaffe of the element of surprise which would be essential for Eagle Assault; Goering's Grand Attack.

Hitler's orders for Eagle Assault went out on 1 August 1940. Two days later, the Luftwaffe decided to put the British radar chain out of action – and then did nothing for nine days. We know that the weather was unhelpful, but the targets were unmistakeable: just fly along the English coastline and look. At last, on 12 August, a squadron of 16 Me110s did just that. The twin-engined fighters acted as bombers. Flying in four sections of four, they swept down the Channel, south of Dover. In Francis Mason's words, 'One by one the sections broke towards the Kent and Sussex coast in a series of brilliantly executed strikes.' They bombed four radar stations and put three off the air.

Immediately, the Luftwaffe sent heavy raids through the blind spots and bombed two airfields. Lympne was only an emergency field and suffered little, but Hawkinge got battered. Then fifteen Ju88s found Ventnor radar on the Isle of Wight, planted their 500-kg. bombs in its signal site, and knocked the station out.

It was a good start, but that was all it was. Within hours, all the Kent stations were working again, some using standby equipment. Ventnor radar was bombed again and dead for 11 days, but neighbouring stations provided overlapping coverage. General Martini's Signals Intelligence detected their output and concluded that Ventnor was still active. Martini lost heart. Two more attacks were made; both failed: and only a week after it began, the attempt to knock holes in Britain's radar chain was abandoned, 'in view of the fact,' Goering said, 'that not one of those attacked has so far been put out of action'.

'Disappointment spread,' Cajus Bekker has written. 'Apparently the "eyes" of the British early-warning system could only be "blinded" for a maximum of two hours.'

The Luftwaffe High Command was too easily discouraged. This was the fruit of ignorance and arrogance. Because it did not fully understand British radar, the Luftwaffe underestimated its importance. Since it was not important, it could easily be destroyed. Then, when a brief attempt failed, the Luftwaffe did not go back with bigger bombs. It decided the task could not be done, and it quit. Yet the Ventnor raid proved that it *could* be done. There can be little doubt that a sustained offensive would have blown holes in Britain's radar cover and made Eagle Assault infinitely easier.

A tribute to British radar came from Adolf Galland, who flew through the Battle:

From the very beginning the English had an extraordinary advantage which we could never overcome throughout the entire war: radar and fighter control.

The advantage was plain to bomber crews. After Eagle Day, when Luftwaffe intelligence officers debriefed the crews on their return, they kept hearing the same thing: the British always seemed to know exactly where the bombers were. Galland again:

For us and for our Command this was a surprise and a very bitter one . . . the British fighter was guided all the way from take-off to his correct position for attack on the German formations. We had nothing of the kind . . . Our planes were already detected over the Pas de Calais while they were still assembling, and were never allowed to escape the radar eye . . . and as a result Fighter Command was able to direct their forces to the most favourable position at the most propitious time . . . When we made contact with the enemy our briefings were already three hours old, the British only as many seconds old . . .

If British radar was a secret in Britain, it was little – if ever – discussed in the Luftwaffe. Diaries, letters and memoirs written by aircrew in 1940 make scarcely any mention of it. Ulrich Steinhilper was both an Me109 pilot and the officer responsible for his air-field's Communications Unit; he was a signals enthusiast. Looking back on July 1940 he recalled 'rumours about new detection equipment that was being developed called Würzburg and Freya, but we couldn't find out much more than that.' Three months later, he was flying frequent missions over the Channel, 'and just like passengers waiting for their scheduled service, the Spitfires would be on station waiting for the next wave'. He blamed this on the predictability of the schedule; he said not a word about radar.

Galland ended the war as a general, commanding all Luftwaffe fighters. Many years later, he admitted that intelligence about British radar was poor, and suggested that the stations were not attacked harder because 'however hard one tries to knock out such stations, one cannot do much harm, and anyway it is easy to repair them.'

This is a lame excuse. The Luftwaffe never tried hard, so how could Galland know? It's true that the 350-foot masts were surpris-ingly hard to knock down: shrapnel went through the holes in the lattice-work structure, as it went through the gaps in the aerials. But the Luftwaffe had two powerful units which specialized in destroying precise targets. Its Stukas had perfected this skill as they knocked out strong points all across France. They were sent to dive-bomb radar stations only twice: Ventnor on 16 August and Poling (near Worthing) on 18 August. Meanwhile, an élite bombing group, *Erbrobungsgruppe 210*, was active all summer, hitting pinpoint targets such as factories and ships. The unit made only two low-level strikes on radars, on 31 August and 4 September. This didn't add up to much. It was scarcely worth the effort. Yet the Luftwaffe knew that the radars mattered to the RAF; later in September – too late – it began trying to jam the chain.

The Luftwaffe need not have toppled the towering masts. There were equally crucial parts of a radar station that could have been more easily destroyed: the nearby buildings – wooden, and above ground – that housed the transmitter and the receiving operators. Concentrated, repeated attacks by the Luftwaffe on those stretches of the radar chain that mattered – the east and south-east coasts – would have placed enormous strain on Fighter Command. The comparison is not perfect, but before the Normandy invasion in 1944, Allied air attacks obliterated enemy radar sites all along the Channel coast. The cost was heavy, but when D-Day came, German radar was blind. In 1940, British radar was wide-eyed, watching the Luftwaffe climbing, assembling, and approaching.

The blunder was Goering's. His senior commanders share the blame. As the weeks and months went by, *someone* should have realized that the British fighters 'always waiting for the bombers' were not there by luck or by magic. *Someone* should have listened to General Martini. A reason for their failure was the very nature of Hitler's war. It was planned exclusively as a quick, offensive war. There would be no need to defend the Reich, and so no thought was given to creating a defensive radar screen. Radar was of no great consequence to Germany. Whatever the British were up to with their topless towers was of no great consequence either, because everyone knew that Britain was beaten.

'All the business of war,' the Duke of Wellington said, 'is to endeavour to find out what you don't know by what you do know;

that's what I called "guessing what was at the other side of the hill."' Goering's mistake was not to endeavour to find out what he didn't know. His Luftwaffe was the best air force in the world. What it didn't know was not worth knowing. Thus arrogance led to ignorance, and ignorance led to failure.

THE BALANCE OF
BLUNDERS

CHAPTER TWENTY-FIVE

A Bonfire of Tactics

RADAR gave Fighter Command the invaluable benefit of time – time to plot the raids and plan the interceptions, time to get the defenders airborne and climbing. Radar helped to guide the fighters. After that, it was up to the pilots. In the early part of the Battle, Luftwaffe tactics were usually good and RAF tactics were often suicidally bad. Tactically, the Luftwaffe showed the RAF how to fight. The new boys beat the old sweats.

The Luftwaffe's public existence (after years of secret development) began in 1935. The RAF was created out of the Royal Flying Corps in 1918. The Luftwaffe grew by winkling officers out of the army, which resisted so much that Goering had to twist arms. The RAF – always independent – had no such problems. Its difficulty was money. From 1919 a succession of governments followed the Ten Year Rule. This stated that Britain would have ten years' notice of any major war in Europe, so there was no need to spend more on the Services than was required to make them ready in ten years' time. The RAF's budget was cut to the bone. The Ten Year Rule was dropped in 1933. By 1937 Hurricanes and Spitfires were on their way, but every squadron in Fighter Command still flew nothing but open-cockpit biplanes: very dashing, highly aerobatic, and not far removed from the types flown by the RFC in 1918. Pilots called the RAF 'the best flying club in the world'. Meanwhile, a part of the Luftwaffe called itself the Condor Legion, and it was in Spain, and at war.

The Spanish Civil War was fought between the elected and legitimate Republican government (too left-wing for Hitler's liking) and the rebel Nationalist army of the eventual dictator, General Francisco Franco. At first Hitler sent unarmed Ju52 bomber-transports and Heinkel 51 biplane fighters to help Franco. So many were cut down by the Republicans' Russian Polikarpov fighters – hard-hitting little monoplanes – that the Condor Legion was reinforced with new types: Heinkel 111 bombers and Me109 fighters. At the same time, its pilots learned from their losses. Close formation flying looked impressive but in combat it was clumsy and inflexible. The Condor Legion opened up its formations to make the most of the Me109's speed and agility. Eventually a formation going into battle might be nearly half a mile wide with perhaps two hundred yards between aircraft.

Trial and error proved that the most efficient formation was a pair (*Rotte*), with the wingman (*Rottenhund*) covering his leader's tail. Two pairs made a *Schwarm*, the basic air-fighting unit of the Luftwaffe. A *Schwarm* flew widespread and at different heights, so that each pair could protect the other, in a format known as Finger Four because the positions were like the tips of the fingers. Space made the aircraft less conspicuous and allowed the pilots freedom to search the sky. It worked. Condor Legion pilots scored heavily.

The Luftwaffe was helping Franco while it helped itself. The Spanish Civil War offered a superb training ground, and Goering exploited it by shuttling his aircrews back and forth on six-month tours of duty. When he was on trial at Nuremburg for war crimes he made no bones about it: 'I had an opportunity to ascertain, under combat conditions, whether the equipment was equal to the task,' he said. The experiment paid off handsomely.

The British government tried to ignore Spain. Certainly the RAF took little interest. In April 1939, when the Civil War was over, an Air Staff officer went to France to interview Spanish Republican pilots in exile. They told him four things. German pilots were very skilful. The cannon-armed Me109 was very destructive. Back-armour on a pilot's seat was essential. And although Luftwaffe pilots attacked at long range with cannon fire they came in close – 200 metres – for machine-gun fire. The Air Fighting Committee at the Air Ministry was not impressed. 'This was noted . . .' say its minutes, 'but it was generally agreed to be unwise to base any very definite conclusions on this report, as the conditions of air warfare in Spain were unlikely to prevail in a general European war.'

Nothing was done. The RAF didn't get cannon-armed fighters until the Battle of Britain was nearly over, and then the weapon often failed to fire. (The Luftwaffe had its share of cannon problems too.) British fighter squadrons went to France without back-armour pilots found it in the wrecks of German machines and installed it in their Hurricanes, without authority. Flying Officer John Bisdee took part in the fighting over Dunkirk; he recalled: 'The Spitfire hadn't got back-armour . . . Some of our pilots were probably shot dead whereas they might have been untouched or only wounded if the armour had been there.' 92 Squadron's Spitfires had back-armour fitted in June 1940, and immediately its pilots felt better for knowing they had a sheet of steel behind them. Others were less lucky. Sergeant Pilot Bill Rolls of 72 Squadron, flying what he called 'clapped-out Spitfires' from Biggin Hill, noticed that some had no back-armour. That was in September 1940, when the fighting was intense.

Fighter Command, and especially its head, Air Chief Marshal Dowding, had no faith in close-range attacks. The recommended range for opening fire was 400 yards. At a meeting of the Gun Sub-Committee at Air Ministry on 5 July 1939, Dowding insisted that 'it was by no means axiomatic that the closer they [the fighters] got to the bomber the more bullets would hit it'. When the Battle began, the eight guns of a Spitfire or a Hurricane had the 'Dowding Spread': they were harmonized (focused) so that the bullets converged at a distance of 400 yards. This was a confession of failure.

'The average standard of shooting in Fighter Command was not high,' wrote Air Vice-Marshal Johnnie Johnson, who was the Allied top scorer in Europe in day fighting, with 38 victories. The low standard of shooting was why 'it was usual for the machine guns to be harmonized to give a fairly large "shot-gun" bullet pattern . . . This area of lethal density . . . gave the poor marksman the best chance of destroying his adversary.' But it handicapped the good shots 'who sometimes closed to excellent killing ranges only to find the area of lethal density was not particularly lethal'. The

Dowding Spread had been a committee decision. Unfortunately, the committee men were not fighter pilots.

In Johnson's opinion, that wasn't good enough: '. . . The essence of leadership in the Royal Air Force was, and is, that every leader from flight commander to group commander should know and fly his aeroplanes.' Instead, in 1940: 'Generally speaking, the only people in touch with tactical problems were the squadron pilots.' The older commanders could be astonishingly remote. Johnson recalled, 'I was mildly rebuked by a senior officer for talking "shop" over a glass of beer when the Battle of Britain was at its climax.' The explanation would be funny if it were not so foolish: 'For some extraordinary reason the best flying club in the world considered it bad form to discuss one's profession after tea.' The Luftwaffe did not take tea.

The best shots changed their guns to suit their attacks. Men like Sailor Malan, of 74 Squadron, and Al Deere, of 54 Squadron, liked to get in close and make sure of a kill. They re-harmonized at 250 yards, sometimes less. Eventually, Fighter Command agreed. But its worst tactic, one that killed many RAF pilots, was the system of Fighting Area Attacks.

This was created in the Thirties by the Air Fighting Development Establishment. It made two assumptions, both wrong. The first was that since Me109s did not have enough range to cross the North Sea, a German bomber attack would always be unescorted. The second was that dogfighting had gone for ever. Spitfires and Hurricanes could not be thrown about the sky at high speed because the pilots could not take the 'g' effects. Therefore, fighters would approach in tight formation and make a formal, pre-planned attack on bombers flying straight and level.

I was fortunate enough to meet Group Captain Myles Duke-Woolley, DSO, DFC and Bar, who led 253 Squadron, flying Hurricanes from Kenley during the Battle. He described how Fighting Area Attacks . . .

> were composed at Northolt in the summer of 1937, largely by Flight Lieutenant 'Tiny' Vasse whose 16½-stone frame was wedged into the gunner's berth of my Demon in 23 Squadron, whilst 111 Squadron's Gauntlets carried out various prescribed attacks against our (also prescribed

and ludicrous) defensive formations. We thought so little of them that we committed our copies to a ceremonial bonfire on 3rd September 1939.

If only every other squadron had done the same.

There were six Fighting Area Attacks in the RAF Manual of Air Tactics, each tailor-made for a specific situation. What they had in common was complexity and rigidity.

The basic RAF unit was the section: three aircraft in vic (i.e. V) formation. Two sections made one flight. If, for example, a flight of fighters met one vic of enemy bombers, the Manual prescribed Number 2 Fighting Area Attack. It would be tedious to repeat the instructions in full. They boil down to this:

(1) The flight forms sections in line astern – one vic behind the other, 100 yards apart.

(2) The leader of the first section 'manoeuvres rapidly' to approach the enemy from astern and gives the warning order for attack.

(3) He picks his target: an outside aircraft. 'At a suitable distance' from the enemy he orders echelon port or starboard 'at about 45 degrees'. The vic changes formation to echelon – i.e., a line angled away from the leader.

(4) 'When steady and about 400 yards from the enemy', he gives the order: 'No 2 Attack, No 2 Attack – Go.' The second and third fighters 'pick up their respective targets', taking care to keep formation, and open fire when in 'optimum range' – or, in one pilot's words, 'wallowing and bucking in the slipstream of the six engines ahead'.

(5) When the leader breaks away, he does so to the opposite side on which the section is echeloned, giving the order thus: 'Breaking starboard, breaking starboard, *go!*' Numbers 2 and 3 'follow in quick succession by the shortest route' and re-form on their leader.

(6) The second section now repeats the attack and then re-forms on the flight leader 'at the termination'.

The other five Fighting Area Attacks are similar: stately, unhurried pieces of aerial choreography. The bombers never return fire or take evasive action, and there is no enemy fighter escort. Johnnie Johnson condemned the official tactics completely. 'These formation attacks were useless for air fighting,' he wrote, adding '. . . the last words too many splendid fighter pilots heard were "Number . . . Attack, go!"'

Even the best pilots could not perform the aerial choreography *and* search the sky at the same time. A Spitfire pilot who was changing formation from vic to echelon, and then watching his leader to be sure of keeping in close formation, was easy meat for 109s falling on him from above and behind. Wing Commander Dizzy Allen, DFC, who flew with 66 Squadron in the Battle, put his finger on the folly of a squadron that kept tight formation:

> . . . eleven pairs of eyes were focused at short range to maintain close formation and only one pair of eyes, those of the squadron leader, was available to scan the skies.

In the Second World War as in the First, most fighter pilots who got shot down never saw their attacker: some never even heard the gunfire that killed them. In May 1940, just after the Blitzkrieg began, Roland Beamont was over France. His Hurricane was one of 36 in immaculate close formation: three squadrons line astern. 'We made a fine sight,' he recalled. Ten Me109s attacked from above. The wing could not be turned fast enough. The 109s dived on the tail section, shot down four Hurricanes, and left. 'None of us fired a shot,' Beamont said. 'We . . . had been soundly beaten tactically.'

The best RAF squadrons in the Battle soon discarded the system of Fighting Area Attacks, but that was no thanks to Fighter Command. In June 1940 it issued a tactical memorandum. Much was unchanged, little was new. In July 1940 Tom Neil, who became a high-scoring Hurricane pilot with 249 Squadron, described the 'standard fighter attacks' as 'like guardsmen on parade'. As late as September 1940, 66 Squadron flew in tight-packed vics, highly disliked by some pilots. Robert Oxspring was one: 'We're trying to fight a battle like an air display,' he said; and when others produced the Manual of Air Tactics, his verdict was bleak: 'That book's a criminal document – the whole formation sticks out like a dog's balls.' Why Fighter Command failed to withdraw the Manual is a mystery. Long after the end of the Battle, it was still official policy. Many years later, when Johnnie Johnson checked the entries in his Log Book, he wrote, 'I see that in 616 Squadron we were still practising the dreaded Fighter Attacks in January 1941!'

CHAPTER TWENTY-SIX

Throw Out These Radios!

EVEN in war, unity against the common foe is not always guaranteed. The Luftwaffe High Command, as we have seen, openly despised the Germany Navy, and the German Army treated the Luftwaffe as a very younger brother. The soldiers' dismissive nickname for airmen was *Schlipssoldaten*: soldiers with neck-ties, a put-down because the Luftwaffe did not wear the traditional, high-collar military tunic. The RAF had its snobberies, too. Anyone in khaki was a brown job, or a pongo. After the Evacuation, a new name for soldiers appeared: the Dunkirk Harriers. There were divisions inside the RAF. Bob Spurdle travelled halfway around the world to fly and fight in the Battle; when he and another pilot reached RAF Uxbridge, this was his welcome:

> 'We have two New Zealand officers to join you, sir,' the batman said as he ushered us into a bedroom.
>
> 'Bloody coloured troops,' the occupant grunted, and he climbed out of bed, piddled in the handbasin, and fell back into his tumbled sheets.

Spurdle joined Sailor Malan's 74 Squadron:

> 74 had a tremendous élan in the air but was a curiously divided and unhappy unit on the ground. With Malan we would have flown anywhere against anything, but 74's curse was, in my opinion, the presence of several Auxiliary Air Force types, who affected longer than regulation hair and who tended to treat menials and pilot officers as they must have treated fags at their public schools. But they knew how to fight.

In peacetime, the Auxiliary Air Force had been a second line of defence, organized in squadrons linked with cities or counties. The pilots were commissioned and flew only at weekends. Private wealth was not essential, but it did no harm. By contrast, the RAF Volunteer Reserve was not formed in separate units; it was a

151

genuine reserve for all the RAF's needs. VR pilots were sergeants. Regular pilots in the RAF were commissioned but most were neither wealthy nor well-connected. The British genius for social barriers produced this definition:

> Auxiliaries are gentlemen trying to be officers. Regulars are officers trying to be gentlemen. VRs are neither trying to be both.

The pressure of combat soon got rid of that sort of nonsense. Within the Luftwaffe, however, there was a more damaging élite: the Spaniards.

These were aircrew who had served in the Condor Legion. Ulrich Steinhilper met some of them in 1938 when he was a trainee pilot, attached to a bomber unit. He was impressed: 'They talked real tactics, learned from experience in the front line.' There was a price to pay for their company. The Spaniards reckoned that heavy drinking went with their status and they made the trainee pilots join them. One night they lined up a dozen trainees. 'They had decided that we hadn't been correctly "tanked-up",' Steinhilper recalled. Mess orderlies brought glasses of beer. An officer ordered '*Gewehr uber!*' (roughly translated as 'Present arms!') and they all drank. 'Then, before the beer had had time to reach our stomach the orderly was pressing another foaming glass into our hand. This lasted until we could hardly stand . . . It was an awful spectacle . . . the cream of the new officer corps, vomiting and crawling over each other like animals. The officers thought it was a great joke, telling us that we'd still got a long way to go before we had finished our real battle training.'

What is significant about Steinhilper's experience is the cocksure confidence of the Spaniards that they had nothing more to learn about air fighting. Steinhilper got a taste of this in 1939, when he joined a fighter group. As the youngest pilot, he was made Group Communications Officer – obviously a job at the very bottom of the totem pole. Already he knew that 'within the Luftwaffe there was a brotherhood of Condor veterans, a kind of old-boy-network, through which it was possible . . . to get things done. They also exerted a stranglehold in many other ways . . .' One way concerned radio. Steinhilper came to the conclusion that, because the Condor

Legion was clandestine, it had avoided using radio in case the transmissions betrayed its existence. Pilots communicated by hand signals or wing-wagging. Back in Germany, the Spaniards disliked the whole idea of radio: it smacked of direction from the ground; they preferred the freedom of the sky. After a Luftwaffe exercise which included an experiment with ground-to-air radio, Adolf Galland blamed Steinhilper's unit for 'bothering' his men: '. . . it would be best to throw out all these damned radios! We don't need them. We didn't need them in Spain and without them we could fly higher and faster!'

Faced with the Spaniards' obstinate resistance to radio, men like Steinhilper (and General Martini, Head of Luftwaffe Signals) made slow progress. Steinhilper flew against Fighter Command throughout the summer of 1940, and in his judgement the Spaniards 'were so entrenched in their views that they, collectively, put the Luftwaffe well behind and may even have cost us the Battle of Britain by their inflexibility.' What is certain is that it was never possible for German fighters to talk to ground control, or for German bombers to communicate with German fighters (or vice versa), or for either of them to communicate with Air Sea Rescue units. Radio discipline was often sadly lacking. During combat, so many German pilots were talking that 'the frequency would be swamped and all that could be heard was a high-pitched whistling as the receivers became overwhelmed.'

Two years passed before the Luftwaffe's air-to-air and ground-to-air radio communications finally caught up with the rest of the war. 'Operationally speaking,' Heinz Knoke told his diary in June 1942, 'it will now be possible for our fighters to be located and directed by ground control at all times' – something that Fighter Command was doing competently in 1940.

Competently but not perfectly. RAF aircraft entered the war with the TR9D HF set. It had a limited range. When Sergeant Pilot Ginger Lacey (later a top scorer in the Battle) took his Hurricane to France, he found that above 15,000 feet his HF radio could receive only the BBC; he made his first attack, on an Me109, with the music of Jack Teagarden and his orchestra in his earphones.

Once the fighting shifted to England and the Channel, HF radio was adequate. Weather changes could affect its quality and range, but in general it worked. VHF radio was far better. Fighter Command began to introduce it in June 1940. The process was painfully slow: by the end of the Battle only 16 of about 40 squadrons had VHF. But many were in 11 Group, where it made a great difference. Clarity of reception was far better, and VHF offered a wider range of channels. This made the task of the controller on the ground and the leader in the air much easier.

The controller's instructions were heard by Luftwaffe pilots, too. They were, at the very least, surprised. When they got back to base, and were debriefed, they mentioned the English voices that had been steering the defending fighters towards them, sometimes even advising how strong the raid was, at what height, on what bearing. German Intelligence analysed the reports and reached a spectacularly wrong conclusion.

General Josef 'Beppo' Schmid was the least successful Head of Air Intelligence in any air force during the Second World War. He had a difficult job. Bad news was never welcome at Luftwaffe High Command: Goering always wanted solutions, not problems. After the war, Schmid recalled the opposition his department faced as Germany began to lose battles. 'Unfavourable reports submitted by intelligence officers at the front were simply dismissed as inaccurate . . .'

Some of this influence may have infected Luftwaffe Intelligence as early as 1940. Certainly Beppo Schmid's version of the air war was strong on optimism. In July he made a detailed survey of British air defences which failed to mention radar, and which described the enemy system as inflexible, with a surplus of pilots, an aircraft industry inferior to Germany's and RAF leadership that was remote and out of touch. On all points he was exactly wrong. On 7 August Schmid reinforced his 'inflexibility' blunder. He reported that, as British fighters were controlled from the ground, 'their forces are tied to their respective ground stations and are thereby restricted in mobility . . . Consequently the assembly of strong fighter forces at determined points and at short notice is not to be expected.' The opposite was true. On 16 August Schmid told

Goering that in the past two weeks his Luftwaffe had shot down 572 British fighters, and so the RAF had only about 300 fighters fit to fly; clearly, the end must be in sight. The reality was that Fighter Command still had over 700 fighters.

Inevitably, reports like this became counter-productive. Luftwaffe pilots, told that the British were down to a handful of Spitfires, saw *and heard* the evidence that Fighter Command was a long way from defeat. The knowledge that combat was inescapable – because the RAF controller could be heard guiding his fighters towards an interception – was at first stimulating to the Me109 pilots (although never to the bomber crews). The novelty soon wore off. As the Battle progressed, the inevitability of interception did nothing for Luftwaffe morale.

After the war, Galland had completely forgotten his Spaniards' disdain for radio. Writing in 1985 about the poor quality of Luftwaffe communications during the Battle, he called it: 'A situation almost unbelievable, which . . . had serious consequences when rendezvous points were missed or escorts/bombers were a little late.'

In Matthew Cooper's words: 'For the German Air Force, war had come too soon.' One vital piece of equipment that it lacked in 1940 was a good radio system. An appreciation of radar would have helped, too.

CHAPTER TWENTY-SEVEN

The Red Light Blinks

THE most rewarding aspects of military history are about what happened, and how, and why. Usually the answers are plentiful. The most intriguing aspects of military history are about what did not happen, and why, and here the answers are skimpy. Sometimes there are no answers. But the non-event can be massively important.

On 22 June 1941 Germany invaded Russia and Stalin did nothing; or rather he refused to believe the first reports, insisted that any attack was a mistake which diplomacy could correct, and ordered the Red Army to stay out of German territory and the Red Air Force not to operate within ninety miles of the frontier. This, at a time when three German army groups were smashing deep into Russia. Stalin was incapable of action. It took him ten days to get his nerve back. It has been suggested that he was in a state of stunned disbelief. But Stalin trusted nobody. He understood power, force. So why did he not immediately fight for his country's life?

On the other side of the world there was disastrous inaction after Hitler declared war on the USA in December 1941 and his U-boat fleet was suddenly free to attack American shipping anywhere. Tankers, especially, were easy victims, silhouetted at night against miles of brightly lit beach resorts. The U.S. Navy Office asked them to turn off the lights; the resorts said that would ruin the tourist trade and they refused. The British convoy system had been working successfully in the Atlantic for more than two years, yet it took America five months to introduce convoys to protect its shipping off the East Coast. U-boat commanders called this their 'Happy Time'. Between January and July 1942 they sank 495 merchant ships and 142 tankers, a total of 2,500,000 tons. Why did it take America so long to respond to such an obvious threat?

Then there was Air Chief Marshal Sir Charles Portal and his conviction that a long-range fighter was an impossibility. Portal was Chief of the Air Staff – the most powerful position in the RAF – for most of the war. In 1941 he told Churchill that the long-range fighter 'will be at a disadvantage compared with the short-range high performance fighter', whether or not it was given increased range by fitting extra tanks. Nothing would change his mind. As the Official History says, he was convinced that 'an aircraft with the range of a heavy bomber and the performance of an interceptor fighter was a technical impossibility.' Soon, in 1942, the American Air Force began its daylight bombing campaign against Germany – with little or no help from Fighter Command. Many Fortresses and Liberators went down in flames before the arrival in December 1943 of the P-51B Mustang, a high-performance fighter which did the impossible: it escorted the bombers all the way, there and back.

Concerning a long-range fighter, Portal said, in effect: 'Never.' A commander should never say never. Portal had allowed a small shutter to fall on his thinking. Its effect was magnified by his power until it made a large impact on the direction of the war. The irony is that Portal was following in Goering's footsteps.

In 1940, with one brief order, Goering could have doubled the fighting efficiency of his single-seat fighters. It never happened. This was the biggest non-event of the Battle, and it made the Luftwaffe's task enormously more difficult.

The arithmetic was simple. The Me109E could stay in the air for about 90 minutes. That gave it a radius of action of about 125 miles. Once he crossed the English coast, the pilot knew he had, at most, 30 minutes' flying time – reduced to 20 minutes' combat time – before he must return. If he left it too late he would ditch in the Channel and probably drown.

It was simple arithmetic, complicated by the luck of war. Combat, foul weather, bad navigation: all were heavy on fuel. This meant that an escort sometimes had to leave bombers that were under attack. Me109 pilots flew with one eye on the sky and the other on the instrument panel. If a red light began blinking, they were down to their last few gallons.

The solution was drop tanks. 'With additional fuel tanks . . . our range could have been extended by 125 to 200 miles,' Galland wrote later. 'At that time, this would have been just the decisive extension of our penetration. As it was, we ran daily into the British defences, breaking through now and then, with considerable loss to ourselves, without substantially approaching our final goal.'

It pays to read Galland carefully. Drop tanks would not have made any 'decisive' difference to Luftwaffe 'penetration', because they could not have changed the British radar and controlling systems. Even with drop tanks, Galland's Me109s would still have run 'daily into the British defences'. What drop tanks would have given the Me109s was time: double the time to protect the bombers, to engage in combat, and still have ample fuel to re-cross the Channel, even if they had to make a fighting retreat.

Portal believed high-performance fighters with drop tanks were a technical impossibility. Goering knew they were not. The first fighter flown by the Condor Legion in Spain, the Heinkel 51, carried an extra fuel tank slung under the fuselage. Japanese Zero fighters had been fitted with drop tanks; in 1939 these aircraft had the longest range of any fighter in the world. Japan and Germany were allies. At the tail-end of the Battle, one third of all available Me109s were converted to fighter-bombers; each carried a 500-pound bomb, which did little damage to England but demonstrated that the 109 was strong enough to take a drop tank. Not that Messerschmitt ever doubted it: the factory was already making a new variant of the 109E, modified for use in the North African campaign, with a jettisonable belly tank that held 66 gallons of fuel.

Why then did the Luftwaffe fight the Battle at such a disadvantage? Several reasons have been suggested, some of them less than plausible. One is that the Luftwaffe did not need drop tanks in the Battle for France because enemy airfields were constantly being captured and made operational, so Me109s were always near the front; thus, when the Battle began, drop tanks were not squadron equipment. This is contradicted by another report. The Luftwaffe *was* supplied with drop tanks during the Phoney War, but they were made of moulded plywood, were stored outdoors, cracked in the wind and rain, and got scrapped. That has the ring of truth about it, yet it still does not explain why metal drop tanks – as used by the Condor Legion – were not made. There was always competition between the Services for supposedly scarce raw materials, but Goering was in charge of the war economy; if he had used his political muscle he could have diverted the necessary metal; after all, drop tanks are not big, and there was a lot of wastage in German manufacturing in 1940. One aircraft maker was using aluminium to build huts intended for German troops in Africa. Another company was making aluminium ladders for Rhineland vineyards. German industry could have turned out a few thousand drop tanks without feeling any pain.

In his memoirs, Galland analyses Luftwaffe failures in the Battle and complains: 'We had always demanded ejectable spare tanks to increase our range.' Demanded from whom? He does not say. There was a brief discussion of drop tanks when Goering conferred with his Air Fleet commanders at Karinhall in August 1940, but it led nowhere. After the war, Field Marshal Milch – Goering's deputy – claimed to have wanted to put drop tanks on Me109s early in the war. Milch's colleagues have described him as 'a veritable storehouse of energy' in 1940, 'untiring in his visits to the front'. Milch wanted drop tanks. Galland wanted drop tanks. Galland had face-to-face meetings with Goering more than once during the Battle. In October he even had a long conversation with Hitler about the air war, followed by three days with Goering, in which they discussed Fighter Command's success. If drop tanks were mentioned, Galland does not say so; and Galland was not one to miss a trick.

By August 1940, Me109 pilots were talking of 'a piece of land on The Island': a neutral strip of England where they could land if they were hit, 'and not have to brave the Channel with a damaged aircraft' – or one running out of fuel. It was only half a joke.

There may be a simple reason for the absence of drop tanks.

Perhaps it all came down to Goering's ego. A massive collection of studies written by Luftwaffe generals for the U.S. Air Force Historical Division has produced some bleak verdicts. One is that 'Hitler and Goering firmly believed that they alone were responsible' for the early military successes; if that were so, Goering needed no advice on how to destroy the RAF. 'He thought it could be achieved in a matter of days or weeks,' writes Sir Maurice Dean in his history of the RAF. 'What were the reasons for this gigantic miscalculation? The main factor was perhaps a heavy sense of victory . . . It must be a push-over . . . There was a delusion about the Me109. No German dared deny that it was the best fighter in the world . . .' As a corollary, no German dared suggest its range was inadequate. The Luftwaffe was afraid of Goering. 'The Battle of Britain was really about fighters,' Dean writes. The best – indeed the only – German fighter was always hamstrung by its short range. The fault was Goering's. Nobody could tell him he was wrong. Such is the nature of dictatorship.

Half the German destroyer fleet was sunk in the Norwegian campaign of spring 1940, and many major ships were disabled. The German navy never recovered. The U-boat effort at Norway was a sorry failure too.

oyal Navy destroyers on patrol. At full speed, their bow wave was enough to swamp a invasion barge. After Norway, German destroyers totalled eight. The British Navy ad forty destroyers ready to fight in the Channel, with as many more in reserve.

The Fuhrer and Admiral Raeder, at the naval review, 1933 – a very rare picture of Hitler in a boat. 'On land I am a lion, he often said, 'but with the water, I don't know where to begin.' He began in 1938 by promising Raeder peace until

Raeder proposes, and Hitler listens, or perhaps not. Fuhrer Conferences were no place for integrated planning; Hitler dealt with each service chief separately. One question he never resolved with Raeder was how the German navy would protect a Sealion crossing.

German paratrooper, fully armed with pistol and small knife, braces himself to dive horizontally, essential because his parachute was attached to straps at the middle of his back. He could not control his descent.

England seen from France. This view, taken by a powerful 35 mm camera, allegedly shows radar towers near Dover being

Converted river barges at a French dockside. Note sandbags to protect the helmsman. Despite bombing, there was no shortage of barges – 2,000 were ready for Sealion, with hundreds in reserve. Whether they were seaworthy for a Channel crossing was a different matter.

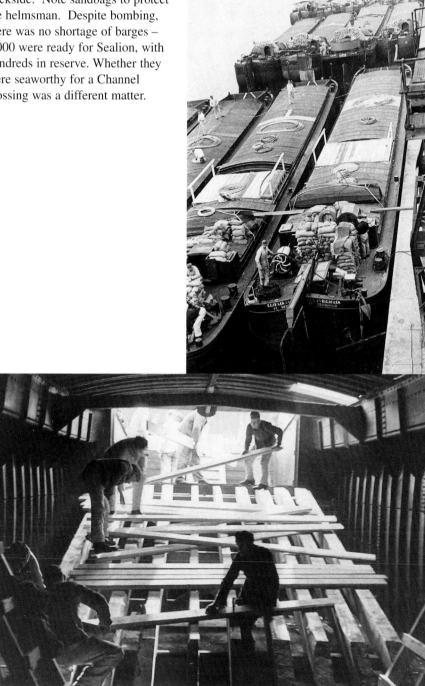

Building an unloading ramp inside an invasion barge. Note the rivets in the steel sides of the vessel. Sealion barges were not naval landing craft, but they were tough enough to withstand bullets.

Airmen reload the machine guns of an RAF fighter with 0.303 ammunition – the same calibre as that used by the British infantry. Effective in air combat, it would have scarcely dented steel-hulled barges.

German tank about to be lowered into the sea for submersible testing. The long tube leading into a funnel was a breathing device, similar to the Schnorkel later used by U-boats. Tests were encouraging, but no underwater tanks reached the invasion forces

Panzers made good pictures, but in fact the bulk of the German army was horsedrawn; and Sealion would have needed thousands of mounts. As this landing exercise on a French beach shows, unloading horses was not easy. If bullets had been flying, the men on the barge would probably have been less visible.

Twelve soldiers struggle to get an anti-tank gun out of an inflatable and onto a ramp, in this invasion exercise. They would have made an inviting target for defenders. Two men at the top seem bemused; two at the bottom, amused.

During invasion training, a German tank is loaded onto the deck of a steamer in a French port. This was the easy part. Unloading it – without the benefit of an English port – would have to be done at sea, winching the tank onto a barge alongside, which would then make for the beach, probably under fire. A slow and hazardous procedure

This rare photograph of elements of an invasion fleet taking part in an exercise for Operation Sealion shows tugs (often trawlers) towing two barges in tandem. The tow units were widely scattered. Many crews were green. No skipper wanted to get tangled up with other craft.

CHAPTER TWENTY-EIGHT

Numbers

NUMBERS alone do not win a battle, but they are a good start. 'Get there fastest with the mostest' was the famous formula for victory of an American general. Hitler had lost his chance to get there fastest. June and July were squandered. Now Britain was armed and alert. The question remained: did Hitler have the mostest?

This has spawned a large family of answers, and these have helped to create one of the most enduring myths of the Battle: the notion that Fighter Command was hugely outnumbered. It is an appealing thought, if you are British, because it makes the Luftwaffe's failure all the more dramatic. Long before that failure, Churchill had endorsed the idea when he described the pilots of Fighter Command as 'The Few'. So they were, in number: from start to finish, just over 3,000 men flew at least one operational sortie in the Battle. Not many more Luftwaffe fighter pilots opposed them; perhaps no more. And the Battle was fundamentally a fight between fighters.

Numbers varied according to the intensity of combat, but the daily average of Hurricanes and Spitfires available, with crews ready for operations, was 608. Often the number of aircraft available for operations was more: over 700 in four different weeks of August and September. With the Luftwaffe it is impossible to be so precise, partly because its record-keeping methods differed, largely because, for the Germans, the campaign was best forgotten. Cajus Bekker claims: 'The German fighter force at the start of the battle disposed of only some 700 first-line Me109s.' This seems low. Churchill, in his memoirs, quotes a rough figure of 850 Me109s 'during the Battle' – but this does not guarantee that all 850 were operational, or were operational against Britain. The Luftwaffe kept many aircraft in Norway, Denmark, Holland, Poland, Czechoslovakia, Austria and Germany. These took no part in the Battle. What mattered was not the total strength of Luftwaffe fighters but the number stationed in Belgium and France. John Terraine has studied the many estimates; he names two in particular. The Air Historical Branch Narrative gives 760 Me109s. Richard Overy gives 893 Me109s but qualifies that by saying only 725 were serviceable.

This matter of serviceability is crucial. In 1940, in any air force, the aeroplanes needed constant attention. Combat doubled the stress on engines, control systems and guns. Airfields were grass, and the narrow, knock-kneed undercarriage of the Me109 led to many landing accidents. Whatever the nominal strength of a squadron of Me109s, the number it could actually put in the air, ready for operations, was usually 15 or 20 per cent less. The Air Historical Branch finds 760 Me109s. Deduct 15 per cent which are in the hangar being serviced and you get 646. That figure may be too low; it is, after all, only an estimate. But increase it by 10 per cent and the overall picture is not very different. It still means that between 600 and 700 Hurricanes and Spitfires fought between 600 and 700 Me109s.

The scene looked very different in June 1940. Churchill described the air war with a kind of grim gusto:

> In the Battle of France we had fought the Germans against odds of two and three to one and inflicted losses in similar proportions. Over Dunkirk, where we had to maintain continuous patrol to cover the escape of the Army, we had fought at four or five to one with success and profit. Over our own waters and exposed coasts and counties Air Chief Marshal Dowding contemplated fighting at seven or eight to one.

Britain believed then that the Luftwaffe was at least three times as big as the RAF. More recently, Cooper has calculated that when the Battle began 'the entire operational aircraft strength of the Luftwaffe in the West (not including Luftflotte 5, in Norway) outnumbered the RAF defenders by over six to one'. This is the sort of statement that bolsters the popular image of the Battle of Britain as a solitary Spitfire squadron climbing to take on an advancing armada of German raiders. Certainly there were days when that happened. There were also days when RAF fighters outnumbered the raiders. How could this happen when, according to the estimates, RAF fighters should have been swamped by six to one?

The devil is in the detail. When Cooper speaks of 'the entire operational aircraft strength of the Luftwaffe in the West' he means all bombers (level-flight and dive) and all fighters (twin-engined Me110 as well as single-engined 109). Other types (reconnaissance, transport, seaplanes) can be ignored. On 10 August – scheduled to be *Adlertag*, Eagle Day – German bombers and fighters in France and Belgium totalled, according to Cooper, 2,733. It was, he says 'a formidable force'. But he also gives the number that were *serviceable* on that day: 2,120. One level-flight bomber in three, and one Stuka in four, was not fit to fly, and about 20 per cent of all fighters were unserviceable – this when the Luftwaffe had had at least ten days to prepare for its grand assault. What's more, Luftwaffe commanders were sensitive of the threat to their airfields from RAF bombers, so they always kept a screen of fighters for their protection. And in any case there is evidence to suggest that Cooper's figures may be too high.

The Germans are great book-keepers. The records of the Luftwaffe Quartermaster General survived the war, and they show that for 3 August 1940 Goering had 1,065 Me109s. Of these, only 878 were combat-ready, and some of those were reserved for home defence. It left 760 available for the Battle.

For twin-engine fighters (Me110s), the QMG's records show that squadrons had 310, but only 240 were combat-ready; furthermore, a shortage of crews brought that figure down to about 230.

According to the QMG, on 3 August the bomber strength of the Luftwaffe totalled 1,458, and according to the QMG 44 per cent of them were not operational – a remarkably high figure. Thus only 818 bombers were combat-ready. Some were based in Norway, which left the Air Fleets taking part in the Battle with between 700 and 800 operational bombers, including 343 dive bombers, soon to be pulled out of the fight.

In short: when Goering announced *Adlertag*, the QMG's records show that he could count on about 760 Me109s and about 230 Me110s to protect 700 to 800 bombers.

As the Battle wore on, both sides were drained of men and machines. On 8 September, Steinhilper's unit was 'short of fully airworthy aircraft . . . for the time being our squadron was flying at one third of its strength'. On 27 September, he was leading the *Gruppe* (roughly equivalent to a wing) but 'because of the losses there were only thirteen fighters from the three squadrons'. The RAF too was being hurt: 21 fighters destroyed on 9 September; 32 on 11 September; 26 on 15 September; 33 on 27 September; and many others damaged. The hidden battle was for replacements, and here the Luftwaffe found itself struggling.

At the root of the problem lay Hitler's hunger for a quick victory. Goering packed his front-line squadrons with aircraft and gambled on keeping a small reserve. Britain reckoned on a long fight: at the time of *Adlertag*, Fighter Command had 289 Hurricanes and Spitfires ready as replacement aircraft. That, as Telford Taylor points out, was 'over a third of Fighter Command's operational strength'.

And more were always being added. British aircraft factories worked harder than the Messerschmitt plants. In June 1940 they delivered 446 Hurricanes and Spitfires. In July the figure was 496; in August, 476. That was double the German rate of delivery of Me109s *and* Me110s. For 109s alone, the monthly rate was about 190, and static. But fighters were no good without pilots.

After the Battle for France, Fighter Command was always short of pilots. Just before *Adlertag* it was 160 pilots short. It was getting 50 trained replacements a week; not enough, even with men transferred from the Fleet Air Arm. Fighter Command's main weakness was always its lack of experienced pilots, and every good historian has pointed this out. Yet the Luftwaffe had the same problem, and this is not always noticed.

There was no lack of pilots: the German flying schools turned out 10,000 in 1939 alone. But flying and fighting are very different skills. As losses mounted, Steinhilper noted that many of them were replacement pilots, sent into action straight from Fighter School.

(His *Gruppe* began the Battle with 36 pilots, all of whom had at least three years' experience; by October 1940 only four survived.) And although both the RAF and the Luftwaffe became desperately short of experienced fighter pilots during the Battle, the RAF had one priceless advantage. Pilots who made a forced landing, and many who baled out, found themselves on home ground; sometimes they flew again the following day. When the Luftwaffe lost a pilot over England, he was lost for good.

Morale cannot be weighed or counted, but low morale can be recognized. Churchill had described his fighter pilots as '. . . undaunted by odds, unwearied in their constant challenge and mortal danger'. That was good backs-to-the-wall rhetoric, but it was a long way from being universally true. Fighter Command knew when a squadron was approaching exhaustion. Dowding revolved his squadrons, moving the tired ones out of the combat zone so that they could rest and rebuild their strength. Goering did not. A German pilot stayed on operations until he died or was wounded or got promoted out of the fight. One result of this policy in 1940 was *Kanalkrankheit* – Channel Sickness:

> A combination of chronic stress and acute fatigue . . . as the battle dragged on, there were to be more and more cases . . . The symptoms . . . usually surfaced as stomach cramps and vomiting, loss of appetite and . . . acute irritability.

Luftwaffe doctors could not advise that an overstressed pilot be taken off operations; if they did 'there would be a flood'.

> So doctors resorted to diagnosing appendicitis. This minor operation ensuring that at least a pilot would be off flying for about two or three weeks.

Nobody liked flying over the Channel. Flight Lieutenant Ian Gleed, DFC, led 87 Squadron during the Battle; he shot down three Me110s. But on a night-time operation to attack a German airfield in France, he could not escape the fear that his Hurricane might have engine failure over the Channel:

> I glance at the clock. One o'clock: halfway. 'If I fall in "the drink" now I haven't a hope of being picked up. I'll shoot myself before we hit . . .'

167

Gleed got back. Many German pilots did not, and the bodies of several were washed up and found to have a single bullet wound in the head. The Channel can be a bitterly cold, sickening, hopeless place. In September 1940 the Luftwaffe deprived its pilots of their last release. It forbade them from flying with any type of pistol.

Clearly, *Kanalkrankheit* gnawed away at the effective strength of the Me109s. Nevertheless, Goering could count on about 1,000 bombers. They would have made a discouraging sight over England. It never happened. The Luftwaffe could never launch all its bombers in one massive daylight raid because bombers needed a strong fighter escort, and there were never enough fighters for that. There were even fewer when the Me110 (called *zerstörer*, meaning destroyer) proved to be no match for British fighters. Increasingly, the *zerstörers* had to be rescued by Me109s. The Stukas – slow and predictable – were an even greater liability. Even with a fighter escort they got shot down in such numbers that they were taken out of the Battle in mid-August. Without Stukas, without Me110s, the strength of Eagle Assault fell by over 600. Now it totalled 1,500 serviceable machines at most: not seven to one but roughly two to one.

Any such mathematical balance is bound to be misleading. There were days when Fighter Command got wrong-footed and its squadrons faced heavy odds; just as there were days when the German bomber crews were dismayed to find so many British fighter squadrons waiting for them. Taking the Battle as a whole, it is clear that Dowding's expectation of 'fighting at seven or eight to one' was far from the general rule. In any case, fighter pilots rarely had time to count the opposition. That was true of both sides. After one German raid, the Luftwaffe report declared that: 'Over the target, huge formations of fighters appeared, with up to eighty aircraft.' The actual figure was 47.

The Battle was like all battles: an untidy, up-and-down affair, with strong elements of luck and guesswork. This does not diminish the courage and skill of the pilots; quite the reverse. But to do them justice, it is necessary to recognize that the sides were more evenly matched than the comic-book stories suggest; and in fighter strength, they were very closely matched.

CHAPTER TWENTY-NINE

Hearsay Is Not Evidence

A LOT of electronic eavesdropping took place across the Channel in the summer of 1940, and very little of it made any difference to the Battle.

There were two kinds. Ultra was secret information gained by decrypting German radio messages sent via the Enigma machine. This was the operation that made Bletchley Park famous. The 'Y Service' was an RAF unit that monitored the Luftwaffe's radio traffic and gathered intelligence about enemy activities. (The Luftwaffe had its own 'Y Service', called *Horchdienst*, which listened to RAF radio traffic.)

Large claims have been made for Ultra's contribution to the Battle, first by Group Captain F.W. Winterbotham in *The Ultra Secret*, published in 1974, and four years later by Ronald Lewin in *Ultra Goes To War*. For instance, Winterbotham (who worked at Bletchley Park) declared that Air Chief Marshal Dowding not only was on the very short list of people who knew the Enigma/Ultra secret, but was actually receiving this intelligence direct from Bletchley Park. Winterbotham also states as fact that the decoding of Enigma transmissions gave warning to Dowding of changes in enemy tactics, and even of changes in strategy, such as the decision to switch the attack to London. He says that Churchill and Dowding had news of Goering's *Adlertag* directive 'within the hour'.

Edward Thomas rejects all of this; indeed he called the last item – the *Adlertag* story – 'fantasy'. Thomas also worked on Enigma/Ultra at Bletchley Park in World War Two; later his career involved strategic intelligence with the Joint and Defence Intelligence Staffs. He was a contributor to the Official History of British Intelligence in the Second World War. So he has been there, seen the papers, done his homework. His version of events is more persuasive than Winterbotham's. Thomas applauds Winterbotham's wartime contribution to the organizing of intelligence, but he points out that Winterbotham was over 70 when he wrote his book, and Thomas says it was 'largely written from memory' because 'he did not have access to any papers', and this explains the mistakes. Lewin, Thomas says, 'simply followed Winterbotham'.

There were three main reasons why Enigma decrypts were of little value to Dowding. The first and largest was that the Luftwaffe sent most of its operational orders by land line or despatch rider, not by Enigma. The second was that Bletchley Park needed time to read the Luftwaffe Enigma cipher, and for Fighter Command delay might have made the information stale and useless; sometimes it was incomplete or meaningless to begin with. For instance, the Luftwaffe identified its targets by code numbers. In 1940, Bletchley could not normally crack that code-within-a-code, and so the rest of the message meant little until the raid had happened. And thirdly, it was dangerous to assume that something would happen just because Enigma said so. As in the RAF, Luftwaffe ops might be 'scrubbed' at any time. Thomas describes how Enigma revealed that a heavy raid on London was planned for 13 September 1940. Nothing came. Then Enigma reported that the raid was now on the 14th. Again, nothing. On 15 September, the raid arrived – but this time Enigma had been silent. It wasn't Bletchley's fault. It was the flux of war.

The RAF 'Y Service' operated at a more front-line level of Luftwaffe communications. It intercepted the Morse messages to and from the bombers, and listened to the plain-language talk between the fighters. Its German-speaking operators became expert at identifying which bomber units had taken off from which bases, where they were assembling, and where they would rendezvous with fighters, sometimes even their height, course, speed and the intended target. On the face of it, this information should have been invaluable to Dowding and his controllers. No doubt some of it was. The Luftwaffe unintentionally helped: radio operators in German bombers routinely tested their equipment half an hour before take-off; that information alone gave early warning that a raid was likely. (Radio operators in RAF Bomber Command did a similar service for listeners in the Luftwaffe's *Horchdienst*.)

The problem with the 'Y Service' was the same as the problem with Enigma: not, could you trust the messenger? but, could you believe the message? As the Battle wore on, the Luftwaffe adopted feints and decoys. A bomber formation might assemble and then fly parallel to the French coast, hoping to lure British fighters into the air, where they would waste their fuel or get bounced by 109s, or both. A formation might cross the English coast and then suddenly split in two, one a major raid, the other a decoy. An attack might be scattered by foul weather, or bad navigation, or garbled orders. The first casualty of war is always the plan.

How much help were Enigma and the 'Y Service' in directing the Battle? Edward Thomas's conclusion is that they were 'never more than a bonus'. They did not influence decisions of strategy. Without them, the Battle would probably have followed much the same course as it did.

Without radar and Fighter Command's control system, on the other hand, the Battle would have been a hugely more difficult struggle for the RAF. Perhaps an impossible one.

11 GROUP:
FINDABLE, HITTABLE
AND BREAKABLE

CHAPTER THIRTY

An Accidental Success

A T the end of June, Goering had issued a General Directive for an assault, but the Luftwaffe wasn't yet ready, its new bases weren't complete, its supply lines weren't up and running, its flying units were still regrouping. So, in the meantime, operations were to be 'confined to nuisance raids by relatively minor forces on industrial and RAF targets'. July saw a lot of small-scale raids over the Channel and the south coast; the Germans called it *Kanalkampf* (a play on words – *Kanalkämpfer* also means 'brawler'). Several British convoys were attacked; the ships were small; few were hit. August saw a crescendo of assault: big formations, bigger escorts, heavy fighting. Yet the impact was scattered. There were too many objectives: the aircraft industry (to starve the RAF), the ports (to starve the people), naval bases (a sop to Raeder), communications (the rail system).

Britain expected an invasion any day, and assumed that these probes by the Luftwaffe had some ominous significance; whereas Goering had no interest in invasion, he was just marking time until he could deliver his knockout blow. Nuisance raids were useful; they gave his aircrew battle practice. From 1 July to mid-August, in combats between British and German single-engined fighters, the Luftwaffe lost 85 Me109s; Fighter Command lost 128 machines: about two a day for the Luftwaffe, about three a day for the RAF. The losses were easily made good by replacements from the factories.

For Germany, this was war at leisure. The summer was half-over and everyone – the army, the navy, the Wehrmacht high command, the Fuhrer – was waiting for the Luftwaffe to snuff out Britain's pointless resistance. On 20 July, the highest Luftwaffe officers came to Karinhall, Goering's palatial mansion on his vast estate north of Berlin. At first he celebrated their promotions to field marshal. Next day, he was in conference with his three western air fleet commanders, the men who would run the assault on England. No final decision was reached. The commanders went away, each to develop his separate proposal. More delay. Hitler lost patience first.

His peace offensive had failed. The British were not prepared to be reasonable. And Hitler recoiled from the brick wall of their stupidity. On 30 July 1940, Goering got a sharp poke in the ribs, in the shape of a telegram that read:

> The Fuhrer has commanded that the preparations for the Grand Attack of the German Air Force against England are to be met with greatest acceleration so that the battle may begin twelve hours after release of the [final] order by the Fuhrer.

Two months had passed since Dunkirk. Now the Luftwaffe was being ordered to *accelerate* its preparations. What had it been doing in all that time? Why wasn't it ready? A large part of the answer lies in the failed leadership of Hermann Goering, who spent much of June and July on holiday, and most of his holiday in Paris, adding to his art collection. The troubles of the Luftwaffe owed a lot to its Commander-in-Chief's vanity, self-indulgence and sloth.

Hitler's mood had swung again. The day after his telegram, a Fuhrer Conference made it clear that Sealion must be ready to go by 15 September, that the Luftwaffe's Grand Attack against England should begin about 5 August and its success should be complete 'after eight or at most fourteen days'. Depending on results, Hitler would decide whether or not to launch Sealion in 1940.

Goering was delighted. On 1 August he was in Holland to preside over a large conference. Theo Osterkamp was there; he commanded JG51, a 100-strong unit of fighters. His record caught both the fact and the flavour of the occasion:

> Everybody of rank and name is present. Because of the good weather the festival takes place in the garden. The 'Iron One' appears in a new white gala uniform.
>
> At first he praised extravagantly the lion's share of the Luftwaffe in the defeat of France. 'And now, gentlemen, the Fuhrer has ordered me to crush

Britain with my Luftwaffe. By means of hard blows I plan to have this enemy, who has already suffered a decisive moral defeat, down on his knees in the nearest future, so that an occupation of the island by our troops can proceed without any risk!'

Luftwaffe Intelligence estimated that in its southern sector the RAF had at most 400 to 500 fighters. Osterkamp went on:

Their destruction in the air and on the ground was to be carried out in three phases: during the first five days in a semi-circle . . . within a radius of 150 to 100 kilometres south of London; in the next three days within 50 to 100 kilometres; and during the last five days within the 50-kilometre circle around London. That would irrevocably gain an absolute air superiority over England and fulfil the Fuhrer's mission!

Osterkamp had flown in combat over England; he could not accept that the battle would be so easily won; but Goering shouted him down. What is truly remarkable about the plan is its timescale: 13 days to destroy the RAF and beat the enemy down on his knees, so that German troops could march into a defeated nation.

Goering's main aim in life was to please and impress Hitler, but there were hard-headed and experienced men on his staff who must have known that the battle could not be won in 13 days. Their problem was twofold. Goering ran the Luftwaffe as his personal air force; what he said, went: he did not tolerate dissent. And the idea of victory by the knockout blow was overwhelmingly strong. Germany had the biggest air force in the world, constantly labelled as 'invincible'. There was an assumption that the Luftwaffe could not be stopped, and that it was a war-winning weapon. Who was to say that Britain would still be standing after 13 days of massive air attack? The war had already shown that fear could be as powerful as fact. Look at Prague. Look at Rotterdam. Maybe the British could be frightened into surrender.

That was a common expectation in Germany. On 17 July, a Berlin newspaper told its readers: 'The whole of England is trembling on the brink of a decision. There is only a slight possibility of England offering any military resistance . . .' German radio stations constantly played and sang *Wir Fahren Gegen Engelland*. One station announced: 'In England, men and women feel the urge to raise their courage by resorting to drink . . . Alcoholic poisoning is increasing by leaps and bounds . . . Press gangs under sergeants are visiting cinemas, cabarets and tea rooms to enrol young civilians as trench diggers . . . Fear in England is indeed terrific . . .'

On 1 August, Shirer took 'two new bets offered by Nazis in the Wilhelmstrasse. First, that the Swastika will be flying over Trafalgar Square by 15 August. Second, by 7 September.' In this sort of atmosphere, it's not surprising that on 4 August, the 22-year-old Ulrich Steinhilper, a fighter pilot newly arrived at an airfield near Calais, should write that he couldn't wait to get into some serious aerial combat: 'Would we actually get the chance to prove ourselves before the British sued for peace or we invaded?' What is surprising is that Steinhilper asked a girlfriend for the address of a family in London. Their daughter, living in Germany, had just had a baby boy. Steinhilper assumed that he would soon be in London, and he wanted to call on the family and tell them about their grandson. This was not so much arrogance as overconfidence. Steinhilper saw no serious obstacle to conquest, except perhaps the weather.

The weather was always the Luftwaffe's bugbear. Final operational plans were completed on 6 August but Goering, hoping for three days of good weather, postponed the offensive to 8 August, then to 10 August. Finally, on 13 August, he launched his Grand Attack. It was *Adlertag*, Eagle Day, the start of the Battle of Britain as Germany saw it. But the Met men got it wrong. Fog and thick cloud rolled in, and *Adlertag* went off at half-cock. 14 August brought rain and wind, as did 17 August, and from 19 to 23 August fighting virtually came to a halt. Flying weather from 25 to 30 August was poor. After that, September was mainly fair. By then, Goering's *Adlerangriff* – Eagle Assault – had lasted, not thirteen days, but a month. This was the month that mattered. He had not achieved the knockout blow he had promised. On the other hand, he had delivered – almost accidentally – what the German navy and army demanded. He had achieved air superiority – not over all of England, that was impossible; but where it mattered, over the invasion area.

CHAPTER THIRTY-ONE

A Perilous State

How can you know you've won if you don't know your goal? What exactly did the Luftwaffe's *Adlerangriff* aim to achieve?

At the time, leaders in Britain and Germany and America assumed that German triumph in the air would automatically bring about a successful invasion. (That belief is strong today.) The idea began early; before Dunkirk. On 21 May 1940, Admiral Raeder advised Hitler that *absolute command of the air over the English Channel* was essential. On 30 June 1940, a memorandum by General Jodl recommended *destroying the RAF*, as this would shatter Britain's will to resist. Two days later, a Fuhrer Directive said that '*air supremacy*' was the most important precondition. On 12 July, a Wehrmacht High Command paper defined it as the *moral and actual defeat of the British Air Force to the point where the opponent no longer exhibited any spirit of attack against the crossing worthy of mention.*

On 21 July, at his Karinhall conference, Goering ordered the *elimination of the RAF.* He used the word *ausschaltung*, meaning eradication. That was clear enough; and on 1 August a new Fuhrer Directive ordered the Luftwaffe to *overcome the British Air Force* – but it also said that once *local air superiority* was achieved, the Luftwaffe should attack British harbours. This echoed a previous Directive, of 16 July, which demanded *elimination of the RAF* but then ordered the Luftwaffe to prevent all enemy air attacks during the invasion crossing – attacks by an air force that had already been eliminated. Something strange here.

Hitler was good at cognitive dissonance: he could announce (and perhaps think) two contradictory ideas at once. Politicians get away with it all the time. When a commander-in-chief does it, the results are likely to be unhappy. What was the real object of *Adlerangriff*? Absolute air supremacy, or local air superiority?

Sloppy speech means lazy thinking. Hitler's generals treated words as if they were interchangeable: command meant supremacy, absolute command equalled total eradication; supremacy and superiority were twin brothers. But this is not so. Air superiority is second-best. It means the enemy is still in the fight: outnumbered, perhaps, but not beaten.

Germany had been spoiled by quick and easy victories. The theory of the knockout blow was still fresh and intoxicating. The Wehrmacht wrote off Britain as a hopeless, helpless mess, stunned by defeat. While the German army waited for the German navy to assemble an invasion fleet, the German air force – best in the world – would overwhelm the RAF (still groggy from its disastrous failure in France) and deliver the knockout blow. Goering promised total mastery of the air, and Hitler agreed; but he also spoke of 'local air superiority'.

Hitler was half-right. In the summer of 1940, absolute command of the air over Britain was a dream, a fantasy. The Me109's range was only 125 miles. The Luftwaffe's best fighters could not get past London. Its bombers faced heavy losses if they went further by day, without fighter protection.

This was self-deception on the grand scale. Throughout the summer, German radio stations signed off their news bulletins with the marching song, *Wir Fliegen gegen Engelland!* But Luftwaffe pilots knew exactly which bit of England they were flying against: its bottom right-hand corner. This seems to have surprised Galland: 'We therefore had to get used to the fact that our offensive could only be directed against a small and extraordinarily well-defended sector of the British Isles.' His fighter pilots, he said, became 'discouraged by a task which was beyond our strength'.

The Luftwaffe had made the classic military mistake of under-estimating the enemy. Goering had written the script for the Battle of Britain: his Luftwaffe was technically superior and therefore it would knock down the RAF fighters and compel Dowding to draw on his reserve squadrons so that they too would be wiped out, until only the Luftwaffe commanded the skies. It was like a game of chess in which Goering played both black and white. But Dowding failed to cooperate. He rotated his squadrons, he kept his reserves outside the main battle zone, and he avoided getting sucked into a gang war in the skies. Nine-tenths of England was beyond the range of the Me109. If Dowding would not come out and fight, the 109s could not go in and make him.

Goering was trapped in a long-range battle with short-range weapons. That meant he had to fight, not as he would, but as he must. His aim was to paralyse Fighter Command by hitting the airfields in the area his Me109s could reach: south-east England. This, by a happy coincidence, was also the planned invasion zone. Goering had no time for Operation Sealion. He believed it was a non-starter, his staff failed to discuss it with the other Services, and there was never an integrated invasion plan. But now, thanks to nobody, harmony broke out. The Luftwaffe was clearing the way.

From 13 August – *Adlertag* – Goering focused on 11 Group and hit it very hard indeed. Bad weather hampered the attack from 20 to 23 August, but the next two weeks saw Fighter Command battling to survive.

Bomb-aiming equipment was primitive in 1940. The attraction of a fighter field as a target was that it was findable, hittable and breakable. From 12 August to 6 September 1940, 11 Group's fields took a hammering, especially the sector stations.

Fighter Command's control system depended on their efficiency. Group HQ ordered the scrambles but the sector stations enacted the orders: they directed the squadrons towards interceptions, they managed the running of the Battle. Knock out its sector stations, and 11 Group would be paralysed. All the radar information pouring into Group would be useless if the sector ops rooms were bombed flat. (Few, if any, were underground.) Increasingly, that is what happened across the length and breadth of 11 Group. Beyond the Channel, the invasion fleets were gathering. The army was ready to load. And over south-east England, the Luftwaffe held air superiority.

To some, this may seem an ungrateful claim, even a subversive one. Surely it was the Luftwaffe that took a hammering? That is not the way it looked to those in command.

Air Vice-Marshal Keith Park, commanding 11 Group, was a very worried man. Later he wrote:

> The enemy's bombing attacks by day did extensive damage to five of our forward aerodromes, and also to six of our seven sector stations . . .

Of the sector stations, Biggin Hill was hit so hard, and so often, that it was near to shut-down: Tangmere, Kenley, Hornchurch and North Weald also suffered badly. Of the forward aerodromes, Manston and Lympne were sometimes unfit for use by fighters. Park went on:

> The absence of many telephone lines, the use of scratch equipment in emergency operations rooms, and the general dislocation of ground organization was seriously felt in the handling of the squadrons . . .

The 'dislocation' affected morale. Some personnel showed great courage (on one airfield a Waaf planted red flags where unexploded bombs lay, so that aircraft coming in to land could avoid them; at another airfield, telephone engineers worked alongside an unexploded bomb as they reconnected the lines to an operations room), but at Manston, which was not only bombed repeatedly but also strafed, some airmen retreated to the shelters and refused to come out. They were the exception. Nevertheless, Park could see 11 Group falling apart:

> Had the enemy continued his heavy attacks against Biggin Hill and the adjacent sectors, and destroyed their operations rooms or telephone communications, the fighter defences of London would have been in a perilous state . . .

And not only London. Fighter Command as a whole was shrinking in strength. Until the middle of August, the RAF could replace fighters and pilots lost in combat, but as John Terraine says, 'It was precisely at this stage that aircraft losses, for four frightening weeks, exceeded production and those in store.' In *The Narrow Margin*, Wood and Dempster offer a bleak verdict: the Command was 'wasting away under Dowding's eyes'. Worse was the loss of men. 'Experienced pilots were like gold-dust, and each one lost had to be replaced by an untried man.' Air Chief Marshal Dowding rotated his squadrons as they tired, but this did not necessarily save men's lives; sometimes replacement pilots died even faster.

As Churchill was to write, 'In the fighting between August 24 and September 6 the scales had tilted against Fighter Command.' If the Luftwaffe persisted with heavy attacks on the airfields, he feared the worst: 'the whole intricate organization of Fighter Command might have been broken down', and that would have meant 'the loss to us of the perfected control of our own air in the decisive area'. The losses in the air were already frightening: in the same fortnight '103 pilots killed and 128 seriously wounded, while 466 Spitfires and Hurricanes had been destroyed or seriously damaged. Out of a total pilot strength of about a thousand nearly a quarter had been lost. Their places could only be filled by 260 new, ardent, but inexperienced pilots drawn from training units, in many cases before their full courses were complete.'

In the first seven days of September, the Luftwaffe destroyed the equivalent of six RAF fighter squadrons. Squadron establishments – the number of pilots on the base – fell from 26 to 16. Of course it was two-way traffic: Fighter Command was taking its toll of the Luftwaffe; in the month from 13 August to 15 September, the crux of the Battle, 729 German aircraft were destroyed in combat, as against 535 British losses. But the German figure includes bombers, whereas the British figure is all fighters; and the Battle was fundamentally a duel between fighters. Air superiority really meant fighter superiority. Matthew Cooper has calculated that in September, at the Battle's climax, the Luftwaffe was shooting down two RAF fighters for the loss of one German fighter. In Mason's words: 'statistically, the Luftwaffe was winning the battle of aircraft attrition'.

This runs against the grain of wartime propaganda, which had Fighter Command as the underdog beating off the massed ranks of the Luftwaffe and shooting down many while it lost few. TODAY'S SCORE, 146 TO 20, a newspaper seller chalked on his board, and that was not the most extreme exaggeration.

The 'numbers game' was played by both sides; both deceived themselves. John Terraine's analysis of the claims is sober, and sobering: he reckons that aircraft losses for the entire Battle – July to October – were: Luftwaffe, 1,882; Fighter Command 1,017. And he identifies a 'serious blemish in existing accounts': they rarely include the losses of Bomber Command and Coastal Command, although both Commands had a hand in the effort to frustrate an invasion. The Air Ministry counted German bomber losses in its claims; common sense says it should have included British bomber losses that were the result, for instance, of bombing invasion barges in the Channel ports. When the relevant Bomber and Coastal Command losses (248 aircraft) are added, the Battle cost the RAF 1,265 aircraft against German losses of 1,882 – a ratio of 2 to 3.

These corrections are the fruit of historical research, far removed from the bodged intelligence of 1940. In any case, the Battle was not being fought on paper. What mattered was how many aircraft Goering and Dowding could call on – not aircraft being serviced or repaired, but operational aircraft, machines ready to fly and fight. At the start of September, Dowding had, in all of Britain, 358 operational Spitfires and Hurricanes. Goering had, in France and Belgium, 620 operational Me109s. He also had 770 operational bombers and 129 operational Me110s, and on the afternoon of 7 September his Luftwaffe demonstrated its superiority over 11 Group by sending the biggest aerial armada ever seen, almost 1,000 aircraft 'massed in a single huge phalanx stepped from 14,000 to 23,000 feet, advancing inexorably on a twenty-mile front', up the Thames Estuary, on its way to bomb London.

CHAPTER THIRTY-TWO

Nothing But German Aircraft

REICHSMARSCHALL Goering's armoured train, codenamed *Asia*, arrived in northern France on 6 September. It was an ambitious piece of work. At its head and tail were open wagons carrying flak batteries. Two massive coaches had been designed for Goering's special needs. In one was his vast wardrobe of uniforms, including a safe for his diamond-studded baton; two bedrooms; a luxurious bathroom; and a small study. The second coach was his spacious saloon-cum-cinema. After that came coaches for his map room and command post, his dining car, and accommodation for his guests and senior staff. It took 171 people to man the train and two of the strongest locomotives in Germany to move it. Goering's coaches 'had been specially ballasted with lead in order that their distinguished occupant might feel as little as possible the jolting which is inseparable from railway travel'.

There is something symbolic about Goering, who now turned the scales at twenty stone, crossing Europe not in an aeroplane of his own Luftwaffe, but in an armoured train whose route was carefully planned so that each night could be spent in the safety of a tunnel.

Next day, his Mercedes limousine (carried in a separate train) took Goering to the forward observation post at Cap Gris-Nez. A recording van was on hand, so he sent a message to the German radio audience:

> I personally have assumed the leadership of this attack, and today I have heard above me the roaring of the victorious German squadrons which now, for the first time, are driving towards the enemy in full daylight . . . Enemy defences were, as we expected, beaten down . . . this is an historic hour . . .

The German public knew that when the Reichsmarschall stepped into the limelight, glory was on the way.

Goering had ordered that London be attacked around the clock. Hitler was pleased with reports that Fighter Command was running out of men and machines. In Denis Richards' terse sentence: '. . . the world's largest air force was now within an hour's flight of the world's largest target.' The capital covered about 800 square miles. Even by night the Luftwaffe could scarcely miss it. Starting on 7 September, the Blitz on London was repeated for fifty-seven brutally destructive nights.

To launch this assault, Goering assembled the biggest air formation ever seen, and he sent it to raid London in broad daylight. This attack was stunningly successful.

In the words of the Official History, 'September 7 amounted to a victory for the German bombers, most of which had reached their targets without much difficulty, dropping more than three hundred tons of high-explosive and many thousands of incendiaries on and around the capital within an hour and a half.'

On that day, Germany certainly had air superiority over southeast England. Pilot Officer Steve Stephen, flying a Spitfire with 74 Squadron, was impressed. 'One German bomber formation stretched from over London right out towards Southend, twenty miles or more and, I suppose, about a quarter of a mile wide. And with an escort of fighters above. It was a breathtaking sight.' Squadron Leader Sandy Johnstone, leading the Spitfires of 602 Squadron, 'could hardly believe it. As far as you could see, there was nothing but German aircraft coming in, wave after wave.' The Luftwaffe made no attempt to evade interception with feints or decoys. 11 Group was simply overwhelmed. The Luftwaffe lost 41 aircraft to Fighter Command's 30, but all the British losses were fighters, while only 14 of the German losses were Me109s.

That night, London was bombed without pause from 8 p.m. to 4.30 a.m., and the docks burned like a beacon. Three hundred bombers took part. One was shot down, by anti-aircraft fire. British night-fighters were few and ineffective. Fighter Command was powerless after dark.

If Hitler had chosen to invade, either then or soon after, the RAF could have done precious little to stop him. Group Captain Tom Gleave commanded 253 Squadron in the Battle. He has identified three essential features of air defence: enough aircraft and good pilots; competent control from the ground; and satisfactory airfields with good communications to fighters and elsewhere. 'Fighter Command,' he wrote, 'came within an ace of being a loser on all three accounts.' So why didn't Hitler strike when his enemy was, if not down, certainly groggy?

One reason was the invasion timetable. The planned date to launch Sealion was 15 September, but on 13 September it was postponed to 21 September. Yet, given the startling triumph of the air armada on 7 September, surely the machinery of preparation could be made to run faster; surely the original date could be revived. The formula for victory taught by every Staff College is: consolidate success. If Hitler was serious about Sealion, he should have seized the moment and battered the RAF, in the air and on the ground, day and night, exploiting success to gain more success. For the air is not the land. No air force can own it while enemy aircraft still exist. At best, an air force can rent the sky by the hour, by the day. Air superiority can be won, but to be retained it must be fought for, again and again.

On 7 September, the Luftwaffe looked well capable of that. 11 Group was in a sorry state, and Fighter Command as a whole was weakening, losing every day experienced pilots it couldn't replace. Hitler had said, often, that the major prerequisite for Sealion was control of the air over the invasion area. Now he had it. The Luftwaffe dominated south-east England. When Hitler, instead of redoubling his assault on 11 Group's airfields, switched his target to London and the other cities, it can be argued that he changed his strategy of attack. Any commander is entitled to do so. But when he postponed Sealion *again*, to 26/27 September, and then on 17 September he called the whole thing off until nobody-knew-when, blaming the persistence of the RAF and the uncertainty of the weather, there could be only one explanation. Hitler lied.

CHAPTER THIRTY-THREE

A Little Help From Upstairs

HITLER lied about most things, to most people. He lied to Europe, promising peace and going to war. He lied to himself, dreaming of German colonies in central Africa. Later, he dreamed that America must lose to Japan, and so he hurried to declare war on the USA. One of his dreams was that Goering's bombers would shatter British morale and make an invasion a formality.

Like many a dream, this one contained elements that were irrational yet curiously persuasive to the dreamer. Until September 1940, the Luftwaffe's orders were not to frighten civilians needlessly but only to hit targets of military value – ports, airfields, factories, shipping. On 24 August, a Wehrmacht High Command document stressed that 'Attacks against the London area and terror attacks are reserved for the Fuhrer's decision.' Hitler played the part of the reasonable man who wished to treat his neighbour as his equal; at the same time he hurled threats of death and devastation at him if he did not come to terms. Part of Hitler admired the British as a force for order in the world, while another hated them for getting in his way. 'He alternately wanted them on his side and at his feet,' Peter Fleming wrote in *Operation Sealion*, 'and in his policy after the fall of France these two strains of purpose coupled to breed a mongrel strategy.'

As late as mid-September, that mongrel was still barking, although weakly: Hitler held out a faint hope that mass hysteria would make Britain crack. The irony of the situation was that if anything was vulnerable to concentrated air attack on 7 September it was 11 Group, not London; and by switching the point of attack from the sector stations to the capital, he gave Fighter Command a breathing-space: a chance to recover.

11 Group gratefully took it. The damaged airfields got repaired, the broken communications restored, the casualties replaced. Squadrons came back up to strength, and if the new pilots were raw, at least their commanders had the rare luxury of time in which to train them. London, and many other cities, took the pounding that had almost broken 11 Group, and this was rough on the civilians. But Fighter Command survived. Before long it was fighting fit.

And the weather helped: first with the usual English autumnal mix of rain, wind and cloud; then with a lucky accident that qualifies as a huge freak.

Goering could not command the weather. In the week after 7 September only one day was 'mainly fine', and the German assault was equally patchy. On two of those seven days, Fighter Command combat losses were 21 and 32; on the other five they were 4, none, 1, 2 and 8 (or slightly more on the last day if three Hurricanes shot down by Spitfires are included). Luftwaffe combat losses were similar.

Sometimes the low scores were the consequence of poor judgement by RAF commanders or controllers, resulting in a failure to intercept raiders. That was not what Goering's staff chose to believe. They reported that Fighter Command was almost finished; that its Spitfires and Hurricanes were too few to cover 11 Group. But Hitler was in a strangely mixed mood. He wasn't ready for Sealion, but he kept saying that the Battle was virtually won. Hitler on 6 September: 'Britain's defeat will be achieved even without the landing.' The Naval Staff Diary on 10 September: '. . . the Fuhrer thinks the major attack on London may be decisive.' Hitler to his commanders, 14 September: '. . . the operations of the Luftwaffe are beyond all praise. Four to five days of good weather are required to achieve decisive results . . . There is a great chance of totally defeating the British.'

General Jodl, Chief of Operations and a great reader of Hitler's mind, wrote that Sealion would take place only 'if it is a matter of finishing off a country already defeated by the air war'. So: one big final assault by the Luftwaffe and Sealion would be a walk-over, a formality – if you believed the Fuhrer.

On 15 September the weather cleared and Goering launched a big assault. This time he did not send his air fleets up the Thames Estuary; he sent them across Kent, straight at London. And he did not send one massive armada; he sent separate waves of raiders – one at about noon, the second at about 2 p.m. The ratio of German fighters to bombers was at least three to one. The remaining Spitfires and Hurricanes must come up to defend London. Then the masses of Me109s would get amongst them and shoot them down. Tactically, it was a straightforward plan. Yet it began to go wrong from the start.

Several historians have commented on this. Mason says that the German bombers, instead of heading for the mouth of the Thames Estuary and picking up their fighter escort on the way, flew west to rendezvous with fighters over France, and this move gave British radar an unusually early picture of the raid assembling, which Fighter Command exploited. Wood and Dempster agree; they write of 'the stupidity of large formations sorting themselves out in full view of British radar'. Telford Taylor, in *The Breaking Wave*, says, 'Whether from carelessness, overconfidence, or a desire to get the show under way without delay, the Germans neglected to carry out the usual diversionary flights and feints . . . This was a principal cause of the Luftwaffe's undoing that day, for it enabled Park to commit his squadrons in good time and at the right places . . .' T.C.G. James, in *The Battle of Britain*, writes: '. . . the success that the RAF squadrons later enjoyed was not least due to the unusually long interval between the first warning of attack and the enemy's advance.' He adds: 'To some extent this was true also of the second attack.' John Terraine agrees: 'Park was able to alert his squadrons to give the enemy a warm reception the moment they crossed the coast.' Len Deighton, in *Fighter*, comments on the way the Luftwaffe experimented with more complex formations, flying higher to avoid interception. 'Both the height and the complexity of the forming-up gave Park a little extra time to position his defences.'

The details vary – lengthy assembly; absence of feints; complex formations at unusual height – but the blame is the same. The Luftwaffe got off to a bad start, and paid for it. That was the accepted wisdom of what happened on 15 September 1940, until Dr Alfred Price gave an address to the RAF Historical Society on 12 June 2002, and blew the accepted wisdom to bits.

Alfred Price is a respected and experienced aviation historian. When he left the RAF in 1974 (after a flying career that spanned fifteen years, in which he logged 4,000 flying hours in more than 40 types of aircraft), he was immediately elected to a Fellowship of the Royal Historical Society. He has written many books – notably *The Hardest Day*, a study of 18 August 1940 – and he is a regular guest lecturer at the Royal Air Force College, Cranwell. He is the last person to debunk the Battle. At the same time, he has a historian's respect for the truth above all things, and his research has rewritten the events of 15 September. Certainly the Luftwaffe made mistakes on that day, but the big reason why so many of Park's squadrons could be up and waiting for the raiders as they reached the coast was the wind.

Alfred Price has looked at the weather charts for 15 September 1940. At 0700 hours there was high pressure over the Bay of Biscay, low pressure off Norway, and a wind from the north-west, high above England, that picked up strength all morning. In the afternoon RAF Bicester, near Oxford, recorded a 90 m.p.h. wind at 18,000 feet, from the north-west. The Met Office at Bracknell reckons that it had reached that strength at 1100 hours.

By then, radar had already seen formations assembling near Boulogne. Before long, these were at height, some above 20,000 feet, heading north-west across the Channel and head-on to a wind of hurricane strength. Bombers and their fighter escorts slogged against it. The first German aircraft took an hour to reach England: from 10.50 when radar first saw them assembling, to 11.50 when RAF fighters began to attack.

'That powerful wind,' Alfred Price said, 'almost on the nose of German aircraft flying on the main penetration route from the Pas de Calais to London, would have a profound effect on the entire action.' The obvious effect was to delay the Luftwaffe as it flew north-west. Another effect was to give speed to the RAF, as it flew south-east.

The first raid was not another air armada. About 60 Me109s were in the lead, freelancing, looking for trouble; they were followed by the bombers, only 25 Dornier 17s but guarded by 60 Me109s, half giving close cover, the other half giving open cover; and lastly a bunch of 21 Me109 fighter-bombers escorted by 21 Me109 fighters. All told, 187 aircraft. Against these, Fighter Command had scrambled 23 squadrons. The German arrival had been so slow that Park was able to request units from 10 Group to the west and 12 Group to the north. Twenty-three squadrons totalled 254 Spitfires and Hurricanes.

Soon the fighter-bombers and their escort, flying high above the rest, passed the Dorniers and pressed on to London. Defending squadrons saw them, assumed they were 109s hoping to decoy British fighters, and let them go. They reached London, tried to bomb rail junctions or stations, a hopeless task from such a height (each fighter-bomber carried only one bomb), caused some minor damage, and went home without loss and almost without having been involved. Their absence reduced the first raid to 145 aircraft against 11 Group's 254 fighters. And the raiders still had to fly 50 miles to London, against a wind that cut their speed in half.

Air combat is often described as a duel. It rarely has that simplicity. All 23 RAF squadrons were never in action at the same time. Three Spitfire squadrons were fully occupied with the free-hunting 109s, but Park harried the bombers all across Kent by sending in eight Hurricane squadrons, in pairs, at five-minute intervals. The escorting 109s, Alfred Price acknowledged, 'fought an excellent covering operation. As a result the Dorniers reached the outskirts of London without losing a single aircraft. But, due to the powerful headwind, the bombers reached the target about half an hour late. By then the Me109 escorts were running low on fuel . . .' Combat had forced them to fly at high throttle settings. 'When the Dorniers commenced their bombing run, virtually all of their escorts had gone home.'

What's more, thanks to the delay, Park had 12 squadrons perfectly positioned to attack the Dorniers, and they did so repeatedly. Nevertheless, the bombing was 'tolerably accurate', Price said, and 'rail viaducts were hit hard and traffic was halted for several hours.' Then the Dorniers had to fight their way back to France, which they did very skilfully. Six had been shot down; most of the rest had been hit. 'Considering the overwhelming concentration of RAF fighters . . . and the absence of escorts,' Alfred Price said, 'it is surprising that any of the Dorniers survived.' He pays credit to the formation leader's 'brilliant fighting withdrawal', to the ruggedness of the Dornier, and to the arrival of thirty 109s, sent to do escort duty. But the Dorniers' greatest saviour was the wind. It was still blowing at 90-plus m.p.h. Now it blew them back to France three times faster than they left it.

So much for the noon raid. The Luftwaffe lost six bombers and nine fighters. Fighter Command lost 13 fighters. Already, the second raid was climbing above the Pas de Calais, bomber formations picking up their escorts, in full view of British radar.

The second force was more than three times the size of the noon raid. There were 114 bombers (Dornier 17s and Heinkel 111s), covered by about 450 Me109s and perhaps 40 Me110s. A total of 600 aircraft.

Again they headed for London, and again the massive headwind dragged down their speed. 11 Group had time to plot the threat, and Park had time to counter it. He put 28 squadrons into the air: 276 fighters.

Three Spitfire squadrons met the enemy force as it crossed the coast. Other squadrons made repeated attacks over Kent. German progress was inevitably slow, but with such a huge shield of Messerschmitts the bomber formations reached London almost intact. There, Park had 19 squadrons in place, waiting. Not all the German fighters were low on fuel; many had flown from France in relays to defeat the headwinds and as Alfred Price said, 'a large proportion of these made it to the target area with the bombers'. Fighter Command would have to smash through the escort in order to get at the bombers. Meanwhile 100-plus Dorniers and Heinkels, keeping tidy formation in three columns, turned on to their bombing runs over three different areas of docks. And that was where the Luftwaffe had its second piece of bad weather luck. The docks were lost under a blanket of cloud.

The cloud had not been there in the morning. The day began

with some mist which burned off. The noon raiders saw London clearly enough. Then, as the second wave laboured over the Channel and across Kent, cloud built up. A lot of cloud. When the raid reached London, 'most of the capital was blanketed by nine-tenth cumulus and stratocumulus cloud with tops at 12,000 feet.' The bombers turned away.

Some RAF pilots claimed that their attacks had forced a Dornier formation to quit. Alfred Price believes otherwise: 'In fact, the Dornier formation had reached the capital intact, having lost only one aircraft on the way in, and it would easily have fought its way through to the briefed target had the crews been able to see it.' On their way out, they bombed targets of opportunity and – like the noon raid – raced home, harassed by Fighter Command but helped by the wind.

In combat that afternoon, the Luftwaffe lost 21 bombers and 12 fighters. The RAF lost 15 fighters. When both actions are combined (noon and afternoon), the Luftwaffe lost 27 bombers and 21 fighters: 48 aircraft. (Losses elsewhere that day bring the total up to 56.) The RAF lost 28 fighters. So 15 September 1940 – now celebrated as Battle of Britain Day – did not produce exceptional scores for either side. The RAF had lost more fighters (31) a week earlier, on 7 September. The Luftwaffe had lost 50 aircraft in two days' fighting on 9 and 11 September. If any single day in the Battle deserves recognition for the severity of the fighting, it is 18 August when, by Alfred Price's calculation, 100 Luftwaffe aircraft and 73 RAF fighters were 'put out of action'. But timing is everything in life, and 15 September proved to be the day when Hitler abandoned large-scale daylight raids in favour of the nightly Blitz: a strategic switch that acknowledged the failure of his air force to defeat the RAF.

CHAPTER THIRTY-FOUR

Spectacular Entry

WRITING in 1985, long before Alfred Price's research into the headwind, John Terraine said of 15 September, 'For Fighter Command, just about everything went right.' Alfred Price counts three large advantages that Fighter Command gained from that torrent of air streaming down from the north-west: the German advance was slowed; the escorts turned back early; and the RAF squadrons got an extra 15 minutes to move into position.

Nevertheless, both raids reached their targets, in 'tidy formation'. The first raid's bombing was 'tolerably accurate'. The second raid began its bombing run, and but for the cloud that covered them, three important London docks would almost certainly have suffered badly; in which case Battle of Britain Day might have been nothing much for Britain to cheer about. It seems reasonable to suggest that, on 15 September 1940, the Luftwaffe was frustrated as much by the unpredictable British weather as by the skill of Park and his controllers, and by the tenacity and courage of his pilots.

And just to ram home the message that this was not the Luftwaffe's day, the high wind delivered yet another boost to Fighter Command. It blew the Big Wing south.

The story of the Big Wing has been told many times, and this is no place to examine all the angles; they have been explored with the greatest clarity and fairness by John Terraine. What matters is that Squadron Leader Douglas Bader commanded 242 Squadron in Coltishall throughout the summer of 1940. That put him 100 miles north of London in 12 Group. The Battle was fought largely in 11 Group.

Bader chafed at inaction. He devised a tactical theory which would send a large formation – three, four or five squadrons – from 12 Group to help 11 Group when massed enemy raids arrived over south-east England. This was the Big Wing, often called the Duxford Wing because the squadrons would rendezvous there. Duxford is about 40 miles north of London. Bader would lead the Big Wing.

Park was not enthusiastic. He thought a Big Wing – assembling and climbing at the speed of the slowest aircraft – would take too long to arrive, could never achieve surprise, and would be inflexible in combat. Ginger Lacey, the most successful British pilot in the Battle, agreed. He described the Big Wing as 'cumbersome and time-wasting'. It was rarely used. However, on that one day, 15 September 1940, the Big Wing and the Big Wind came together and shocked the Luftwaffe.

Goering had assured Hitler that Fighter Command was broken. A few battered squadrons, half-strength and weary, were all that remained to be knocked out of the sky. So Luftwaffe Intelligence said. So Luftwaffe crews were told. The noon raid met 23 squadrons, full-strength and far from weary. The afternoon raid met 28 squadrons. None of these made a more spectacular entry than the Big Wing.

Five squadrons had assembled at Duxford and raced southwards, hustled along by a mighty tailwind. As the first raid reached London, the bomber crews – already hounded across Kent – saw a single formation of 55 RAF fighters heading for them. This was a shock. Later, the crews of the second raid had the same unhappy experience. Merely the sight of the Big Wing dealt a hammerblow to Luftwaffe morale. The more they looked, the more they saw. Alfred Price quotes the official Luftwaffe report of the action: 'Over the target huge formations of fighters appeared, with up to eighty aircraft.'

After such an emphatic entry, it would be satisfying to be able to celebrate equally big victories. In both actions, the Big Wing claimed to have destroyed 52 enemy aircraft. That was nearly 30 per cent of the total RAF claim for the day. Alfred Price has studied the evidence: 'In my analysis, I could confirm only five victories claimed by the wing, plus two more that it shared with fighters of No 11 Group . . . On that day, the Duxford Wing lost five Hurricanes and one Spitfire destroyed.'

Both sides over-claimed on 15 September. It was an inevitable feature of the high-speed confusion of air combat, not helped by the demands of propaganda. The Air Ministry – reacting too rapidly, and too hopefully – claimed 185 German aircraft destroyed, and that is where the figure remained until the end of the war brought about an uncomfortable correction to less than 60. But certainly the Prime Minister knew at the time that 185 German wrecks were not to be found in the south of England, and they could not all be in the Channel. He had prodded the Air Ministry to explain this anomaly once before. That didn't stop Churchill congratulating Dowding on 15 September (in what was really a press release) by saying that the Royal Air Force, aided by Czech and Polish squadrons and 'using only a small proportion of their total strength', had cut the Luftwaffe assault 'to rags and tatters'. Churchill knew that this was not true. That afternoon he had stood beside Park at 11 Group Operations Room and asked: 'What other reserves have we?' Park had said, 'There are none.' Churchill's 'small proportion' and 'rags and tatters' were wide of the mark, but they were justified because he was speaking not only to Dowding but to the British people, to the world, especially to America, and propaganda is a valid weapon of war. On the same day, Goebbels' Propaganda Ministry told *The New York Times* that 'in spite of tremendous numbers involved in the present battles, only part of the forces of the Reich's air army has been sent into action'.

Churchill's statement reminds us not to believe everything a nation's leader says. Churchill cheerfully bent the truth. Hitler went much further. He was dishonest by instinct, by nature. To understand Hitler's war, it pays to assume he was lying to everyone unless proved otherwise. This is certainly true of Sealion. He blamed the air battle, and he blamed the weather. He did not tell the truth.

The meat in the sandwich of the Battle of Britain was just one month: from *Adlertag*, 13 August, to Sealion stand-down, 17 September. Before that month there was skirmishing; afterwards, withdrawal. It did not seem so brief at the time, and all those Fighter Command aircrew who flew on operations between 10 July and 31 October certainly deserve their Battle of Britain clasps. They helped win two great victories in the summer of 1940. First, the RAF surprised and shocked the Luftwaffe, gave it a bloody nose over Dunkirk and a hammering over the south of England. This was not a total victory. As we have seen, neither side could claim that. But it was a psychological victory: it showed the world that the Luftwaffe was not invincible. For the first time anywhere, a courageous, resolute, well-organized defence had rebuffed a German attack, sent it home to mourn its dead, nurse its wounds, and wonder at the apparently endless numbers of Spitfires and Hurricanes waiting to hack at its flanks.

The second victory was strategic. Sealion died. This is not to say that the RAF could have prevented Sealion; far from it. But the Luftwaffe's failure to smash Fighter Command gave Hitler a convenient exit. In Britain it certainly *looked* as if the RAF killed Sealion. Hitler did not win the Battle of Britain and then he did not invade; surely one prompted the other? But war is not always as simple as that.

A MIGHTY RIVER CROSSING

CHAPTER THIRTY-FIVE

Sawing the Baby in Half

O_N 4 June 1940, the last day of the Dunkirk evacuation, Churchill sent a remarkably bullish memorandum to General Ismay, who was Chief of Staff to the War Cabinet. He asked: '. . . if it is so easy for the Germans to invade us, in spite of sea-power, some may feel inclined to ask the question, why should it be thought impossible for us to do anything of the same kind to them?' As he wrote, Churchill's enthusiasm grew: 'How wonderful it would be if the Germans could be made to wonder where they were going to be struck next . . .'

He dusted off a plan he had made in 1917 for an amphibious assault on the Frisian islands. Bulletproof landing craft would put the infantry ashore, and tank landing craft with wire-cutters in their bows would penetrate the defences. Churchill also proposed that barges or caissons made of concrete be towed across the North Sea and sunk to make a torpedo-proof harbour for warships. Advanced thinking, for 1917.

In October 1940, four months after Churchill's memorandum, the first British LCT (Landing Craft Tank) was being tested. Four *years* later, concrete caissons were towed across the Channel and sunk to make Mulberries: artificial harbours for the Normandy invasion. In the years between, the Allies had learned from amphibious landings in North Africa, Sicily and Italy. D-Day took four years to plan and prepare.

The German navy and army had about two months to make Sealion ready. The target date for S-Day of 15 September was later moved to 21 September. By then, the army was trained for the assault and the navy had created an invasion fleet – several fleets, in fact. The set-up wasn't perfect, but for Sealion to be ready at all was an amazing achievement.

Operation Sealion is a maddening story. Hitler cannot seem to make up his mind, contradicts himself, leaves everyone guessing. His commanders-in-chief seem not to be on speaking terms, and when they do speak, it is with forked tongues. Time seems to drift by, slowly, and then it races away: too many tasks, not enough days.

Many gifted writers have ploughed this rocky field, and I need not do their work again. One lesson they reveal is that there was almost no blunder by the various High Commands that could not be rescued and put right by the sheer hard work and competence of the junior ranks: a German characteristic that helped keep the war going for another five years.

The junior ranks had little to do in June, the month after Dunkirk. Hitler had peace on his mind and the Armistice in sight. On 20 June, the day before Compiègne, he summoned Admiral Raeder to a conference. Generals Keitel and Jodl (from Wehrmacht High Command) came too.

Raeder ran through a long agenda. Invading England came so far down that it was almost Any Other Business. The reason was simple: no boats. The navy had no landing craft. Give it two weeks and it could collect 45 seaworthy river barges, maximum. All Raeder's talk of landing zones and mines and (of course) air supremacy was just noise. The Fuhrer didn't like the sound of it: high risk, he said, heavy casualties.

So he said; but the High Command knew from experience that, with Hitler, all things were possible: remember how suddenly he ordered the army to stop outside Dunkirk. It paid to second-guess Hitler's mind, to display quick footwork. Jodl was skilled at that. On 30 June his memorandum on the war against England listed a three-stage strategy for victory. Invasion came a poor third. Once the Luftwaffe and the navy had brought England down, an armed landing would apply the *coup de grâce*. Invasion would be no more than a symbolic gesture. But even a gesture must be convincing. Therefore, there must be an operational plan and all suitable preparations made. Hitler agreed. Two days later, his Directive ordered planning to start. The document was secret; only five copies were made, and circulation was tightly restricted.

All those on the list could have gathered in one room, and still have had space for maps and blackboards. They could have agreed on a coherent, integrated plan. It never happened. The Luftwaffe turned its back on all invasion planning. In any case, the Fuhrer had command of all three Services. The last thing he would do was raise one man to be controller of a combined operation. There was only one leader in Germany.

So the navy and the army went their separate ways, and eleven days later – 13 July – von Brauchitsch, C-in-C of the army, presented Hitler with a plan to send three attack groups across the Channel, one each from Calais, Le Havre and Cherbourg, and land 31 divisions (plus eight in reserve) on a stretch of the English coast more than 225 miles long, from Ramsgate in the east to Lyme Bay (near Weymouth) in the west. This would ultimately involve moving over 500,000 men, thousands of horses and hundreds of tanks. The army's term for the operation was *grossen Flussüberganges*: a mighty river-crossing. Brauchitsch aimed to invade Britain on 15 August. Hitler approved the plan there and then.

The navy was stunned. Three weeks earlier, Raeder had told Hitler that he hoped to have 45 barges for use as landing craft by mid-July, and Hitler had nodded. Now it was mid-July and Hitler expected him to transport half a million men across the Channel, starting on 15 August. What, in God's name, was the army thinking of? The answer became obvious when General Jodl explained that the landing was to be:

> . . . a mighty river-crossing on a broad front, where the air force takes the role of artillery; the first wave of crossing forces must be very strong and . . . bridge building will be replaced by the creation of a sea transport road, completely secure against attack from sea, in the Dover Narrows.

So Germany would invade Britain just as she had invaded Poland, Holland, Belgium, France: by crossing rivers. The Dover Narrows were to be treated like a mighty river – yet the invasion was still to be 'on a broad front', which meant 225 miles. How could the navy deliver the troops to all those beaches? How could the air force protect them? Of course it was preposterous, and of course Raeder was not about to tell Hitler that. He played for time.

There were more conferences. The term 'river crossing' was abandoned. The navy pulled the invasion plan apart and scrutinized each piece. In the first wave, the army wanted to land 90,000 men, 4,500 horses and 650 tanks. The second wave would carry 160,000 men and 50,000 horses. The men must be fully equipped to fight, which added to the load. Reinforcements would follow, with more horses.

Analysis made the picture worse. The army wanted all the landings to be made on beaches. Every barge, tug and motorboat in Germany and Occupied Europe would be needed. After the first wave had crossed the Channel, the empty fleet would return to France to pick up the second wave, and return again, and so on.

More conferences. Raeder said the 15 August target looked highly uncertain. And then, on 28 July, the navy sent a memorandum to the army which created a minor *Donnerschlag*. Halder – Chief of Staff to von Brauchitsch – took the news very badly; it upset all the army's draft plans:

> . . . it states that Navy needs ten days to put the first echelon across. If that is true, all previous Navy statements were so much rubbish and we can throw away the whole plan of invasion.

It was like a bad marriage, both sides insisting, neither side budging. The army knew that a broad front assault was essential for success. Winning was the army's business. Let the sailors stick to *their* business, which was transport. The navy knew ships and it knew it couldn't collect enough ships for a broad front. Its alternative was a narrow front landing, between Folkestone and Beachy Head, less than 50 miles. The navy said it could put ashore a first wave of three divisions on this narrow front. Totally unacceptable, the army replied. British defenders would be waiting on high ground which the German soldiers could not outflank. 'Sheer suicide,' Halder called it. 'I might as well put the assault troops straight through a sausage machine.'

The army couldn't win with anything less than a broad front. The navy couldn't supply anything bigger than a narrow front. Only Hitler could break this logjam. For most of August he showed great skill at ducking and dodging, waiting for Goering's *Adlerangriff* to bring England down. Grudgingly, army and navy made concessions: Raeder found more ships, Brauchitsch gave up Ramsgate at one end and Lyme Bay at the other; now his front was only 80 miles wide. The operation had a codename, Sealion. The target date was moved to September. But it wasn't until 26 August that Hitler ruled that the army must take what the navy could give, and spelled it out in a directive from OKW (Wehrmacht High Command). In Telford Taylor's words:

> Thus OKW sawed the baby in half, giving to the Army a landing force which it thought inadequate, and saddling the Navy with a transport responsibility which it thought excessively dangerous.

In this new, slimmer operation, the first wave of the invasion would land nine divisions. Add other forces (Luftwaffe, paratroops, specialist units) and the total is in the region of 300,000 men and 50,000 horses. The second and third waves would bring 400,000 men and 75,000 horses. 125,000 horses eat a lot of hay: about 1,250 tons a day, which would have to be transported too. It is time to take a closer look at all those German horses being shipped to Britain.

Chapter Thirty-Six

Bold Arrows

WHEN Germany attacked the West in May 1940, its army had one horse for every four infantrymen. If he was lucky, the infantryman was on the horse, or at least in its wagon. If not, he walked. Most walked. There were only six motorized divisions of infantry, compared with 118 footslogging divisions.

Germany conquered France no faster than her infantry, kitted out for combat, could walk, which was no faster than the horses could pull the infantry's guns and its supply wagons. If every German horse in France had suddenly gone lame, the Blitzkrieg would have stopped dead. Tanks can win battles, but they cannot occupy a country.

The legend says otherwise. On the historians' maps, bold arrows mark the armoured thrusts. In the cinema newsreels of 1940, panzers always sped across the screen. In television documentaries today, the Blitzkrieg is all dash and crash, the armoured vehicles of the German army charging through holes it has blasted in the Anglo-French defence. Very rarely do we see an infantryman trudging forward. No news photographer or cine-cameraman would waste film on the Poor Bloody Infantry (unless they were surrendering) when he could get dramatic shots of tanks at high speed or of artillery belching flame.

There is no doubt that the ten panzer divisions were crucial in 1940, but France could not have been overrun and occupied without the 118 German infantry divisions – almost two million men – and those divisions could not have moved without horses. That was why the Sealion planners aimed to load 125,000 horses on the invasion fleets. They had no option.

Motor vehicles were never the strong suit of the German army. Its trucks weren't rugged enough, they wore out quickly, and factory output was painfully slow. When war began, it was army policy to use *more* horses: to replace written-off trucks not with new vehicles but with new horses. By the time the war ended, the Wehrmacht had used 2,700,000 horses, nearly twice as many as in the First World War.

In theory, the standard German infantry division had about 17,000 men and 900 vehicles. In reality, natural wastage and the stress of battle whittled away at the motor transport, which made the division's 5,000-plus horses all the more valuable. Wherever it went, the bulk of the German army travelled by horse. It rode into Paris on horses in 1940, and it rode out on horses in 1944.

Motor vehicles drank diesel or petrol, which meant carrying or finding fuel. The German army rejected the idea of carrying large amounts of fuel across the Channel and unloading it on the beaches: too hazardous. The chances of capturing British fuel dumps were slim. So 125,000 horses would be essential. You could always find a field where a horse could graze.

How to ship them over the Channel and put them ashore was another matter. The same question applied to landing the troops. They wanted to practise landing on beaches – something they had never done before – but for this, they needed boats. Hitler could order an invasion fleet, but when he whistled, would it come?

By the middle of August 1940, Sealion was looking sluggish. Some might say comatose. Only 12 per cent of the invasion fleet was in place and ready to go, and S-Day was a month away.

The navy had done its sums; it knew how many transport craft it needed to lift the first wave. In declining order of size, the list was:

165	steamers
390	tugs
140	trawlers
120	motor coasters
1,130	barges
1,500	motorboats

If they all turned up, that totalled 3,445 vessels.

The barges carried the infantry; without them, nothing. Tugs, trawlers and steamers towed the barges from shore to shore. Steamers carried supplies, heavy weapons, reserves. Some coasters were lightly armed to protect the fleet and support the landings. The motorboats had a complicated task that can safely be left until later.

Europe, and especially Germany, had a lot of barges, and that was why the navy requisitioned them: because they were there. It was certainly not because they were ideal for the job. They were made for canals and rivers, not for the heaving, surging, changing waters of the Channel. Two-thirds of them were not powered; the remainder were underpowered; all would have to be towed to England. The navy rejected many barges, powered or not: too old, too rusty, too stinking. Barges were not passenger vessels: they carried coal, chemicals, timber, potatoes, sand, cement, iron ore, fertilizer. Guano, maybe.

Those considered seaworthy went through a brief but brutal conversion. The wheelhouse was cropped. A concrete floor was poured, the hull strengthened and degaussed as a protection against magnetic mines. The pointed bows were hacked off and replaced with flat, batwing doors and a rudimentary ramp. This was the only entrance and exit. The barge had a sectioned roof, removable for loading cargo, but if all the sections were not in place the troops might have been drenched by spray, until they would be wading in seawater. River barges, when loaded, lie very low in the water. It would not take a large wave to slop over the gunwales. In any sea heavier than a flat calm, a river barge was liable to roll like a pig. Enclosing the troops would keep them dry. The price would be the stench. Good soldiers don't always make good sailors. Being unable to see the heaving horizon would not help their queasy stomachs.

It was a choice between hearing the waves thumping on the roof, and being seasick; or seeing the restless Channel, and being seasick. This is an occupational hazard of all amphibious operations. Probably, Sealion would not have suffered more than most, except for one thing: the barges would be at sea for a very long time.

But first the Germany navy had to bring them *to* the sea. The assembly area stretched from Rotterdam to Le Havre, 250 miles, and reached 100 miles inland, from Paris to Koblenz. Barges crammed the waterways and dockyards, and they could not be rushed. Barges were not built for speed. Meanwhile, the navy was searching for manpower. The barges alone would need 16,000 men, the whole fleet 24,000. The navy had 4,000. It recruited strenuously, mainly from merchant ships and yacht clubs. On top of all that, the harbours at Dunkirk, Calais, Boulogne, partly or wholly wrecked in the fighting, were still under repair.

Raeder's men were being ordered to do the impossible and so they tried harder. They worked night and day and proved that it wasn't entirely impossible after all. By the end of August, the shipping that was moving towards the Channel ports, ready for Sealion, made impressive numbers: 168 steamers, 1,900 barges, 221 tugs, 221 steam trawlers big enough to work as tugs, and about 1,600 motorboats. Tugs were still scarce, but they were being sent from as far afield as the great naval bases at Kiel and Wilhelmshaven, now left with only two tugs; which gives an idea of the urgency of the matter. When Sealion was postponed for a further week, to 21 September, the signs were that the navy could do the trick, could get Sealion afloat and meet the army's minimum demands. In mid-September the German commander of one Channel port said, 'I walked for miles from prahm to prahm [barge to barge]; a patch of open water was hard to find.'

Schwerpunkt

O PERATION Overlord – the Normandy invasion – began with an attack by five seaborne and three airborne divisions. Operation Sealion would have attacked with nine divisions by sea and three airborne regiments. So the numbers hitting the beach, and the silk, in each operation, would have been about equal.

The German army has always prided itself on its good staff work. Its middle-ranking officers must have toiled to complete the planning of Sealion. A measure of their progress is the way they sought to anticipate failure, and even to exploit it. As D-Day was to show, amphibious operations inevitably result in some confusion: boats get scattered, units land on the wrong beach, regular formations become split, mixed, leaderless. The German army was ready for this. Command on the beaches was to be highly flexible. Troops that got lumped together by accident – never mind their original units or their planned tasks – were ordered to combine in *ad hoc* fighting forces and to press home the attack. There was nothing rigidly Prussian about the Sealion plan, but this was partly because there was never a single plan for Sealion.

Blame the splintered nature of the Wehrmacht. Its High Command – Hitler's poodle – should have integrated the orders for all three Services. It failed. So: not so much a Sealion, more a performing seal keeping three balls in the air. Army High Command issued invasion orders on 30 August, Navy High Command on 20 and 30 August, and Goering on 5 September. This cannot have helped those staff officers who were putting together detailed plans for an intricate operation that would distribute an army and its horses throughout several transport fleets, always remembering that these fleets would leave from widely separated harbours at different times and sail at different speeds in order to attack England simultaneously at different points. This was a massive undertaking. Others have tracked its twists and turns and recorded them in detail. Fortunately we can leapfrog that process and jump to what matters: the launch of Sealion.

For ten days before S-Day, elements of the transport fleets would have been leaving Rotterdam, Antwerp and Ostend, working their way down the Dutch and Belgian coasts, reporting for duty at the Channel ports assigned to them. On the morning of S-Day minus 1, perhaps earlier, these ports would have begun loading men and animals. All day, the Port Commanders would have hustled the craft out through the locks and set about the devilishly difficult business of shepherding the tugs and their barges into tidy formations that matched the army's pattern of attack. By 4 p.m., most of that work would be done.

'The numerous proposed landing craft flotillas, with their neatly planned formations, indeed looked magnificent on paper . . .' wrote Vice-Admiral Otto Schulz. 'How, in practice, this mass of loaded craft could be sailed in the evening on time from the ports, could take up their prescribed formation . . . and . . . could make the Channel crossing in this complicated formation, by night, across the current, was a problem to any seaman.' And that was before 'one then took the enemy countermeasures into consideration.'

Sealion would go. Streams of barges and steamers, escorted by minecraft, would snake into the Channel from Dunkirk, Calais, Boulogne and Étaples. Other steamers would be moving to rendezvous with them. Further down the coast, at Le Havre, a mass of motorboats would embark on the long haul to Brighton.

The targets were four landing zones. From right to left, they were labelled B to E. (Zone A, at Ramsgate, was long since cancelled.) Zone B and Zone C each had its own transport fleet and army commander, but in fact the zones butted against each other, so B/C made one target area. This stretched from Folkestone, which is six miles west of Dover, around the sharp bulge of Dungeness, to Cliff End, five miles east of Hastings. Zone B/C was about 30 miles long. Zone D went from Bexhill westward around

Beachy Head to Newhaven: about 20 miles. Beyond it was Zone E, from Brighton westward to Worthing: about 13 miles.

Nobody was in any doubt that Zone B was the most important landing area. It was nearest to France. In army jargon it was the *Schwerpunkt*, the main thrust of the assault, where the crack troops would storm the beaches, and where the big break-out must happen. First secure the beachhead, then get the rest of the first wave ashore to consolidate the position, and surge inland. This success would create a great hinge in Kent so that the forces advancing from Zones C, D and E could revolve on the hinge and cut off London.

There were four landing zones, so there were four invasion fleets, here labelled B, C, D and E. First they had to cross the Channel. It is worth leaving Sealion, with its enormous convoys of tugs and barges and steamers and escorts forming up for the first time – there had been no chance of rehearsal – while we look at the English Channel. There is no stretch of water quite like it.

CHAPTER THIRTY-EIGHT

Problems for Cross-Channel Traffic

THE Admiralty *Dover Straits Pilot* is not an excitable book. It tells the mariner the facts, simply and soberly, as it has done since 1856. It describes far more than the Dover–Calais Narrows. On the English coast it reaches a hundred miles west, as far as Bognor Regis, near Portsmouth. On the French side it just fails to include Le Havre. It also covers a healthy chunk of the North Sea, up to and beyond Rotterdam. Sealion could have learned a lot from the *Dover Straits Pilot*. Under the heading *Sea and Swell*, it says:

> Dover Strait, and the sea areas on either side, have a very distinctive sea disturbance with the area to the W of the Dover Strait greatly affected by rough to very rough seas with SW to W gales. During these periods, conditions on both sides of the English Channel can cause serious problems for cross-Channel traffic as there is only limited natural shelter available along most of its coastlines.

Two things make the Dover Strait so distinctive: the shape of the Channel, and the depth of the sea.

Twice a day, the Atlantic tide floods into the Channel. At its mouth, between Normandy and Dorset, the Channel is 100 miles wide. Move up-Channel to Brighton–Dieppe, and the width is much the same. Then it starts to close. By Boulogne–Folkestone the width has halved. By Dover–Calais it has more than halved again. Now, what was a 100-mile-wide tide is forcing itself through a gap which at its smallest is only 18 miles across. Then the charge is reversed as the ebb tide drains from the North Sea back into the Channel. At Dover, sea level can rise and fall by 20 feet or more. It is the massive pressures and contortions of these colossal shifts of water, twice every day, that make the Dover Strait such a challenge to the mariner, who cannot even depend on getting ample deep water wherever he goes. There are banks, shoals, rocks, and worse, hiding in the Narrows.

Nobody sings of the White Cliffs of Fécamp except the *Dover Straits Pilot*. Between Fécamp and Dieppe and between Dieppe and Le Tréport, it tells us, the coast consists of sheer chalk cliffs, as much as 280 feet high. This 50-mile stretch is opposite Beachy Head: a standing reminder that a land bridge once joined England and France.

Its remains have not been scoured out by the tides. 'The whole area is shallow,' the *Pilot* says, and warns that the Dover Strait 'contains a number of dangerous banks lying NE–SW in mid-channel. These banks are composed of coarse sand and broken shell.' It adds that, because of these banks, navigation is restricted. In plain English: the banks are no-go areas. The seabed is also littered with wrecks – victims of the hazards of peace and war – and in 1940 both sides laid minefields. (Some – especially in the Dieppe area – have still not been swept.) But the shallow banks are the biggest hidden hazard. They are to mariners what bunkers are to golfers, only less visible, far bigger, and deadly to the trespasser.

Typical is The Ridge, in mid-Channel between Cap Gris-Nez and Dungeness: 'a dangerous steep-to shoal', the *Pilot* calls it, 'which runs 10 miles N–S and should not be crossed, even at High Water'. North of The Ridge, and also in mid-Channel, is The Varne: eight miles of dangerous narrow shoal, 'with strong tide rips in its vicinity, and, in bad weather, a heavy sea breaks over it'. The Varne, too, should not be crossed; neither should nearby Bullock Bank, six miles long and 'generally marked by strong tide rips'. There are others: Sandettié Bank, between Belgium and England, 15 miles of wide shoal, a trap for the unwary; Royal Sovereign Shoals, the biggest of a whole family of shoals that confront anyone sailing between Dungeness and Beachy Head; and more.

The escort vessels commanding the transport fleets would be crewed by German navy personnel who could read a chart; it's fair to assume they would lead their followers into safe waters, even if they couldn't guarantee that all of them would stay there.

What the escorts could not do is draw a straight line on their charts and sail direct to the landing zones, even if the hazards allowed it. The barges were too slow.

Four knots – four and a half m.p.h. – was an optimistic speed. Three knots was more likely. But even at four knots, the tugs and trawlers hauling the pairs of barges could not battle the tidal flow. If they tried to hold their course, butting against the tide, they would be lucky to make one knot. Accept the inevitable, go with the tide and make what headway you can across its enormous stream. When it turns, turn with it and let it sweep you back to your original crossing. With luck, you should be within striking distance of your target. For a sailor with only three or four knots of power, the shortest route across the Channel must always be a crooked course.

All this assumes helpful weather. If the weather turns foul, it might be a very crooked course indeed.

The problem was not insoluble. Britain could be invaded. The Romans did it. In the summer of 1940, German officers with time on their hands read Caesar's commentaries, *The Conquest of Gaul*. The book has chapters on his two British campaigns. They were not entirely encouraging. Caesar had a lot of trouble with the weather and with the tides, sometimes both together. They almost destroyed his first invasion in 55 BC.

This operation had much in common with Sealion. 'It was now near the end of summer, and winter sets in early in those parts,' Caesar wrote. He took advantage of some favourable weather. Ten thousand men in 80 transports and warships sailed from Boulogne to Dover. Cavalry in 18 transports left from a different port. The foot-soldiers crossed safely, but the cavalry transports made a hash of the tides and got swept back to France.

Caesar badly needed those cavalry. The British fought hard, and the Romans had a desperate struggle to win the battle of the beaches. Four days later, the cavalry transports set off again, 'before a gentle breeze'. They were in sight of Caesar's camp when 'such a violent storm suddenly arose that none of them could hold its course'. They were scattered. (Some got blown back to France again.) The original fleet, at anchor or beached, was so badly knocked about that the ships were 'unusable, which naturally threw the whole army into great consternation'. Food was short. Caesar hadn't planned on wintering in Britain. Bad weather persisted. The enemy reneged on a peace deal. The equinox was close. Caesar patched his ships, saw a window in the weather, and got his men off this soggy island before winter trapped them all.

Caesar had suffered as much from storms and the fickle rise and fall of the Channel as from the treacherous British. He went back again next year with a huge force, 20,000 men and perhaps 800 ships, of which 600 were genuine landing craft, built to his design for quick loading and easy beaching. The landing was unopposed. Caesar set off to do battle, 'feeling little anxiety about the ships because he was leaving them anchored on an open shore of soft sand'. He knew how to spin a yarn. We can sense doom.

Two days later, as his men were about to pounce on the fleeing enemy, news came 'of a great storm in the night, by which nearly all the ships had been damaged or cast ashore; the anchors and cables had not held . . . so that many vessels were disabled by running foul of one another'. Bloody weather. Bloody Channel.

Caesar spent the rest of the summer campaigning, hounding the British, while a massive repair programme went on. Then something odd happened. He was short of ships and he had a lot of prisoners, so he decided to make the return voyage in two trips; but, inexplicably, 'very few of the vessels coming over empty from the continent' reached Britain. It was every invader's bad dream: being isolated on the far shore. Caesar waited 'a long time' and then packed his men tightly into what ships he had. He was due some good luck, and he got it. The sea was calm.

Rome eventually got Britain, and eventually lost it. A little more than a thousand years after Caesar, came the only other conquest. Sealion's planners might have taken heart from William the Conqueror. First he had to win over many of his council in Normandy, men who respected both the Channel and the English army and who thought invasion was a reckless idea. Leadership and determination swung the argument for William, but it couldn't change the wind. His fleet left Normandy in August 1066, crawled up the coast and got no further than the little port of St Valéry-sur-Somme. In the end, William arranged a religious procession to pray for a change in the weather. Either divine intervention or the greatest of good luck sent him a favourable wind that put him ashore in Sussex on 28 September, just as King Harold was doing battle with his brother Tostig in Yorkshire. Thus William had two untroubled weeks to prepare for Harold's return. Soon he was king: the reward of drive, courage and skill. The Wehrmacht could claim all three qualities. But could it expect the British army to be in Yorkshire when it landed?

Seven hundred-odd years later, Napoleon fretted at the difficulty of the Channel – 'a ditch that shall be leaped when one is daring enough to try', he called it in 1803. His aim was to gather up more than 3,000 vessels to carry 100,000 men, 3,000 horses and 125 guns. The British navy was in the way, but Napoleon had a new idea, a dodge to beat the Channel winds *and* the enemy ships. All his oar-powered transports were to make a dash for England as soon as a total flat calm left the sails of the British warships limp and put their guns out of range. 'Celerity is better than artillery,' Napoleon said. Months passed. A total flat calm was in no hurry to arrive. He never had a chance to prove his epigram in the Channel, and eventually he invaded Russia instead.

Napoleon – like Hitler and Caesar – was a landsman. The restless, mischievous sea puzzled them all. Caesar wrote that he 'had found that owing to the frequent ebb and flow of the tides the waves in the Channel were comparatively small' – this, after storms had twice wrecked his fleets. Two thousand years later, General von Manstein, then commanding 38 Corps, left his car on the beach and went swimming in the Channel with his driver and ADC. They were far out to sea when they saw the waves lapping around their Mercedes. 'Only in the very nick of time did we succeed in getting a tractor to tow it out of the incoming tide.' Manstein – at the very heart of Sealion planning – understood the Channel no better than Caesar.

At least the German navy could accurately predict the tides. Predicting the weather was a gamble. At the end of July, naval operations staff produced a 15-page document that spelled out some hard truths about the crossing. Weather, it said, was a decisive factor. The barge tows must have calm conditions. Any seaway of more than Force 1 could bring disastrous consequences.

Admiral Francis Beaufort had the fine idea, in 1805, of devising a Wind Force Scale for the Royal Navy by classifying the strength of the wind according to its visible effect. Force 1 is a 'light air' of no more than three knots. The sea has no waves, but 'ripples with appearance of scales are formed'.

As the wind rises, the Beaufort Scale climbs through the breezes (light, gentle, moderate, fresh and strong) and the gales (moderate, fresh, strong and whole) to Force 11, which is storm, 56–63 knots, wave height 30–45 feet ('small- and medium-sized ships might be for a long time lost to view behind the waves') and finally Force 12, hurricane, 64 knots and above, waves over 45 feet high ('sea is completely white with driving spray').

Nobody can forecast the weather in the Channel with any confidence when the need is to promise sea conditions no worse than Force 1. Even a maximum of Force 2 is beyond any Met man to guarantee. The Channel is too volatile for that. A yachtsman can put to sea at dawn with a shipping forecast of Winds Variable, Force 3 or Less and at 11.30 hear the Coastguard tell him 'Southeasterly Gale 8 Imminent'. What Imminent means is Immediate. On the other hand the Channel can be unpredictably calm too. Look at the Dunkirk Evacuation: a week of flat seas.

Sealion might get lucky. The German navy might get the Force 1 seaway it wanted. What was certain was the weather would eventually change for the worse because, in the Channel, it always does; and then the empty barges – like Caesar's empty transports – might be blown to oblivion.

Or they might not. Bad generals (and admirals) seek reasons for not attacking, and always find them. Men like the Duke of Normandy think only of victory, take a risk, and sometimes – against the odds – they triumph. In the first year of his war, Hitler had attacked when his generals predicted failure, and he won. Maybe Sealion would be another surprise victory.

THE HEART OF THE LEGEND

CHAPTER THIRTY-NINE

Long Shot

LENI RIEFENSTAHL might have filmed the launch of Sealion. Her *Triumph of the Will* had celebrated the Nazi Party rally at Nuremberg in 1934, her *Olympia* had glorified the Berlin Olympics of 1936, and she had followed the Wehrmacht into Poland, filming its victories. Now she would be out to capture a spectacle beyond the reach of Cecil B. de Mille, something greater than Nuremberg, braver than the Olympics, more historic than Poland: the setting-forth of the biggest invasion force ever seen, and the beginning of the end of Britain. Mile upon mile of ships, backlit by the setting sun. Hundreds of funnels pumping black banners of smoke.

The best place to film would be from the glazed nose of a Ju88 bomber, cruising over the Channel. Riefenstahl would need an aerial view to capture the scale of the great transport fleets, but even so she would never get an entire fleet in one shot. Well, some things are best left to the imagination.

By sod's law, the crucial fleet would come out of the worst ports. The force aiming to go ashore on landing zone B – the *Schwerpunkt* – would sail from Dunkirk, Ostend and Rotterdam, the most easterly ports of the whole operation. Dunkirk was 19 miles from the cross-Channel route to zone B; Ostend, 43 miles; Rotterdam, 120 miles. Invasion vessels would have to load and leave those ports long before the rest of Sealion, or they would never join their fleet. The worst port was the nearest: Dunkirk.

Fighting during the Evacuation had left it in ruins. There were 80 wrecks to be seen in its waters, and probably more hidden under the surface. Barges – over 150 of them – had assembled for loading in the inner harbour. All but two of the locks leading to the outer harbour had been smashed. The port commander reckoned he would need four days to ease all the invasion traffic out to the open sea.

So, after some bumping and grinding in the crowded locks, the fleet would start to form up at sea on S-Day minus 1. This demanded space.

Each tug (*Schlepper*), whether it was a genuine tug or a steam trawler, would tow two barges in tandem. The preferred arrangement was an unpowered barge first, leading a powered barge. (There were too few powered barges; in any case, they lacked the thrust to master the Channel, let alone to haul a second barge.) Tug skippers would keep a safe distance, using long cables to separate all three vessels. Nobody wanted any bumping and grinding in the chop of the Channel.

So a tug unit (*Schleppzug*) might have occupied two hundred yards of water, or more. A group of tug units made a *Schleppverband*. They would form up in columns, two, three, even four abreast. Crews were new. This would be the first time they sailed in formation. Skippers would allow generous space between tug units and columns. Nobody wanted a rogue barge fouling somebody else's tow-line.

The Sealion timetable required one *Schleppverband* (25 tugs, 50 barges) to leave Ostend about midday on S minus 1, early enough to rendezvous with the second *Schleppverband* (75 tugs, 150 barges) which would have left Dunkirk at 4 p.m. Together they would carry advance detachments of two infantry divisions – the 17th and the 35th, of the 16th Army. The rest – from Ostend and Rotterdam – would be coming along behind in a *Geleitzug*, a group of steamers, here 57 strong, towing 114 barges.

Slowly. River barges could not be rushed down the North Sea. Three or four knots, in the churning wake of a steamer, would be a good average. From Rotterdam to the rendezvous might mean the best part of three days and nights: a long time for a soldier to sit in a barge. Its sanitary arrangements would be minimal. Perhaps the sailor's maxim of 'Bucket and chuck it' would apply. Certainly the army grooms looking after the infantry's horses would have been kept busy with shovel and broom.

By 8 p.m. on S minus 1, the two *Schleppverbaunde* out of Dunkirk and Ostend – 100 tug units – should have met, linked up, and begun nudging their way into the Narrows. With the *Geleitzug* from Ostend next and the Rotterdam *Geleitzug* following – 57 steamers in all – transport fleet B would stretch over ten or 12 miles of sea. At its head would be the men to storm the beaches in minecraft. Next would come 200 barges, carrying the assault troops; then 57 steamers, towing 114 barges. This was the First Strike of the First Wave. The hope was to get 60,000 men ashore by the end of S-Day, and 110,000 men (and 24,000 horses) into the Zone B Beachhead by the end of S-Day plus 3.

Transport fleet B – the key formation – would be one of four fleets, some even bigger.

From Calais, 100 tug units would go to sea, in columns three abreast, loaded with forward units of 16th Army's 7th Infantry Division and the 1st Mountain Division, heading for Landing Beach C: Dungeness to Cliff End. From Boulogne, transport fleet D's mass of barges would be so great – 330, making 165 tow units – that they would form up in rows four abreast. Their target was Bexhill–Newhaven. By the time the last tug unit cleared port, the first would be halfway to England.

Finally, Le Havre would send transport fleet E, the weakest force, with the longest route. Two regimental groups – 3,000 men and equipment – would cross in 200 motorboats and 100 motorized sailboats, to land at Brighton–Worthing. If they got ashore and dug in, 25 steamers with tugs and barges would follow. Meanwhile a further 25 steamers would make a massive detour via Boulogne, for reasons that make very little sense. They might reinforce the Brighton attack or they might not: nobody knew for sure. From Le Havre to Brighton is 85 miles; more, when the winds and tides have their say. The motorboats would do well to average 7 knots. Landing Beach E was an awfully big task. Nevertheless, the fleet – 20 boats wide and 15 boats long, with minesweepers and picket boats to screen them – would make an impressive formation.

Then there was Sealion's bodyguard. For ten days, minesweepers would have been out in the Channel, sweeping mines from the fleet routes; and for ten days the navy and the Luftwaffe would have been laying minefields to block any interference with the invasion. These mine barriers were codenamed Caesar, Bruno, Anton and Dora. Minefield Caesar, off the Goodwin Sands, was designed to stop the British navy entering the Straits from the North Sea. The purpose of minefields Bruno and Anton was to flank the route to be taken by transport fleet E, from Le Havre to Brighton. Minefield Dora, 150 miles further west, was designed to fend off any threat from the big naval base at Plymouth. Raeder reassured Hitler that his navy could do the job. In the event, German minelaying failed to deter the Royal Navy. What Hitler was most interested in, however, were the big coastal guns, the bigger the better. He could never get enough of them.

As early as 30 May, when the Battle for France still occupied his generals' minds, Hitler was thinking of shelling deep into England from Calais. Army High Command asked the Navy to nominate targets up to a range of 80 miles (calling for a very big cannon indeed, and one which didn't exist, although there is evidence that the German army kept trying, and failing, to make it). On 12 July, when invasion was still just a plan on paper, Hitler gave high priority to coastal artillery. The army kept two batteries, K5 and K12, for hurling shells deep into England, but the navy had fire control over all the others, which existed to 'command the straits of Dover under all circumstances'. Next day the chief of naval ordnance urged that Hitler be told that these guns could not be much help to an invasion, but his advice seems to have been unwelcome, because three days later Wehrmacht High Command demanded installation of 'the largest possible number of heavy guns' to protect the crossing and 'to cover both flanks against enemy interference from the sea'. The Fuhrer's passion for big guns – shelling the enemy always made him feel more secure – quickly gave the Calais area the firepower of several battleships.

By mid-September, 13 massive weapons had been mounted in huge concrete casemates. Four 11-inch guns were ready to fire from Cap Gris-Nez by early August. Three 12-inch, north of Boulogne, were ready in mid-August. Four 15-inch, south of Gris-Nez, were scheduled for mid-September, just as two 11-inch near Blanc-Nez came into action. And these were just the battleship-calibre guns.

August also saw the arrival of 35 heavy and medium batteries from the army and seven heavy batteries, formerly French. All told, the navy controlled over 150 pieces of big artillery. Its first task was to make the Straits too hot for British shipping to pass through in daylight. This was a large, determined effort, and a total failure.

The British convoys were big (up to 25 merchant ships) and slow (5 or 6 knots). Coastal batteries began shelling them on 12 August. Soon every convoy the gunners could see was being shelled. Between August and December 1940 they fired at least 1,880 rounds. The results can be found in Admiralty records: 'No British or foreign merchant ship was sunk by the enemy batteries throughout the war. No foreign merchant ship was damaged. Seven British merchant ships . . . were damaged.' Churchill, too, was excited by coastal guns. The Admiralty installed several near Dover. 'Many long-range duels were fought between the batteries which faced each other across the Straits,' the Official History says. 'But in fact neither side did appreciable damage to the other's batteries or to his shipping.'

Hitler's big guns were a dictator's toys. If they could not hit a slow convoy by day, how could they hit a fast destroyer flotilla by night?

CHAPTER FORTY

Bullets Versus Barges

THE promise of a canopy of shells was welcome, but for solid reassurance nothing could beat the very visible umbrella of the Luftwaffe.

Goering's indifference to Sealion would vanish like smoke as soon as Hitler said the fleets would sail. All summer the army and the navy had demanded air superiority for Sealion; all summer the Luftwaffe had boasted that the RAF was battered, shattered, on its knees, out of the battle. Now the Luftwaffe must prove that point. It must keep the skies clear above the embarkation ports while the fleets assembled, and then guard them as they headed into their crossing routes.

That shouldn't be difficult. Despite the tenacity and courage of Fighter Command's pilots, and for all the British wizardry of radar and control, by September 1940 the Luftwaffe was stronger than the RAF. On 1 September Fighter Command had 650 machines on squadron strength but only 358 Spitfires and Hurricanes were serviceable, and losses exceeded production to such an extent that, if the rate continued, in three weeks reserves would be nil. On 7 September, Luftwaffe Air Fleets 2 and 3 (Belgium and northern France) had 787 operational Me109s and 129 operational Me110s.

Northern France and Belgium were thick with Luftwaffe bases. Their organizational skills had been polished by a summer of combat. Whenever he wished, Goering could summon fighter squadrons from Occupied Europe – nobody else was fighting Germany – and saturate his airfields with more 109s and 110s. Numbers like that would allow him to order standing patrols from dawn to dusk in the build-up to S-Day. High-flying squadrons could watch over the Channel, to intercept intruders. Freebooting Me109s could raid Kent and Sussex and keep Fighter Command busy. On 7 September, when Goering put nearly 1,000 aircraft (350 bombers, more than 600 Me109s) over London, he still had a healthy reserve. In all, his fighters flew 1,000 sorties that day. A week later they did the same again.

By then, of course, the Luftwaffe had shifted its aim from the sector stations to London (mainly by night, when no fighter escort was needed). This change relieved the pressure on 11 Group but it made no difference to operations above the Channel. On 20 September, S minus 1, there would be nothing to stop the Luftwaffe keeping a vast umbrella of 109s over the invasion fleets. And with airfields close at hand, they could land, refuel, rearm and return to the sky in 15 minutes – the RAF's tactical advantage in the Battle now being reversed.

It is hard to see how British fighters – outnumbered, and using up fuel and ammunition in combat – could reach many barges, and harder still to see how they could damage them, or the steamers.

The Spitfire and the Hurricane were not tankbusters, let alone shipbusters. Their eight guns fired a maximum of 13 seconds of rifle-calibre 0.303 bullets. These were designed to smash the alloy skins and the engines of enemy aircraft. They were not meant to hammer holes in the steel hulls of barges. Even wooden hulls would be thick enough and rugged enough to absorb bullets. Sealion's barges were made to hold heavy cargo and to take the thousand shuddering thumps and bashes that river traffic endures. No doubt strafing would be a frightening experience for troops inside the vessel, but it is hard to believe that a 200-ton (some were 600-ton) Rhine barge could be sunk by a Spitfire in 1940.

The hard fact is that Fighter Command would have been the wrong weapon to send against a German invasion fleet. The combats above the Channel would have damaged both air forces. They would not have sunk a single ship. Fighter Command won a great victory over the Luftwaffe, simply by refusing to be beaten. It did not stop Sealion, because it could not stop Sealion.

Nobody in Fighter Command – certainly not Dowding or Park – ever claimed that it could. That myth has been added by others who have not paused to think how fighters firing rifle-calibre bullets could sink an invasion fleet.

This goes to the heart of the legend of the Battle of Britain, which declares that Germany could not invade Britain as long as Fighter Command survived. The reality is that, if Sealion had sailed, Fighter Command alone could not have stopped it or even slowed it; especially as most of the Sealion crossing would happen at night. In 1940, almost all fighter aircraft ceased to fight at night.

Bombers, of course, did not. What could Bomber Command do against Sealion?

CHAPTER FORTY-ONE

The Great Shield

BOMBER HARRIS – Marshal of the RAF Sir Arthur Harris – was not slow to make big claims for Bomber Command. God knows, his men deserve all praise and thanks: they alone carried the fight to the Nazi homeland during the years between Dunkirk and D-Day, and they paid a grim price for it. More's the pity, then, that Harris went too far in 1946 when he wrote: 'It was definitely Bomber Command's wholesale destruction of the invasion barges in the Channel ports that convinced the Germans of the futility of attempting to cross the Channel.' Those who have looked at the facts believe otherwise.

Terraine reckoned that 'RAF bombing crippled about 12 per cent' of invasion craft. Grinnell-Milne reckoned that 'less than 10 per cent of the assembled shipping' was 'sunk or damaged . . .' Walter Ansel's estimate was smaller. He reported the totals of invasion craft in the Channel and Lowland ports by 27 September – 1,859 barges, 397 tugs, 68 command boats, 1,000 motor boats, 100 coastal motor sailers, and 159 steamers (of 2,000 to 8,000 tons). This was *after* RAF bombing had knocked out 79 barges, five tugs, seven motorboats and seven steamers. Peter Fleming reckons the damage was worse: 21 steamers lost (of 170), 214 barges (of 1,918), five tugs (of 386), 3 motorboats (of 1,020). Pick whichever report you like; the result is a very long way from the wholesale destruction 'definitely' claimed by Harris.

'Every port from Antwerp to Dieppe was packed like lumber floating in a river with thousands of these invasion barges,' wrote Guy Gibson, a Hampden pilot in 1940. The barges were moored inside the basins of these ports. Bomber Command raided them on twenty-three nights in September. Six of those raids involved over

50 aircraft; five involved over 100 aircraft – major efforts for those days. Claims were high (Gibson believed he sank 100 barges in Antwerp docks one night) but photo-reconnaissance evidence soon punctured those claims. In 1940, Bomber Command was small and poorly armed: Gibson's aircraft carried 'many small bombs, even hand-grenades, which would, at least, do the job if they hit the right spot.'

Viewed from England, the packed rows of invasion barges might seem a simple and inviting target. All too often the bombers became the target, as men like Gibson discovered the hazards of flying at night into the heart of a port that was heavily protected by a ring of flak, searchlights and barrage balloons. 'The RAF disturbed rather than disrupted the German preparations,' Fleming wrote. No doubt a lot of German army orders got torn up and rewritten. But the loss of 79 barges (or even 214) would never stop Sealion. The German navy had 700 barges in reserve, waiting to fill the gaps.

If Bomber Command found it difficult to hit invasion barges when they were tied up in port, row upon row, it is reasonable to ask what success the Command would have had against single barges at sea, separated from each other and from their tugs by perhaps 100 yards of water. Bomb-aiming equipment was not designed for such small and scattered targets. Moreover, RAF bombers sent to attack the transport fleets in the last hours of daylight on S minus 1 would meet massed patrols of Me109s, and this would lead to a very one-sided contest. Nine months previously, Bomber Command had called a halt to all daylight raids, after two disastrous operations had proved that bombers without fighter escort were easy meat for Me109s. Any bombers not shot down would be hounded and harassed. The transport fleets were long; some bombs might strike home; but it would be a lucky strike.

The German fighters would land at sunset. Bomber Command might try again. Its target would be no easier to hit by night than it was by day. The experience of Dunkirk provides good evidence of this. Then, evacuation in daylight had to stop because Luftwaffe attacks had become too dangerous, but evacuation began again successfully at night, when darkness shielded the beaches and the ships.

Darkness was the great shield over Sealion. As the fleets churned slowly along their invasion routes, Bomber Command would be hunting for strings of small dark ships on a black sea in a black night. And Fighter Command would be grounded. The fact of a night crossing takes all the steam out of the argument that Fighter Command alone would have stopped an invasion. For all that Fighter Command and Bomber Command could do, the Sealion assault troops would have been hitting the beaches of Sussex and Kent as dawn broke on S-Day.

THINGS THAT GO BUMP
IN THE NIGHT

Chapter Forty-Two

Dawn or Nothing

THE German navy wanted to ship Sealion to England in daylight. The crossing would be something between a headache and a nightmare; all sailors agreed on that. The transport fleets were slow and clumsy and they trailed to the horizon. Just to lead them around the hazards of banks and wrecks – unmarked in wartime – while making allowance for tides and currents would test the most competent navigator. The tug units might bunch up or scatter or lag behind; perhaps all three. The crews were raw and they had few radio links. Air cover was essential, but rain or cloud might interfere. So it followed that the escort vessels must have daylight to marshal their untidy force, and to identify the landing beaches on the other side. Even in daylight (which might include mist or fog) the task was massive. The navy knew that without daylight, without such peacetime aids as buoys and lightships, approaching a blacked-out coast, confusion and error was guaranteed.

The German army insisted on a crossing by night. It had one good reason for this and one was all it needed. The army always attacked at dawn. Its soldiers had a clear view of their targets and all day to capture them. Compel the army to attack in late afternoon or at dusk, and when night fell who could be sure who was doing what and where? The soldiers would dig in and wait. The enemy would rush in reinforcements. By dawn the attackers would be the defenders. So: no debate, no compromise. It was a night crossing and a dawn landing, or nothing.

The navy won a small concession: moonlight. It must have some light to help it shepherd the great ungainly fleets. Everyone agreed that high tide was essential in order to lift the barges over rocks

241

and sandbanks and to put the soldiers ashore well up the beaches. But the barges must return to France, and reload. To make sure that they would refloat easily at the next high tide, it was essential to beach them two hours *after* high water.

So the formula wrote itself: S-Day must have a quarter-moon and a high tide two hours before dawn. The German navy calculated which days in September met those needs, and told the army. Across the Channel, the Admiralty put itself in the Wehrmacht's boots, made the same calculations, and told Churchill's War Cabinet just when Germany was most likely to invade.

CHAPTER FORTY-THREE

Hit the Beach

To the British, there is something clanking and ponderous about jawbreakingly long German words created by butting several short words together, such as *Himmelfahrtskommando* and *Vorausabteilung*. In fact, both were accurate labels for the same part of Sealion. The official term for the spearhead – the first men ashore – was *Vorausabteilung* (Advance Detachments). Unofficially, it was known as *Himmelfahrtskommando*: Heaven-Travel Command. The humour of front-line troops is usually black, but the Germans spearheading the beach landings must have known the chances were that half would die; like all front-line troops, each man assumed he would be in the other half. Which is not to say that the assault would fail. An amphibious landing at dawn is an unpredictable business.

Some things were known. The *Vorausabteilung* must arrive well ahead of the main body of the fleet. Tug units could not anchor offshore; tides, currents and winds would turn the barges into a cat's-cradle of confusion. The tugs must keep moving, keep the force in shape, hope that the advance units could seize the beaches and make them safe for the barges to approach, slowly, and to unload, quickly, with nothing to hide behind.

The *Vorausabteilung* for each landing zone was 2,000 picked men. Their orders were to storm the beach. They would arrive at speed on 16 minecraft (minesweepers or minelayers) and transfer to motorboats and sturmboats a few hundred yards from shore. The sturmboats were true army craft: small, fast, open, unarmoured; made for river crossings. There were never enough of them; hence the motorboats. There was also talk of using rubber dinghies, which would be paddled ashore; photographs exist of troops practising this. There was even mention of pneumatic rafts. Raked by shore fire, they would be the forlorn hopes of the operation. Each sturmboat carried only six or eight soldiers. There would be much shuttling back and forth between minecraft and beach. Inevitably, some sturmboats would be sunk.

There could be no surprise. The defences would have been tracking the invaders for some hours, with patrol boats, with flare-dropping aircraft, and at first light, by eye from the shore. Now would be the moment for Fighter Command. Strafing could do great damage, both to the thin-skinned sturmboats and to the men struggling ashore.

The troops had some help in the shape of motor coasters and small ferries fitted with ship-to-shore artillery; but in training, German army gunners had found that a rolling, lurching ship made a poor gun platform. And these gunships were scarce. On 17 August 1940, the 16th Army laid on a big demonstration landing south of Boulogne, for the benefit of Field Marshal von Brauchitsch. Fire from ships at sea was represented by exploding charges that had been planted beforehand on the beach. General Halder, the army's Chief of Staff, was not impressed. Where are the ships to throw the shells? he asked. Good question. In the end the navy had 27 coaster gunships. Six or seven per landing zone. Not enough.

There was always the Luftwaffe. German fighter pilots would have had an early night on S minus 1, knowing that they would be airborne again in the grey of pre-dawn, back in the business of keeping the sky clear over Sealion. British fighters – low-flying at high speed – would be hard to stop; bombers less so, unless there was cloud cover in which they could hide.

The assault force for Landing Beach B – nearest to the Pas de Calais – had high hopes of the Stuka squadrons based there. From the beginning, Sealion plans had divided the tasks: the navy would act as engineers, getting the army across, and the air force would act as artillery, knocking out enemy strongpoints. The Stukas had taken a beating over England, and the Luftwaffe had been slow to rebuild. General Wolfram von Richthofen commanded the Stuka force. He believed he had too few squadrons to cover the 16th Army's front. He proposed that it be narrowed; a First Wave of only one corps seemed right to him. This would have been even narrower than the navy's suicidal sausage-grinder of a Narrow Front. The army dismissed the idea.

With luck, constant dive-bombing would keep the defenders' heads down. Smokescreens, bad weather and groundfire might interfere. There was no radio link between assault units on the beach and aircraft overhead; collateral damage from friendly fire was to be expected. It had better not be from the big coastal batteries in France. A 15-inch shell in the wrong place might wipe out a large part of a *Vorausabteilung*

Alongside minefields and air cover, these coastal batteries – so the plans said – would protect the transport fleets. This was Hitler's fantasy. By S-Day, the fleets were out of the gunners' sight. There was no pre-arranged fire to help the assault on Beach B. All other landing areas were out of range. This had been obvious from the start. The coastal batteries were Hitler's folly, but nobody dared say so.

Clearly, the assault troops needed more help than the Luftwaffe and the batteries could give. Sealion would arrive late in the year. The beaches were staked and wired. The beaches were mined. The beaches were covered by crossfire. To get from the waterline and capture a beachhead the troops would need tanks, and perhaps they existed.

General Reinhardt had had a good Blitzkrieg, leading an armoured corps. Early in July he was put in charge of an experimental team to solve the problem of landing over open beaches. Underwater tanks were a top priority. He took his team, and some navy advisers, to the island of Sylt in the North Sea. By 22 August he had 210 underwater tanks, boosted to 250 by September. This was a remarkable achievement. It was an impressive weapon. Reinhardt's team had taken the standard German medium tank, waterproofed it, and added an air intake in the form of a large flexible tube whose end was buoyed to make it ride on the surface. The critical moment would be the launch. Reinhardt urged the Luft-waffe not to bomb the shallow waters beside the landing areas: he wanted a smooth seabed for his tank-tracks.

Specially adapted barges would bring the tanks across the Channel, approach the landing area and lower their ramps. The tanks would drive off, sink, settle on the bottom, and crawl to the beach. Fifty or sixty German tanks churning out of the sea on to Beach B, crushing the wire, giving the infantry protection, shelling the defences, might have thrown back the enemy long enough for self-propelled barges to rush the beach and release a thousand infantry.

All the tests, however, were done at places like Sylt, where the waters were shallow and the seabed was smooth sand. There was no such guarantee off the Kent and Sussex coasts. Each underwater tank weighed about 23 tons. Its greatest operating depth was 25 feet. Its crew, once they had sunk to the bottom, would be driving blind. The tank might struggle in clay or lurch into a hole or bounce off rocks; it might be swung by the tide or currents until it was driving parallel to the shore, as happened to some Allied 'swimming' tanks at D-Day. Or the crew might be lucky and reach the shore, perhaps on friendly sand, perhaps on steep and unfriendly shingle. Nobody knew, especially General Loch, com-manding the 17th Division. No underwater tank ever reached him.

And nobody knew how the great fleet of barges would have succeeded in landing. Here was another horribly complex opera-tion that could never be rehearsed in full. Such small rehearsals as were made were not encouraging. Early in September 1940, Cap-tain Puttkamer, Hitler's naval adjutant, reported that he had wit-nessed a recent exercise near Boulogne in which landing barges drawn by tugs had been thrown into complete disorder by the tide.

The German navy worked out – on paper – a move that was brutally simple. A transport fleet approaches England, following the swept route that takes it parallel to the coastline and about ten miles out to sea. When its commander calculates that the fleet is opposite its landing zone, he orders every tug unit to turn right simultaneously. (Few tugs had radio. The order would be given by the blinking of green lights and by megaphone.) The tugs now are battling the falling tide.

Walter Ansel has made a study of this manoeuvre. His comment:

> Imagine turning one hundred tandem barge tows, three or four abreast, from column into line, off a hostile shore in the dark of night, with a raging power of three or four knots at your command!

The tows would take at least two hours to approach the shore, under fire all the time. To avoid grounding, each tug would have to release its barges well offshore; this would leave one underpowered barge chugging to the beach while the unpowered barge accepted what help it could find. One suggestion was that cutters or motorboats be lashed alongside the barge. Its final approach would be desperately slow, and painfully exposed to shore artillery.

What Sealion needed was a port in which to unload its ships, and that was impossible. There were only three harbours of any size on the invasion coast: Dover, Folkestone and Newhaven. Ansel's verdict on German planning for the use of English ports is 'weak and slow'. He adds: 'There were few good ports on England's south coast, but, such as they were, they deserved a higher combat priority than is given in the orders.' Yet this begs the question that any port would have been usable.

All were heavily defended. Sooner than let them be captured, the British would block the entrances and demolish the docks. The Official History describes the installation of 'guns and torpedo tubes to defend the harbours' and preparations 'to immobilize the ports by destroying the docks, wharves, cranes and other equipment . . .' The invaders' urgent need for a port is obvious; and so is the defenders' absolute determination to deny him, by turning every port into rubble.

Writers who believe in the possibility of a successful German invasion of Britain in 1940 imagine a second Blitzkrieg, carried out by an overwhelming force of panzers and heavy artillery and motorized troops, all arriving in harbours which the British have stupidly abandoned. The reality is that Sealion depended entirely on using converted river barges for landings on open beaches. The heavy weapons were on the steamers, waiting out in the Channel, and the only way to get them ashore was by off-loading them on to barges waiting alongside, a slow and difficult business, especially in a combat zone and with choppy weather and a strong tide. Also lowered into the barges would be horses: essential to haul the artillery up the beach.

Finally, that great British fear: airborne landings. It is difficult to measure the size of their threat. Goering's indifference meant that it wasn't until mid-September that the Luftwaffe definitely committed its airborne troops to Sealion; and even then the plans had many holes in them. The final decision seems to have been to make the main drop on high ground behind Folkestone. To save the Ju52s from massacre, they were to release their gliders at considerable height over the French coast. The gliders would proceed slowly across the Channel. Yet British radar would have detected the mass of Ju52s; the gliders' prospects would not have been good. British defences, already on invasion alert, would have been waiting for paratroops.

The German navy never had any faith in the ability of airborne forces to swing an amphibious assault. An internal memorandum in August reminded Raeder that 'airborne troops can influence neither the weather nor the sea; they cannot prevent the destruction . . . of the few harbours, nor hold off the enemy fleet or even a small part of it.'

There's the rub. Who was to hold off the enemy fleet? It was a question that very few German officers wished to ask, and even fewer tried to answer.

CHAPTER FORTY-FOUR

Salt Horse

A T the outbreak of war, everything about the Royal Navy was impressive. Consider:

> five battleships
> six aircraft carriers
> 19 cruisers
> 52 flotilla leaders and destroyers

Those were only the warships that the Admiralty was *building* in September 1939. The size of the true fleet – of operational ships – was massive. Today it strains the imagination:

> 12 battleships
> three battlecruisers
> six aircraft carriers
> 23 heavy cruisers
> 29 light cruisers
> six anti-aircraft cruisers
> 69 submarines
> 51 escort vessels
> 165 destroyers
> and hundreds of smaller vessels.

This fleet was spread around the globe. There were separate Commands for the Mediterranean, the China Station, the North Atlantic and South Atlantic, the West Indies and East Indies. Nevertheless, the Royal Navy was strong enough to meet all those demands *and* have a Home Fleet in July 1940 that amounted to five capital ships (3 battleships and 2 battlecruisers), 11 cruisers and 80 destroyers – not counting 10 cruisers and 52 destroyers on escort duties in the Atlantic. The Home Fleet outnumbered the German navy by over ten to one.

In fact the odds were even longer. After Norway, Hitler ordered Raeder not to risk his few big warships in battle. Some were still under repair. The Admiralty could not be absolutely sure of this; perhaps the battlecruisers *Scharnhorst* and *Gneisenau*, and the heavy cruiser *Prinz Eugen*, would be back in action sooner than Naval Intelligence thought. Even so, the bottleneck of the Channel, at night, with four transport fleets straddling it, was no place for a big ship to manoeuvre. Sealion's fate would depend on the work of destroyers and cruisers.

So protection for the Sealion crossing came down to this: the coastal batteries around Calais, which were largely ineffective; the mine barriers, which were incomplete; and eight destroyers plus E-boats and U-boats to fight off the Royal Navy. The shallow waters of the Channel are not helpful to submarines, which is why the navy planned to keep its U-boats outside the mine barriers: six to the east of the Dover Straits, 15 in the western approaches. Little more is said about U-boats in Sealion planning. This is understandable. The boats were adequate, the crews were good, but the torpedoes had failed again and again.

The trouble began two weeks into the war. U-39 found the carrier *Ark Royal* and fired three torpedoes. All three exploded – prematurely. U-39 was depth-charged, forced to surface, and abandoned by her crew. German torpedoes were fickle. Some worked – the carrier *Courageous* was sunk three days later – but on 13 October 1939, when U-47 got inside the enormous navy anchorage of Scapa Flow, it had to fire seven torpedoes before the last two sank the old battleship *Royal Oak*.

And so it continued. At the start of the Norwegian campaign, Herbert Schultze, a veteran U-boat commander, fired a spread of three torpedoes at a heavy cruiser, and missed. That evening he found another cruiser; now his torpedoes exploded too soon. Later he attacked two destroyers and a battleship; all escaped. In U-47, Günther Prien, the hero of Scapa Flow, fired eight torpedoes at two British cruisers; only one torpedo exploded, and that was because it hit a rock. Two days later his torpedoes missed the battleship

Warspite. Prien went home. 'I can hardly be expected to fight with a dummy rifle,' he told Dönitz, the commander of U-boats.

In 28 U-boat attacks on British warships, and 15 on transports, the torpedoes failed. Dönitz withdrew all his submarines from Norway. Raeder ordered an inquiry. It found that depth regulators, magnetic detonators and impact pistols were all faulty. Members of the Torpedo Experimental Command were court-martialled for procedures that (as Dönitz wrote) 'can only be described as criminal . . . In all the history of war I doubt whether men have ever had to rely on such a useless weapon.' Even in 1942, the problems were not completely solved.

In 1940, Sealion stood little chance of being saved from British warships by a screen of U-boats. The opposite was more likely: the tracks from faulty torpedoes would betray the U-boat's presence, and a pack of destroyers would hound it to death. It had happened before.

Destroyers were well named. They were a feral breed, wolves of the ocean, hunting for prey. British destroyers were small, averaging in 1940 about 1,500 tons; very agile; fast, with a maximum speed of about 36 knots – say, 40 m.p.h.; and well armed, typically with four 4.7 inch guns and 8 torpedo tubes.

Because it was lightweight, had a low freeboard and narrow lines, a destroyer that was hammering through heavy weather could be uncomfortable to the point of misery. (German destroyers performed even worse in big seas. With a short forecastle and carrying a great weight of guns, the bows plunged deep and waves often reached the bridge.) Yet it was said of British destroyers: 'There never was a class of ship that seemed to be more at home on its natural element, the sea.' And, it might be added, 'doing its natural job, hunting the enemy'. Morale in British destroyers remained high. Danger was the spur; action was the pay-off. Four hundred and fifty-six British destroyers took part in the war, and 164 were lost: odds of slightly worse than one in three. A destroyer commander had to be a good leader.

He was known as the 'Salt Horse', navy jargon for an officer who chose not to specialize (for instance, in gunnery or navigation) as the best route to a command. The Salt Horse had a ship with no specialist executive officers to solve his technical problems: he solved them himself; he specialized in everything. The reward has been described as: 'the thrill of handling a destroyer, of manoeuvring at high speed in close company . . . of fighting such a ship when fast reactions are essential'.

Destroyer commanders had a killer instinct, an appetite for havoc. They were similar to fighter pilots: skilled, intelligent, a little mad, dedicated to combat. The first two Victoria Crosses won by the Royal Navy in the Second World War went to destroyer captains. Both awards were posthumous.

This was what Sealion faced. The Royal Navy had 70 or 80 destroyers in home waters. German naval intelligence guessed – quite accurately – that something like 40 destroyers would attack the transport fleets: 20 from the west, 20 from the east. There might also be three or four light cruisers to stiffen the flotillas.

The Salt Horses against the Sealion. It would be an interesting collision.

CHAPTER FORTY-FIVE

Clean Sweep

Assume that S-Day was 21 September 1940. Sealion would have sailed on 20 September in order to make the crossing by night. What would have happened?

Of the British naval forces on alert in the Channel, the Plymouth destroyer flotilla, six strong, was the most distant: almost 200 miles from Brighton. It would have sailed at midday on S minus 1. By then, all the activity in and around the invasion ports of Dunkirk, Calais, Boulogne and the rest would have made it clear that this was no training exercise.

The German navy kept six (of its last eight) destroyers, and a bunch of E-boats, at Cherbourg. They might have come out and challenged the Plymouth flotilla, but first they would have had to know that it had sailed. In August 1940 a door had been slammed in the face of German Naval Intelligence when the Admiralty (better late then never) changed its codes and ciphers. Until then Raeder's men had been reading all British naval signals with a fluency gained by long practice. Now, suddenly, there was nobody to tell Cherbourg what orders had been sent to Plymouth. No doubt the German destroyers would have done their best to seal off the Channel against enemy warships, but no navy can block 100 miles of sea, day and night, with only six destroyers and with no up-to-date intelligence on enemy movements. Furthermore, the German attempts at creating mine barriers would have had little effect, as evidenced by the fact that the Royal Navy patrolled the French and Belgian coasts by night, almost at will. For example, on 13 September British warships bombarded four Channel ports and returned home without loss.

By late afternoon, the Plymouth flotilla would have joined the Portsmouth flotilla – 16 destroyers – off the Isle of Wight. Now the 4 p.m. departure of the transport fleets would have signalled Sealion's intention to make a night crossing. The Luftwaffe umbrella was there for all to see. Common sense dictated that the flotillas should wait until night to attack.

After 4 p.m. the transport fleets would have about four hours of daylight. Certainly from 9 p.m. onwards they would be sailing in darkness. The most westerly fleet was the rectangle of 200 motor-boats and 100 motor-sailers out of Le Havre, heading for Beach E at Brighton, and now approaching mid-Channel. It is not impossible that the fleet could slip past the two flotillas – in fog, perhaps – but the chances of avoiding 22 British destroyers (and countless small patrol craft), all searching for an invasion force, must be considered slim, and, once found, the motorboat formation would be rammed and smashed, cut to pieces by the bows of only a few destroyers, swamped by their bow-waves, all in a few minutes. A destroyer making 36 knots can throw out a highly destructive wall of water. It would be carnage. This was the weakest of the transport fleets. (Some thought it was a deception, meant to distract attention from the main invasion.) When the destroyers charged out of the night, searchlights flickering across the columns of motorboats, there would have been a long moment of terror and a few bursts of fire from the escort vessels, before the boats were left wrecked and the troops drowning. Some escorts might escape. More likely, they would run into the rest of the destroyers. If any part of Fleet E reached Brighton, it would be as splintered wreckage and bodies, washed up on the beach.

The tide would have started ebbing when transport fleet B – the key fleet, carrying the crucial assault force – left Dunkirk and met its steamer element from Ostend. Twelve hours later, the tide would have risen again and started ebbing again, and dawn would be breaking as the barges ran on to the beaches at Folkestone and Hythe, two hours after high water. This was the iron grip that time and tide had on the scheduling of Sealion.

Transport fleet B would hug the French coast at first. There was no profit in using the rush of the outgoing tide to steer for the middle of the Strait and offer the long convoy as a target to the Dover batteries. Those big guns would hurl some battleship-type shells in any case. The chances of hitting a tug unit were remote, but the heaving fountains of near misses might upset formation-keeping.

By sundown the fleet would be well past Calais. Now the ebb had ended, and the fleet commander had the tricky job of turning his ships towards England and using the flood tide to steer them on their way. Then, with luck, everybody would be well positioned at about 2 a.m. when – give or take half an hour – the tide turned again, and the ebb would help the fleet work down the English coastline.

The nearest Royal Navy base was Dover, but enemy bombing had forced the Admiralty to empty it of warships. Next nearest was Sheerness, on the south side of the Thames Estuary. Harwich was about 40 miles to the north. Both were less than 100 miles from Folkestone. Together they made up the Nore Command: three heavy cruisers, two light cruisers and 20 destroyers. Leaving base at mid-afternoon and cruising at half-speed, they had ample time to meet up and wait for night, before hustling through the Straits – always assuming they got past *Caesar*, the German mine barrier laid in the North Sea.

The German navy was skilled at minelaying. In the first winter of the war it carried out 11 operations off the English coast, notably in the Thames Estuary, and sank 67 Allied ships, including some destroyers. The Admiralty moved quickly. 'Between February and September 1940 the minesweeping force increased from 400 to 698 ships,' the Official History recorded. A large proportion would have been at work in and near the Channel, and Raeder knew it.

'The preparations for a landing on the Channel coast are extensively known to the enemy, who is taking more counter-measures,' wrote the German naval staff in their War Diary on 19 September. German minecraft worked for ten days before S-Day, sweeping the crossing routes and laying mine barriers. Hitler's Directive No. 16 had ordered that these barriers make the Channel 'completely inaccessible' to enemy warships. But the Admiralty – with 'over a thousand armed patrolling vessels, of which two or three hundred are always at sea' – kept track of the work. Royal Navy minelayers repaired British minefields, and minesweepers tackled the German barriers. Minecraft was not a precise science. There was a constant risk to both navies: rogue mines might get washed into 'safe' channels; mine barriers that had been swept could be restored, partially or wholly. The Nore Command might well have lost destroyers or cruisers, sunk by mines on their way to the Strait. What is certain is that the loss of two or three ships would not have deterred the others. Britain was threatened with invasion. The Royal Navy had only one intention: to attack.

It would have faced another threat when it left port: bombing by the Luftwaffe during the hours of daylight on S minus 1. The bombers were capable of sinking warships. They had done so off Norway. On the other hand, Dowding and Park would be ready, when radar gave warning, to send fighter squadrons from the nearby airfields of Hawkinge, Manston, West Malling, Biggin Hill, Hornchurch, North Weald and others.

And perhaps the most significant evidence came from Dunkirk. In the ten days of the Evacuation, when thirty-nine Royal Navy destroyers carried to safety about a third – over 100,000 – of the troops that were rescued, the Luftwaffe sank only six of these ships. By the nature of the operation, the destroyers were often close to shore, and slow-moving or motionless. If the Luftwaffe could sink only six out of thirty-nine in ten days, it was unlikely to score highly against a flotilla at sea, capable of 36 knots, free to manoeuvre, and defended by fighters. By day, in a bombsight, from 5,000 feet, a destroyer was as thin as a pin. By night it was virtually invisible from the air.

The Nore flotillas and cruisers would overhaul the steamers first. British naval radar was not very clever in 1940, but it could hardly fail to pick up such a crowd of shipping. If the wind was blowing up-Channel, it might even be possible for the Salt Horses to smell the sulphurous smoke pumping out of so many funnels.

These steamers were merchant ships. There had been no time to armour them. Some carried a few machine guns or pieces of small-calibre artillery, meant for the beaches. The ships would be heavily laden with troops, tanks, artillery, horses, and all the thousand stores an invading army needs, from bullets to stretchers.

The steamers were best left to the three light cruisers out of Sheerness. Each had six 6-inch guns. Some had four 4-inch guns, some had eight. Their first salvoes would set ablaze enough steamers to illuminate the others. After that the ships would be sunk as fast as the gun crews could reload.

This could not be called a battle. To defend Fleet B, the German navy had only two destroyers and some E-boats, based at Ostend. If they escorted the steamers and turned on the cruisers, they would find themselves outgunned by the bigger ships and outnumbered by twenty British destroyers.

The slaughter of the steamers would have the grim, lopsided, brutal efficiency of an abattoir. They were defenceless. They did not have the speed to scatter. Within minutes, many would be holed, listing, sinking, burning. The sea would be a tangle of barges, some cast off, some dragged down by the mother ship. When the cruisers reached the head of the convoy they would turn and steam along the other side, picking off surviving steamers. There would be no mercy, no pity and certainly no chivalry. These were invaders, come to do to Britain what they had done to Poland, Norway, Holland, Belgium, France. No lifeboats would be lowered. Let them drown.

Before the final shell killed off the last steamer, the destroyer flotillas would be racing ahead to find the tug units.

The American admiral Walter Ansel was a D-Day planner. He had this to say about the Sealion soldiers:

> Think too of the lowliest amphibian, battened down below in the stale hold of an ex-Rhine grain barge. He might have gulped his seasick pills hours ago. His life jacket and the straps of sundry impedimenta bind him round in crouching-room-only company of 69 companions. There are yet hours to go; he may grip his piece and think, once over, all will be well! Did he but know.

Then he would hear the distant boom and crash of the cruisers' guns: a boom when they fired, a crash when they hit. The firing would double and redouble until it made a continuous roll of thunder. The soldiers would know that this was not the sound of their coastal batteries, lending support to Sealion. This was the enemy and he was near.

The destroyers would easily find the miles-long sprawl of tug units. River barges, narrow and lying low in the water, would not make profitable targets for a destroyer's 4.7 inch guns; even less for its eight torpedo tubes. Better to shell the tugs. The escort vessels, mainly minecraft, would interfere. Shell them too. And charge through the columns at full speed. A destroyer making 36 knots would ram a towing cable with terrible effect. The barge would be dragged sideways, rolling on its axis, until the cable was sawn through. By then the barge would have capsized.

Throughout the transport fleet, the high bow waves of 20 zig-zagging destroyers would compete to rock the barges, flood some, sink others. The bigger barges might survive. They would be worth shelling. A few small barges might drift away. Powerless, unable to steer, they would be carried by the tides until they ended up somewhere: France, if they were lucky; on rocks, in a minefield, in the Atlantic, if they were not.

Finally, the destroyers would discover the *Vorabteilung* – mine-craft with motorboats and sturmboats – and they would shatter it.

The Salt Horse was a single-minded, some would say bloody-minded, commander. Admiral Ansel knew the type:

> To wreck invasion at sea must have been the fond hope of every destroyer. These light craft attacking in close-knit units would have held the rare advantage of open season, with every object sighted fair game and no limit on the bag. Think of tangled tows by the dozen, sitting-duck steamers, and hundreds of confused small boats! The night promised a veritable destroyer sailor's dream. Fulfilment lay easily within their capability. Disaster portions could have been dealt *Sealion* in one grand orgy, his wretched bubble whipped into a red froth on the sea.

Ansel did not exaggerate. There is evidence of the havoc caused when warships meet an enemy supply convoy at night.

The Battle of Crete began with landings by German airborne troops. They took heavy losses, and seaborne reinforcements were urgently needed. However, the Royal Navy had three squadrons patrolling the waters to the north of Crete.

At midnight on 21 May 1941, Rear-Admiral Glennie's Force D (three cruisers and four destroyers) intercepted a German flotilla off the north coast of Crete. The flotilla consisted of about 20 caiques (sailing vessels) and four or five coastal steamers escorted by an Italian destroyer and four torpedo boats. The ships carried an anti-aircraft regiment, heavy weapons (including tanks) and artillery, plus two battalions of an Alpine regiment: 2,330 troops in all. Glennie reported that his ships charged into the flotilla 'with zest and energy'.

'A wild melee followed, with the English destroyers ramming one after another of the caiques, sinking by gunfire the steamers, and threshing this way and that in water crowded with drowning soldiers and enemy crews who were clinging to rafts and pieces of wreckage. The whole area was brilliant with flares and criss-crossed with tracer and pom-pom fire. For two and a half hours the enemy convoy was hounded, until it had been thoroughly shattered and dispersed, and then Glennie called his ships together and they turned west, with a good night's work behind them.' Of the two Alpine battalions, only 52 men reached Crete.

Early next morning, the squadron commanded by Rear-Admiral King found another convoy of caiques escorted by destroyers, and sank or burned most of them. Other enemy craft were intercepted.

There were no RAF aircraft on Crete, and by day the Royal Navy squadrons were repeatedly bombed. Some ships were lost. Nevertheless, the German attempt to send an invasion fleet ended in total disaster.

After the slaughter of Fleet B, the destroyers and cruisers of the Nore Command would seek out Fleet C: 200 barges in tow, and 57 steamers pulling 114 barges. To the west, the flotillas of Plymouth and Portsmouth would have no difficulty in finding Fleet D: a long and curling column of 330 barges in tow. Somewhere behind it came 25 steamers and 50 barges from Le Havre via Boulogne. The Royal Navy still had work to do.

CHAPTER FORTY-SIX

Trapped on a Far Shore

THE Sealion crossing and its destruction form one of the great what-ifs of history. It is reasonable to suggest that things might have worked out differently. Dense fog might have hidden the transport fleets. The British flotillas might have lost many more ships to mines; others might have been disabled by engine failure or damage to steering; a few might have been rammed by German destroyers determined to go down in glory. Friendly fire and freak collisions were always a risk in high-speed close-range operations at night. War is a violent business, and violence has a habit of exploding the expectations of both sides. What then?

Suppose that half the Sealion fleets evade the Royal Navy. Half the barges and steamers are sunk, but half are not. They reach England on schedule and begin feeding troops into the assaults on the beaches. The British army has had ample warning: it is ready and waiting, and it lays down a storm of fire on the invasion area. By now full daylight has arrived. This gives a further chance to the British warships. They can cruise offshore and bombard the beaches and the nearby waters, which are thick with barges. Further out they can shell the steamers, now even better targets than they were at night.

Luftwaffe bombers may well sink some warships. Overnight, however, the Admiralty has had time to order more destroyers and cruisers south, and no doubt Fighter Command has inflicted much damage on the Luftwaffe. But the crucial struggle would be on the beaches, where the invaders are caught between the guns of the army and the navy. Reinforcement is vital, and the chances are bleak.

In theory, the barges that had been run on to the beaches will refloat at the end of the afternoon of S-Day. The tow lines must be made good – not easy, under fire. Tugs will set off for France. So will any steamer that has unloaded. They face another night in the Channel, which means they face the Royal Navy. If they survive the journey, reach port and load up with supplies and stores and reinforcements, they then face a *third* night in the Channel, with no more protection than they had on the first. It is hard to believe that they will be third-time-lucky. Sealion, like Caesar, will be trapped on a far shore.

This was the enormous gamble of Sealion. Its planners assumed that all would go well, or at least fairly well. They could tolerate losses of 10 or 20 per cent in the crossing, but they must have enough shipping to get back to France, re-load, return, and hustle reinforcements to the men on the beaches who, after 48 hours of fighting, must be running out of strength and hope and ammunition. The Royal Navy existed to shatter that plan. Even if it sank only half the enemy ships each night, that was enough to kill off Sealion.

Germany did not have command of the Channel, but German failure was no guarantee of British success. What evidence is there that the Royal Navy was competent to find and to smash Sealion at night? Here is what it did in September 1940.

From the start of the month, there were nightly patrols in the Channel by destroyers and motor torpedo boats (MTBs) from the Nore and Portsmouth. On 6 September, for instance, they skirted the Belgian and French coast, saw no activity in the ports, met no enemy ships, and came home. Next night a similar force headed for France. Four MTBs searched the port of Boulogne (despite very heavy weather) and moved up the coast to Calais. In the total blackness they identified some ships, torpedoed two of them, machine-gunned a tug, and left.

8 September saw a more vigorous search. Two cruisers, five MTBs and eleven destroyers crossed the Channel and split into five groups. One went to Ostend. Two MTBs got into the harbour, circled the shipping and torpedoed four steamers. The other MTBs

went up the entrance channel to Dunkirk but found nothing. Visibility was bad that night, yet a cruiser and three destroyers went into Calais, right up to the inner harbour, without being detected. The fourth group – same strength – looked into Boulogne and briskly shelled the inner harbour. The fifth group, five destroyers, inspected the coast as far as the Seine. A thunderstorm did not help. All ships came back safely.

Next night, six destroyers and four MTBs carried out the same operation again, and bombarded the harbours at Calais and Boulogne. (That was enough for German Naval Group West, which decided that those ports were too unsafe to keep transport ships in.) The attacks got heavier. On 10 September, destroyers swept the enemy coast and sank trawlers and barges. This was the day when the German naval staff wrote that weather conditions were 'completely abnormal and unstable' and impaired preparations for Sealion. They did not impair the Royal Navy. On 11 September, every port from Holland to Cherbourg got entered and shelled. Next night, British destroyers, MTBs and fast gunboats from the Nore, Portsmouth and Plymouth 'carried out what was almost a tour of inspection, entering the mouth of the Maas, Flushing and the Scheldt, Ostend, Dunkirk, Calais, Boulogne, Le Touquet and even heavily fortified Cherbourg, surveying them for signs of invasion preparations and shelling . . . any vessels . . . they encountered . . . All the attackers got back to England unharmed.' And so it continued. The biggest operation was in the early hours of 11 October. The battleship *Revenge*, with an escort of seven destroyers, bombarded Cherbourg harbour and left it in flames. A week later Calais got similar treatment; a total of 45 salvoes hit the harbour. No British ship was lost.

If the Royal Navy, night after night, in fair weather or foul, could penetrate the invasion ports and sink enemy ships, there can surely be no doubt that the same British warships could find the Sealion fleets in mid-Channel, and reduce them to wreckage and corpses. The German army and navy expected to land 60,000 men on S-Day. Few would have lived to see the dawn.

CHAPTER FORTY-SEVEN

The Chameleon of Truth

WINSTON Churchill set the tone for future historians of 1940. Writing of 'the stamina and valour of our fighter pilots' he concluded, 'Thus Britain was saved.'

Why did Churchill ignore the Royal Navy, and give the credit to Fighter Command for preventing a German invasion attempt? Why did Hitler not admit that the Royal Navy was the major reason why he postponed – cancelled, in effect – the launch of Sealion?

Hitler's is the easier case. Hitler lied because he could not be honest about his failure, since that would diminish his stature as Fuhrer, Commander-in-Chief, and 'the greatest Field Commander of all time'. He had a dream that Goering's *Adlergriff* would destroy British morale, bring down Churchill's government, and result in a plea for peace, after which Sealion would be unopposed. None of that happened.

Hitler knew the truth about a Channel crossing. Back in July 1940, at a Fuhrer Conference, he was reviewing the Sealion project with his army leaders. (Admiral Raeder had left.) 'Our little Navy,' Hitler sighed, 'only 15 per cent of the enemy's . . .' The true figure was less than 10 per cent, but nobody argued. Hitler was no sailor; nevertheless, he knew the difference between a battleship and a barge; he knew that the Royal Navy was massive and that it could, and would, sink his unprotected invasion fleets in a night: an intolerable humiliation. He could not blame his Services without losing face, which is why, at an OKW conference on 14 September, Hitler flattered the Luftwaffe – 'accomplishments are beyond all praise' – and told the navy it had reached 'all targets set for it in preparation for the Channel crossing'. Three days later he postponed Sealion indefinitely.

Hitler knew enough about the air forces to know that the Luftwaffe could not ensure a night crossing by an invasion force, and that the RAF could not prevent one. Neither fact was a reason for cancellation. He also knew that the Royal Navy would destroy a night crossing. That fact was unmentionable – if the Royal Navy was supreme, then Sealion was bound to fail and Hitler was a fool ever to think otherwise. So, instead, Hitler blamed the only non-military element, the only thing that he could not be expected to control. He blamed the bad weather which, he said, had hindered the elimination of British fighters. Yet he knew that they could never be eliminated. He knew that the Luftwaffe had given him what he wanted: local air superiority. So his excuse was an evasion. Hitler lied.

All the staff at Naval High Command were relieved to hear it, none more so than Admiral Raeder. From the very beginning, he feared that Sealion would be a catastrophe. Long before it raised its head, when war broke out (four years earlier than he expected), he had written an unhappy memorandum about his navy:

> The surface forces are so inferior in number and strength to the British fleet that, even at full strength, they can do no more than show that they know how to die gallantly . . .

So Raeder, too, had lied throughout the summer of 1940; or, if not lied, at least had dodged the truth. At meeting after meeting with the Fuhrer, he said the Luftwaffe must achieve supremacy over the RAF as a precondition of invasion. The navy had no great admiration for the Luftwaffe. But Raeder could not openly admit to Hitler that his navy was a weakling. Such talk was unacceptable. Hitler would have sacked him. So Raeder sidestepped the problem. By insisting that the Luftwaffe's task came first, he avoided revealing the grim situation of the German navy. If the Luftwaffe failed, the navy was off the hook; if it triumphed, Britain would seek peace, invasion would be a formality, and the navy would not be put to the test.

The Wehrmacht had won such huge victories in 1940 that it is tempting to treat its commanders' statements with more respect than they deserve. The three Services never formed an integrated whole. Each competed jealously with the others in order to protect its own interests (and to stay in Hitler's favour). On the surface, there is agreement about the need to win air supremacy over Britain and the Channel; but each commander had a different motive. Raeder wanted to save his navy. The Army C-in-C., Brauchitsch, was lukewarm about Sealion but, as Hitler had begun to talk about invading Russia, it might be worth keeping Sealion alive if this distracted Hitler from the horrifying idea of a war on two fronts. As for Goering: a triumph for his Luftwaffe was his big chance for glory after all the laurels won by the army. Goering was locked into the battle.

Raeder, Brauchitsch and Goering each said that the Luftwaffe must defeat the RAF for invasion to succeed. But just because they said it didn't make it true. Each had his own agenda: he wanted to survive.

Churchill gave all the kudos to Fighter Command and scarcely mentioned the Royal Navy because, in 1940, Britain desperately needed a visible victory. The Spitfires and the Hurricanes were visible; so were the wrecks of Dorniers, Heinkels and Junkers. As Peter Clarke has written in *Hope and Glory*:

> At the time the heroism of young fighter pilots in engaging the Luftwaffe, day by day above the fields of Kent, was what captured the imagination. It was Churchill's best-remembered speeches which focused these images of 1940 and invested them with his own thrilling sense of history in the making.

That piece of history – thanks to some creative accountancy by the Air Ministry – was a victory which Churchill made the most of, knowing how vital it was to give America a reason to continue her support. Then, when Hitler seemed to endorse Fighter Command's achievement by abandoning Sealion, the influence of the Royal Navy became even more ghostly.

Yet Churchill always knew the reality of Britain's defences, even if he found it politic to say otherwise. On 11 June 1940, during a flying visit to France, Churchill was asked by General Weygand what he would do if a hundred German divisions invaded Britain:

On this I said that I was not a military expert, but that my technical advisors were of the opinion that the best method of dealing with a German invasion of the Island of Britain was to drown as many as possible on the way over and knock the others on the head as they crawled ashore. Weygand answered with a sad smile: At any rate I must admit you have a very good anti-tank obstacle.

Churchill knew that, without the Royal Navy, Germany would have at least attempted an invasion. Fighter Command could not sink a ship or even seriously damage one. Air power was irrelevant to a night crossing.

The only relevant force was the Royal Navy. That was why Hitler quit. There was no battle in the Channel, and that was the Royal Navy's 'silent victory'. It was not loud enough for Churchill's needs. The pressures of the hour cried out for laurels to be won by heroes. The RAF had proved that Nazi Germany was not invincible. Fighter Command had denied victory to the Luftwaffe. For that, it deserved all praise. But it was also praised (and still is) for what it could not do: preventing an invasion by sea – and that tribute belongs to the Royal Navy.

Notes

Chapter One – Two Powerful Myths

3   Quotes: Keegan, *The Second World War*, p. 102.
    A.J.P. Taylor, *The Second World War*, p. 72.
    Churchill, *Their Finest Hour*, p. 279 PB.
    Roy Strong, *The Story of Britain*, p. 498.
    Roberts, *The Penguin History of the Twentieth Century*, p. 416.
    Richards, The Fight At Odds, p. 197.

5   *'Undertaking essentially to be ...'* Ansel, p. 137.

5   *'a mighty river-crossing'* ibid., p. 131.

6   *'Luftwaffe knocks out the English ...'* ibid., p. 236.

6   *'Formation Pigpile!'* ibid., p. 262.

6   *'Preparation for Sea Lion requires ...'* ibid., p. 287.

6   *'poor little shallop'* ibid., p. 138.

6   *'It was weak because ...'* Porten, pp. 23–4.

6   *'all the grandiose plans ...'* Becker, *The German Navy*, p. 38.

7   *'If the German figures ...'* Wright, p. 204. Dowding repeated this exchange in his 1941 *Despatch on the Battle of Britain* – a 28-page document which makes only one mention of invasion (saying that German air supremacy was essential to protect an invasion by sea) and no mention of the Royal Navy or the German navy.

Chapter Two – Sugar Umbrellas

11   *Europe had not recovered from* ... Figures for the death tolls appear in Esposito, *A Concise History of World War One*, Appendices; also Terraine, *The Smoke and the Fire*, pp. 35–39.

12   *... The* Daily Mirror *and* Sunday Pictorial *thoroughly approved of Oswald Mosley's* ... Article in *The Independent Review*, 11 November 2003.

13   *... A Luftwaffe pilot who was based* ... Ulrich Steinhilper, p. 114.

13   *... They knew that trenches were being ...* For air raid precautions during the Munich crisis, see A.J.P. Taylor, *English History 1914–1945*, p. 524 PB; Angus Calder, *The People's War*, pp. 25–6; Virginia Cowles, *Looking For Trouble*, p. 174.

14   *'I have now been informed by Herr Hitler ...'* Toland, p. 488.

14   *... There was a moment of anticlimax ...* Cowles, pp. 191–2.

14   *This was the 'piece of paper' ...* Churchill, *The Gathering Storm*, chapter 17.

14   *... Crowds cheered him all the way ...* A.J.P. Taylor, *Origins of the Second World War*, p. 186; Toland, p. 493; *London Review of Books*, David Reynolds, 7 August 2003, p.14.
The French premier, Daladier, got a similar reception when he flew back from Munich to Paris. The crowd's welcome startled him. 'Are they all mad?' he asked a colleague. (Charles Wheeler in a television documentary, *From 1914 to D-Day*.) Mussolini too came home to an ovation, 'perhaps the greatest, in his own opinion, of the entire twenty years of Fascism. At every station and grade crossing multitudes awaited his train, many on their knees, to acclaim him. (Toland, p. 494). The Empire (as it was usually called) would not have rallied behind Chamberlain if he had rejected the Munich Agreement. Telegrams from the Prime Ministers of Canada, Australia and South Africa sent their warmest congratulations on the success 'which has crowned your unremitting efforts for peace'. South Africa's Hertzog told him the news 'was received in the Union with immense relief'. In 1938, war with Germany was the last thing the Empire wanted. (Macleod, p. 269)

15   *'No conqueror returning ...'* Toland, p. 493.

15   *... The exception was Reynolds News ...* Also: *... 'Great Britain will not be involved ...'* A.J.P. Taylor, *English History 1914–1945*, pp. 501–527 PB.

15   *'Peace was the important thing ...'* Also the Punch cartoon and Chamberlain's Christmas cards: Cowles, pp. 193–197.

16   *'As Priam to Achilles ...'* Toland, p. 476.

Chapter Three – Serial Liar

17   *'The Prime Minister has confidence in ...'* Churchill, vol. 1, p. 293 PB.

18   *... Hácha ... and ... Chvalkovsky were met at Berlin ...* TIME/LIFE *Prelude to World War Two*, pp. 198 and 206.

18   Hitler *'felt almost ashamed ...'* Bullock, p. 484.

18   Goering: *'I should be sorry...'* *'might accelerate ...'* Toland, p. 517 footnote.

18   *'Hácha asked for another ...'* and *'They literally hunted ...'* ibid., p. 517.

18–19 *'From Berlin, Hitler declared ...'* TIME/LIFE, ditto, p. 198.

19   *Sugar umbrellas disappeared ...* Cowles, p. 245.

19   *Compulsory military service ...* Churchill, vol. 1, p. 319 PB.

19   *... Chamberlain abandoned appeasement ...* Taylor, *English History*, pp. 542–3 PB.

19   *As it happened ...* Toland, p. 516.

Chapter Four – The Knock-out Myth

21   *as Chamberlain finished ...* Goldsmith-Carter, p. 4.

21   *... the British Air Staff reckoned ...* Alfred Price, *Blitz on Britain*, p. 10.

21   *The Ministry of Health ...* ibid., p. 10.

21   *Upwards of 300,000 hospital beds ...* Taylor, *English History*, p. 531 PB.

22   *By 1939 even Liddell Hart ...* ibid., p. 536 PB.

22   *... Baldwin at the microphone ...* ibid., p. 301 PB.

22   *'I think it is well also ...'* Terraine, *The Right of the Line*, p. 13.

22   *(reinforced in 1934, when ...)* Zimmerman, p. 18.

23   *... Japanese naval bombers ...* World War II Almanac, p. 10.

23   *'One group of horsemen gave me ...'* TIME/LIFE *Prelude To War*, p. 155.

23   *'We will bomb you ...'* Gilbert, *History of the 20th Century*, vol. 2, p. 214.

24   *Besides, the raid took place ...* Taylor, *English History*, p. 535 PB.

25   The *'sacred oak tree'* lived for a further 67 years. It died of natural causes in 2004. *The Times* marked its passing with a report (22 April 2004) that said its correspondent in 1937, George Steer, 'took shelter under the tree as Guernica fell to a *blitzkrieg* attack by Nazi warplanes'. In fact Steer reached Guernica in the night after the raid. The calibre of his reporting can be judged by the way he described how German fighters 'came down in a line, like flashing dancing waves on shingle. They burst in spray on the countryside as they merrily dived.' Steer reported that the 'famous oak of Guernica' was 600 years old. At its death, *The Times* said the tree was 146 years old, making it 79 in 1937. As for the death-toll: the new Peace Museum in Guernica 'suggests a figure of 250 dead'. (Peter van Dungen, University of Bradford: Letter to *The Times*, 29 March 2005).

25   *'This is how I can deal ...'* Gilbert, p. 278.

25   *The next victim was Rotterdam* ... A.J.P. Taylor, *The Second World War*, p. 51; and Gilbert, p. 304.

25   *'It seems the reason ...'* Shirer, *Berlin Diary*, pp. 268–9.

26   *Luftwaffe made a feature film* ... Encyclopaedia of World War II, p. 243.

26   *'It makes one shudder ...'* Vassiltchikov, p. 16 PB.

26   *Some of the miscalculations* ... Also: *Germany would drop 100,000 tons* ... Taylor, *English History*, p. 535 PB.

26   *Bad was made worse* ... Harry Flannery, a CBS correspondent in Germany in 1940, reckoned that a bomb on Berlin had a 1 in 5 chance of hitting a building because four-fifths of the city was open space. Flannery, *Assignment to Berlin*, p. 41.

27   *... dropped only 73 tons* ... Reynolds, p. 163 PB.

27   *... Allied bombing of Germany* ... *London Review of Books*, 21 August 2003, p. 28.

27   *When Germany invaded Poland* ... Middlebrook, p. 19.

Chapter Five – Only Fishbait

31   *Goebbels turned Freiburg* ... Telford Taylor, pp.114–117.

32   *'We have done it!'* Toland, p. 609.

33   *'Only fishbait ...'* Toland, p. 610.

33   *When William Shirer visited* ... Shirer, *Nightmare Years*, pp. 570–1.

33–4   Hitler, on (a) Dunkirk evacuation, (b) to naval adjutant, (c) to valet, (d) to Frau Troost, (e) to Bormann: Toland, p. 611.

34   *'They are not buried ...'* TIME/LIFE *Battle of Britain*, pp. 18–20.

34   *His plan was an airborne extension* ... Wood & Dempster, pp. 220–1 PB. They claim that Goering rejected Milch's plan. This seems unlikely.

35   *'the blueprint for victory ...'* TIME/LIFE *Battle of Britain*, p. 19.

Chapter Six – Small War in Europe, Not Many Dead

37   *... when sixteen European nations were neutral* ... They were: Sweden, Norway, Finland, Belgium, Holland, Denmark, Luxembourg, Spain, Portugal, Rumania, Bulgaria, Hungary, Greece, Turkey, Ireland, Italy.

38   *Fuhrer Directive No. 6* ... Ansel, p. 40.

38   *As General Keitel said* ... Ansel, p. 92. Siegfried Westphal translates *der grösste Feldherr aller Zeiten* as 'Lord of the Field', an obsolete military term. Later in the war, disrespectful German officers shortened it to Gröfaz.

38   '*The British won't come back* . . .' Thompson, p.148. The general was von Kleist.

Chapter Seven – Die At Our Posts

41   *In May 1940, a Gallup poll* . . . Thompson, p. 178.
41   *Another Gallup poll asked* . . . Fleming, p. 91.
41   *His courage failed him* . . . Hamilton, p. 326 PB.
41   '*It might lead to all* . . .' Fleming, p. 91.
42   '*My own impression,*' *he recalled* . . . Hamilton, p. 344 PB.
42   *Five days after the invasion* . . . Thompson, p. 180.
42   *As the air raids got worse* . . . Hamilton, p. 347 PB.
42   . . . *nights in a country mansion* . . . ibid., pp. 324, 332, 343.
42   . . . *primarily a businessman* . . . Thompson, p. 179.
42   . . . *sold his shares* . . . Hamilton, p. 332 PB.
42   . . . *daffodils were yellow* . . . Thompson, p. 180.
43   . . . *General de Gaulle assembled* . . . Harman, p. 224.
43   *Britain had 29 divisions* . . . Thompson, p. 144.
43   . . . *Luftwaffe was believed to outnumber the RAF* . . . Churchill, vol. 2, p. 234 PB.
43–4   . . . *his 7th Panzer Division had captured* . . . ibid., vol. 2, p. 134 PB.
44   '. . . *by my estimate* . . .' Bishop, p. 48.
44   . . . *Churchill told the American ambassador* . . . Thompson, p. 152.
44   . . . *hope of prompting aid* . . . Parkinson, p. 24.
44   *Halifax wrote in his diary* . . . Thompson, p. 152.
44   *(At the landing ports* . . .) Parkinson, pp. 2–3.
44   '*second-hand cars purchased at fantastic* . . .' Parkinson, pp. 9–10.
44   *The* New Statesman *magazine* . . . Thompson, p. 142.
45   '*it is extraordinary,*' *he complained* . . . ibid., p. 141.
45   *The hunt for German spies* . . . Masterman, pp. 48–9; also his Foreword PB.

There was also a hunt for Italian spies – easier, because there were so many Italians, ten thousand in London alone; but less productive, because none got up to anything sinister. In 1938–9, London had an Association of Italian Café Keepers which the Home Office suspected was the front for a Fascist organisation. MI5 knew that hundreds of children of Italian parents were attending Fascist summer camps in Italy (report, *The Times*, 8 May 1999); no doubt they enjoyed the holiday in the sun. When war came, the Double-Cross System 'turned' and handled about 120 agents, who came from all over Europe – except Italy. If an Italian spied in Britain I have yet to hear of it.

45   . . . *six agents were sent to Eire* . . . Fleming, pp. 182–3.

46   'We are divided from England . . .' Fleming, p. 178.
46   Churchill's memoirs reveal . . . Churchill, vol. 2, p. 142 PB.
47   'if we were deserted by the United States . . .' Martin Gilbert, Churchill: A Life, p. 325 PB.
47   'The vast mass of London . . .' Thompson, p. 154, footnote.
47   'With what appeared to be . . .' ibid., p.150.
47   'Certainly everything is as gloomy . . .' Parkinson, p. 36.
48   The story circulated of an elderly . . . Thompson, p. 139.
48   . . . report descending parachutists . . . Fleming, p. 55.
48   . . . hurl the grenades . . . ibid., p. 54
48   'parachutists may sweep over . . .' Churchill, vol. 2, p. 204 PB.
49   'imminent peril may descend . . .' Fleming, p. 67.
49   'their purpose being to put the fear . . .' Luftwaffe, p. 150.
49   'worked upon the nerves . . .' Thompson, p. 111.
49   Not a few Allied units . . . Terraine, The Right of the Line, p. 132.
49   'fury of personal hostility' Richards, vol. 1, p. 119 PB.

Chapter Eight – Hitler Hops

53   'Hitler is now the gambler . . .' Bishop, p. 35, footnote.
53   His staff were astonished . . . Ansel, p. 92.
53   (Hitler's cameraman recorded . . .) Toland, p. 614 and photographs pp. 524–5.
54   'I shall come to an understanding . . .' Ansel, p. 93.
54   'a force for order in the world' ibid., p. 93.
54–5   Ribbentrop biography: see Encyclopaedia of World War Two, p. 525; also Toland; and Fest, The Face of the Third Reich.

Ribbentrop's Nazi salute to George VI was unwise. On the other hand, the England football team 'had given the Fascist salute in Rome and that had gone down well' – so well that the Football Association decided that before the 1938 match against Germany, the team would give 'the Hitler salute', and it was photographed doing so. Appeasement had a long arm. (R.W. Johnson, London Review of Books, 24 July 2003)

55   'He does not hesitate . . .' Ansel, p. 94.
55   'We take the field . . .' and 'Even Michelangelo . . .' World War Two Almanac, p. 118.

Chapter Nine – Hitler Declares Peace

57   The Luftwaffe's war on Britain . . . Telford Taylor, pp. 118–9.
57   'A night raid was like a boxing match . . .' Telford Taylor, p. 119.
57   '. . . call me Meyer.' Encyclopaedia of World War II, p. 243.

57   . . . *offensive killed more RAF aircrew* . . . Taylor, *The Second World War*, p. 79.

57   For Bomber Command operations, June 1940: Middlebrook, pp. 50–52.

58   . . . *certainly bombed Switzerland* . . . Shirer, *Berlin Diary*, p. 316.

58   *'Give them back ten bombs . . .'* Toland, p. 613.

58   *Hitler dismissed the idea* . . . Toland, p. 613.

58   . . . *Warlimont . . . was present* . . . Toland, p. 624.

58   *'senseless bombings . . .'* Ansel, p. 113.

58   *'He thought it quite possible . . .'* Toland, p. 624.

59   *Directive No. 13 ordered a large-scale air war* . . . Telford Taylor, p. 49.

59   *'For the British, Dunkirk and Compiègne . . .'* Telford Taylor, p. 46.

59–60   *The German navy had always* . . . Telford Taylor, p. 51.

60   *Raeder liked the look of Dakar* . . . Ansel, pp. 101–102.

60   *'to use Madagascar for settling . . .'* Telford Taylor, p. 51.

60   . . . *offensive telegram from Goering* . . . Ansel, p. 102.

60   . . . *a high-risk, heavy-loss operation* . . . Ansel, p. 103.

60   *'How can we take on . . .'* Fest, *Speer – The Final Verdict*, p. 139.

60   *'taking such action soon'* Telford Taylor, p. 51.

60   . . . *forty-five seaworthy barges* . . . Telford Taylor, p. 206.

60   *'On land I am a lion'* Ansel, p. 143, footnote.

61   *One of the more exotic* . . . Thompson, p. 155.

61   (*'I am not going in with this gang . . .'*), ibid., p. 158.

62   . . . *a giddy plan of Ribbentrop's* . . . ibid., p. 149.

Chapter Ten – That's My Meat

63   For Hitler's postponed invasion of the West: Cooper, pp. 103–6.

63   *Goering sought the help* . . . Toland, p. 598.

63   *16 in all* . . . Westphal, p. 79.

64   *'You've got to have bayonets . . .'* Flood, p. 334.

64   *'The receptivity of the great masses . . .'* ibid., p. 588.

64   *'with a dunce's cap on its head . . .'* Fest, *Speer – The Final Verdict*, p. 19.

64   *'Reparations hit every German . . .'* Taylor, *The Origins of the Second World War*, pp. 46–7.

65   . . . *new scale of food rations* . . . Shirer, *Berlin Diary*, pp. 149–50; 162 (petrol).

65   *A Berliner recorded* . . . Vassiltchikov, pp. 4 (baths), 12 (toilet paper), 9 (queues). PB.

Chapter Eleven – Afire With Scorn

67–8   For Armistice ceremony at Compiègne: Shirer, pp. 328–333.

68   ... *German army engineers* ... ibid., p. 335; and ... *they dynamited* ... TIME/LIFE *Battle of Britain*, p. 21.

68   *Hitler left his Belgian village* ... Telford Taylor, p. 53.

68   ... *ten happy days* ... Fleming, pp. 114–5.

68   *Picnics and monologues; Meissner visit.* Ansel, p. 122.

69   *Between June 23 and July 11* ... Telford Taylor, pp. 53–4.

69   '*I want to come to terms* ...' Toland, p. 620.

69   ... *Jodl* ... *wrote a six-page memorandum* ... Ansel, pp. 116–7.

Chapter Twelve – Neutral Gear

71   ... *Straits of Dover are 18 miles wide* ... Admiralty Sailing Directions: Dover Straits Pilot, p. 23.

71   ... *von Lossberg recalled the feeling* ... Ansel, pp. 101 and 115

72   ... *severe shortage of motor transport* ... Telford Taylor, p. 56.

72   '*The English have lost the war* ...' ibid., p. 52.

Chapter Thirteen – Heil Germania!

75   *In his biography of Hitler* ... Bullock, p. 804 PB.

75   ... *full to overflowing with plans* ... Fest, *Speer*, p. 83.

75   '*Magnificent building ideas* ...' Fest, ditto, p. 368, Note 55. Hitler's words must be judged by his deeds. To set his building plans in motion, in September 1941 he ordered granite to the value of thirty million Reichsmarks from quarries in six countries. Speer planned to build a thousand small cargo ships to transport the stone. (Speer, p. 247 PB)

75   '*an heroic battle* ...' Ansel, p. 96.

76   ... *his old sergeant* ... Toland, p. 620.

76   *With him he took to Paris* ... Fest, *Speer*, pp. 112–3.

76   ... *Hitler wore a snow-white topcoat* ... ibid., p. 114 (picture).

76   *They saw the usual sights* ... ibid., p. 113.

76   '*Wasn't Paris beautiful?*' Speer, p. 237 PB.

77–9   Summary of Speer's rise to power, 1933–37: Speer, pp. 57–9; 92–3; 96–7; 107–9. PB.

78   '*For a commission to build* ...' ibid., p. 31 PB.

78   *Hitler gave him an office* ... Fest, *Speer*, p. 66.

78   '*seem like toys*' ibid., p. 76 (quoting Genoud, *Libres propos*, p. 81.)

78–80   Descriptions and dimensions of proposed new buildings in Berlin/Germania: Speer, pp. 114–5; 187; 190–4; 115; 212–3; 216–7. PB.

Chapter Fourteen – Thunder in the Mediterranean

85   *'Never has a great nation . . .'* Churchill, vol. 2, p. 129 PB.

85   *The army had almost no field artillery* . . . ibid., vol. 2, pp. 129 and 215 PB.

85   *. . . President Roosevelt ordered the American army* . . . Churchill, vol. 2, p. 127 PB.

85   *'The more I see the nakedness . . .'* Alanbrooke, p. 90.

86   *(Germany had its own 18b . . .)* Christian Schutze, *London Review of Books*, 21 August 2003, p. 29.

86   *'The weather still remains fine . . .'* Thompson, p. 145.

86   *'a considerable body of evidence . . .'* Also: *. . . the public was jumpy . . .* Parkinson, pp. 42–3.

86   *The U-boat war was going badly* . . . Churchill, vol. 2, p. 565 PB.

86   *. . . asked America to release . . . destroyers* . . . ibid., vol. 2, p. 194 PB.

86   *'In three weeks England will have . . .'* ibid., vol. 2, p. 182 PB.

87   *'talking to the void'* ibid., vol. 2, p. 185 PB.

87   *The German navy was quick to see* . . . Ansel, p. 94.

87   *A small part of the fleet was at anchor* . . . Churchill, vol. 2, pp. 198–9 PB.

88   *'It would be disastrous if . . .'* Glen St J. Barclay, pp. 8–11.

88   *He gave his guarantee* . . . Ansel, p. 94.

88   *Admiral Darlan . . . sent a coded signal* . . . Thompson, p. 187.

88   *. . . the Chiefs of Staff in Washington* . . . ibid., p. 189.

89   *On the evening of 2 July* . . . Churchill, vol. 2, p. 200 PB.

89   *'You are charged with one of . . .'* ibid., vol. 2, p. 201 PB.

89   *'It is impossible for us . . .'* ibid., vol. 2, p. 200 PB.

90   *His ships were trapped* . . . Thompson, pp. 188–9.

90   *By one account, the British had mined* . . . Glen St J. Barclay, p. 11.

90   *. . . discussion was described as 'frigid'* . . . Churchill, vol. 2, p. 201 PB.

90   *His crews cheered* . . . Thompson, p. 188.

90   *Dunkerque was hit in both* . . . W.R. James, pp. 55–56; Glen St J. Barclay, pp. 9–10.

91   *'We all feel thoroughly dirty . . .'* Glen St J. Barclay, p. 11; also Thompson, p. 189.

91   *There was talk of declaring war* . . . Churchill, vol. 2, p. 203 PB.

92   *Franco stonewalled . . .*

Spain's neutrality may have been helped along by Churchill's policy of bribing Franco's advisers and generals with millions of pounds to stay out of the war. Report, *The Sunday Times*, 3 August 1997.

92   *'immensely impressed Roosevelt . . .'* Warren Tute, *The Deadly Stroke*, p. 17.

92   *'It was Oran, he said . . .'* Kenneth S. Davis, *FDR: Into The Storm*, p. 590 Random House, 1993.

Chapter Fifteen – Fuhrer Knows Best

93   *That was how Hitler's naval adjutant* . . . Ansel, p. 123.

93   *The Nazi press urged* . . . ibid., p. 125.

94   *Then he went to his sprawling chalet* . . . ibid., p. 127.

94   *Hitler soon found comfort* . . . Thompson, p. 189.

Chapter Sixteen – The Fuhrer is Puzzled

95   *'In the eyes of the people . . .'* Speer, p. 186 PB.

95   *'by night at the Berghof . . .'* Ansel, p. 127.

95   *Hitler spent the next six weeks* . . . Telford Taylor, p. 58.

96   *'If political command demands . . .'* ibid., p. 56.

96   *. . . the German navy built nothing bigger than a destroyer* . . . ibid., p. 64.

96   *. . . an armchair tour of the new German empire* . . . ibid., p. 64.

97   *(Admiral Canaris, head of the Abwehr . . .)* Höhne, pp. 428–9.

97   *. . . plans for the French and Belgian Congo* . . . Ansel, p. 141.

97   *(William Shirer noted next day . . .)* Shirer, *Berlin Diary*, p. 354.

97   *Mussolini kept offering* . . . Telford Taylor, p. 65.

97   *'The Fuhrer is greatly puzzled . . .'* ibid., p. 64.

97   *'If Hitler invaded Hell . . .'* Churchill, *The Grand Alliance*, pp. 370–2 PB. Also Tolland, p. 674.

98   *'. . . a military defeat of Britain . . .'* Telford Taylor, pp. 64–5.

Chapter Seventeen – Hitler Does the Decent Thing

99   *He 'monologued ideas'* . . . Ansel, pp. 114–5.

99   *'He is rather inclined . . .'* ibid., p. 126.

99   *We await undismayed* . . . Gilbert, *Churchill: A Life*, p. 668 PB.

100   *Perhaps he had got wind of* . . . Hamilton, p. 541.

100   *'Kennedy told me Hitler had . . .'* ibid., pp. 370–1.

100–1 *'A very magnanimous peace offer . . .'* Telford Taylor, p. 59.

101   *Soon, Ribbentrop predicted* . . . Toland, p. 621.

100–2 The Reichstag speech: Shirer, *Berlin Diary*, pp. 356–7.

101   *'It is solemn and theatrical . . .'* Parkinson, p. 68.

101   *'Hitler became the Napoleon . . .'* Shirer, ditto, p. 357.

Hitler's decision to make so many high-ranking promotions in such a public manner may have been prompted by Stalin's appointment of 479 officers to major-general in June 1940 – 'the largest mass promotion in the history of any army'. (Keegan, *The Second World War*, p. 177)

101   *Hitler revived memories of the 'atrocity'* ... Telford Taylor, p. 60.

102   *'Mr Churchill ought for one ...'* TIME/LIFE *Battle of Britain*, p. 26.

102   *'jumped up constantly like a jack-in-the-box ...'* Shirer, ditto, p. 358.

102   *'I can see no reason why this war ...'* Telford Taylor, p. 61.

102   *BBC Radio sent the first answer* ... TIME/LIFE *Battle of Britain*, p. 26.

102   *'Can you understand those British fools? ...'* Parkinson, p. 165.

103   *'such a meaningless, purely rhetorical ...'* Telford Taylor, p. 61.

103   *... was cancelled 'for political reasons'* ... ibid., p. 119.

Chapter Eighteen – A New Use for Cheese-cutters

105   *On 9 July, the first convoys* ... Churchill, vol. 2, pp. 224–5 PB.
The first delivery of weapons was followed by much more. In 1940, the U.S. War Department sent Britain half a million Enfield rifles, 130 million rounds of ammunition, 50,000 machine guns, and 900 75mm artillery guns with a million shells – all the result of Roosevelt's order. It amounted to a huge act of support. If an invader had got ashore in the summer of 1940, he would soon have discovered that Britain was no longer 'naked before her foes'. (Conrad Black, *Franklin Delano Roosevelt, Champion of Freedom*, Weidenfeld & Nicolson, 2003)

105   *'... when I arrived there Ironside had already gone!'* Alanbrooke, p. 93.

106   *75,000 Ross rifles were coming* ... Parkinson, p. 18.

106   *'You can always take one with you.'* Churchill, vol. 2, p. 232 PB.

106   *'might reach these shores ...'* ibid., vol. 2, p. 240 PB.

106   *'the invading strength seemed even in July ...'* ibid., vol. 2, pp. 240–1 PB.

106–7   *A German invasion force would need* ... ibid., vol. 2, p. 246 PB.

107   *Every port and harbour on the east* ... ibid., vol. 2, p. 147 PB.

107   *'Such attacks should be hurled ...'* ibid., vol. 2, p. 242 PB.

107   *'They would have used Terror ...'* ibid., vol. 2, p. 232 PB.

107   *That included incinerating the invaders* ... Alanbrooke, p. 142.
Sealion's planners discussed the possibility that defenders might use oil to set the English beaches on fire. The German navy thought it would take too much oil; nevertheless, the navy proposed sending fire-fighting tugs with the assault troops. Each tug would tow a log chain; it would circle the conflagration, thus enclosing it in the chain; and it would then tow it out to sea. (Ansel, p. 245)

107   *'thousands of tons of various types ...'* Churchill, vol. 2, p. 559 PB.

107	*142 Squadron of Bomber Command* . . . Bomber Command Assoc. Newsletter No. 31, March 1996, p. 12.
107–8	*. . . poison gas should be used* . . . Weinberg, p. 146.
107	*Home Guards were taught how to garrot* . . . Goldsmith-Carter, p. 59.
108	*. . . thrusting a crowbar into its track wheels* . . . TIME/LIFE *Battle of Britain*, p. 42.
108	*5,000 Tommy guns a month* . . . Bishop, p. 21.

Chapter Nineteen – The Jolt was Violent

109	*A German paratrooper jumped without* . . . Lucas, pp. 17 and 40 (caption). Some paratroopers carried a few grenades.
109	*With a conventional parachute* . . . ibid., p. 19 (caption) and p. 27 (caption). See also picture preceding title page, showing a paratrooper descending.
110	*If he landed unhurt* . . . ibid., p. 17.
110	*Four years later* . . . Keegan, *The Second World War*, p. 382.

On the night of 5/6 June 1944 the successes, and the losses, of Allied airborne forces varied widely. Some British paratroop units were almost wiped out; others assembled in largely intact formations. Similarly, the 82nd and 101st Airborne Divisions of the US Army had very mixed fortunes. The Official History (*The Army Air Forces in World War II*, pp. 186–9) records that 'after the enemy coast had been crossed, difficulties swiftly multiplied . . . only the leading planes of any formation escaped continuous and heavy anti-aircraft fire as they flew inland. Fog and cloud made visual observation uncertain. Formations tended to break up, and even the trained pathfinders experienced difficulty in identifying their drop targets. Some paratroop formations dropped accurately; some gliders accomplished 'little short of a miracle' in making 'hazardous landings in small and obstructed fields'. But the main drops – made between 0016 and 0404 hours – were 'generally scattered', and by dawn only 1,100 of the 6,600 men of the 101st Airborne Division had found their reporting points. By the end of 6 June, 1,400 had joined them. Thus more than half the 101st were missing on D-Day. Many were dead, wounded or captured. One estimate is that 40 per cent of the Division's paratroops (about 2,600 men) became casualties on 6 June (*The D-Day Companion*, pp. 191–2). Yet enough survived to accomplish most of their missions, especially securing the causeways across the flooded marshlands west of Utah beach, so that seaborne assault troops could move inland. The formula for manning a successful airborne operation would seem to be: think of a number, double it and double it again.

110 *They might capture Liverpool* . . . Churchill, vol. 2, p. 204 PB.

111 *. . . Germany invaded Denmark and Norway* . . . Lucas, pp. 14–15 and Cooper, p. 110.

Germany did not declare war on Norway; but then, neither did Britain, and an Anglo-French force was poised to invade Norway when Hitler beat them to it by 24 hours. The Allies' justification would have been the necessity to cut off Swedish iron ore supplies to Germany, claiming that the extreme needs of war supercede the normal rights of other states. Britain had used this argument in 1807, when Nelson attacked the neutral Danish fleet. Germany used it in World War One, to justify unrestricted submarine warfare. Presumably Britain used it in both Gulf Wars, since war was never declared against Iraq; but war is rarely declared nowadays.

111 *The Germans used their entire airborne forces* . . . Cooper, pp. 93 and 113.

111 *. . . the huge fortress of Eben Emael* . . . Lucas, p. 20.

111 *It guarded the bridges* . . . Price, *Pictorial History of the Luftwaffe*, p. 22.

111 *Nine Luftwaffe gliders, carrying 71 paratroops* . . . Lucas, p. 19, and Bekker, *Luftwaffe War Diaries*, p. 123 PB.

112 *Contrary to legend, Eben Emael* . . . Bekker, p. 129 PB.

112 *Belgian engineers blew three bridges* . . . Lucas, p. 25.

112 *They captured Waalhaven airfield* . . . ibid., pp. 28–9.

112 *(They bombed it anyway . . .)* Macksey, *Kesselring*, pp. 71–2.

112 *. . . General Student, was in hospital* . . . Ansel, p. 112.

113 *Of 22,000 airborne troops* . . . Lucas, p. 58.

113 *Taking Crete cost Germany* . . . Humble, p. 92 PB.

113 *The Luftwaffe lost 220 aircraft* . . . Cooper, p. 200.

Chapter Twenty – Hacking Down Auntie Ju

115 *Tante Ju was the Luftwaffe's workhorse* . . . Cooper, p. 119.

115 *'Some were hacked down . . .'* Macksey, *Dunkirk*, p. 71.

115 *. . . the Luftwaffe had lost 213 of the 475* . . . Cooper, p. 119.

116 *. . . Luftwaffe commanders simply raided* . . . *Luftwaffe*, p. 145.

116 *Yet when he invaded Poland* . . . ibid., pp. 94–5.

116 *. . . concrete bombs, filled with shrapnel* . . . ibid., p. 103 and Irving, p. 83.

116 *Instead of expanding the Luftwaffe* . . . *Luftwaffe*, pp. 144–8.

116 *When war came, 20 per cent* . . . Cooper, p. 94.

Chapter Twenty-One – No Picnic in Poland

121   *Four months before the Second . . .* Caidin, p. 58 PB.

121   Data of fighter maximum speeds: from Jane's *Fighting Aircraft of World War Two*; also, re Dewoitine, *Encyclopaedia of World War Two*.

122   *'down on his knees in the nearest . . .'* Telford Taylor, p. 130.

122   *'They almost pity us . . .'* Parkinson, p. 92.

122   *'You've got to shoot down four . . .'* Gelb, p. 120 PB.

122   *In the event, Wareing got one . . .* Mason, B.O.B., p. 536.

122   *In August 1940, when the monthly output . . .* Richard Collier, p. 99. Also Cooper, p. 148. Cooper says the output of Me109s was 190 per month.

122   *'the fighter arm represented a* quantité . . .' Galland, p. 14 PB.

123   *. . . according to the Luftwaffe Quartermaster-General . . .* Bekker, L.W.D., p. 466 (Appendix 2) PB.

123   *'In addition to obsolete Hurricanes . . .'* Galland, p. 3 PB.

123   *'The enemy air force was heavily . . .'* ibid., p. 7 PB.

123   *It is true that the French air force . . .* Terraine, TROTL, pp. 162–3.

123   *In the same campaign the Luftwaffe lost . . .* Cooper, p. 119.

123   *'At the end of the Polish campaign . . .'* Bekker, L.W.D., p. 32 PB.

124   *. . . he had sold the skin before he shot the bear . . .*
Hitler could be just as cocksure. On 12 November 1940, Molotov visited Berlin. Ribbentrop wanted the Soviet Union to join the Axis (Germany, Italy, Japan) and turn it into a four-power pact. Molotov said nothing. Then Hitler made an offer. 'After the conquest of England, the British Empire will be apportioned as a gigantic worldwide estate in bankruptcy of forty million square kilometers.' Russia would get 'access to the ice-free and really open seas.' Still Molotov did not respond. Next evening, Ribbentrop attended a banquet at the Russian embassy. RAF bombers attacked Berlin, and Ribbentrop took Molotov to his own air-raid shelter, where he again tried to sell a four-power pact to Molotov. England, he said, was beaten but didn't know it. 'If that is so,' Molotov replied, 'why are we sitting in this air-raid shelter? And whose bombs are those that are falling so close that their explosions are heard even here?' (Toland, pp. 643–6)

Chapter Twenty-Two – The Warhorse and the Thoroughbred

125   *'Luftwaffe pilots insisted that . . .'* Steinhilper, p. 314.
Similarly, RAF pilots reckoned that yellow-nose Me109s were especially dangerous, as the Luftwaffe knew from monitoring their radio reports. The 'Abbeville yellow-nose 109s' were often singled out for mention. But the truth was that many Luftwaffe bases flew yellow-nose 109s,

which were not an elite in any way. (Steinhilper, 288) That was the situation in 1940; it might have been different later.

125   *'were credited with four-fifths ...'* Mason, *The Hawker Hurricane*, p. 560. Also: Encyclopaedia of World War Two on 'Hurricane'.

125   *Throughout the Battle, 11 Group always ...* Mason, *Battle Over Britain*: 11 Group strength tables; also *Hurricane*, pp. 84–5.

126   *Sergeant Josef Frantisek ...* Mason, *Battle Over Britain*, p. 540.

126   *... in a remarkable piece of research ...* Mason, *Hurricane*, p. 211.

127   *... called the Hillson Slip-Wing.* Mason, *Hurricane*, p. 100.

127   *Mackenzie lost three feet of wing ...* Masters, pp. 106–110, and picture on p. 112 facing.

128   *'For the sheer joy of flying ...'* Scott, p. 89.

128   *In fact negative-g made the Merlin cough ...* The Merlin in Perspective, Appendix VI, The Rolls-Royce Heritage Trust.

129   *Comparative trials showed that ...* Terraine TROTL, p. 165.

129   *'... consisted of putting everything ...'* From Appendix VI, quoted above.

130   *'my feet were like lumps ...'* Deere, p. 133 PB.

130   *'my hands invariably turned to ...'* Neil, p. 134.

130   *'a formidable opponent to be treated ...'* Terraine, TROTL, p. 165.

Chapter Twenty-Three – Hitler's Merlin

131   *Daimler Benz got 1,150 horsepower ...* Caidin, p. 75. See also Wood & Dempster, p. 460 PB, and Mason, B.O.B., p. 573.

131   *... Merlin III produced a maximum of ...* Mason, B.O.B., p. 562. See also Vader, p. 39; Wood & Dempster, pp. 432–3 PB; and Bill Gunston, *The History of Military Aviation*, p. 67.

131   *... the altitude, the temperature ...* Caidin, p. 85 PB.

131   *When an RAF pilot tested a 109 ...* ibid., p. 92 PB.

131   *Daimler Benz scored again.* Rolls-Royce designers did improve the performance of the Merlin supercharger, but by then the Battle was over. (Hooker, pp. 50–51) Early in 1941, Spitfire squadrons got the new Merlin. 'Increase in all-round performance is truly tremendous ... it gives us a much higher ceiling,' Geoffrey Wellum recorded. His squadron patrolled at 'just a fraction under 40,000 feet ...' Then: 'We were all shattered ... when a pair of 109s described a couple of wide circles round our formation about 1,000 feet above us.' (Wellum, pp. 250–252) The 109s were probably photo-reconnaissance aircraft, stripped of arms and armour to reduce weight.

131   *'Mate the most powerful engine ...'* Caidin, p. 15 PB.

132   *... an 88-gallon fuel tank ...* ibid., pp. 102–3 PB.

132   *... he could 'slam' the 109 ...* ibid., p. 90 PB.

132   *Above 400 m.p.h. – which means* . . . ibid., p. 90 PB.

132   *'. . . positively frightful lateral . . .'* ibid., p. 90.

132   *Calculations on the drawing board* . . . Deighton, *Fighter*, p. 113.

133   *A combat report by Heinz Knoke* . . . Caidin, p. 87 PB.

133   *'. . . the G-force draining the blood . . .'* Steinhilper, p. 307.

Chapter Twenty-Four – Radar: A Muddled Picture

135   *'Bomber' Harris . . . looked on the bright side* . . . Terraine, TROTL, p. 102.

136   Graf Spee *had gun-ranging radar* . . . Price, *Instruments of Darkness*, pp. 15–16; also Haines, pp. 129 and 44.

136   *It would have been bad news* . . . ibid., pp. 15–16 PB.

136   *(a British mobile radar . . .)* ibid., p. 82 PB.

137   *. . . Britain's chain of radar stations* . . . Richards, *The Fight at Odds*, map facing p. 152, PB.

138   *. . . General Martini suspected* . . . Brian Johnson, pp. 63–4; and numerous other sources.

138   *. . . they operated on short wavelengths* . . . Bekker, LWD, p. 187 PB.

138   *Two days later, the Luftwaffe decided* . . . ibid., p. 188 PB.

139   *Flying in four sections of four* . . . Mason, B.O.B., p. 230.

139   *Ventnor radar was bombed again* . . . Terraine, TROTL, p. 188.

139   *. . . neighbouring stations provided overlapping* . . . Brian Johnson, p. 81.

139   *'in view of the fact,' Goering said* . . . TIME/LIFE, B.o.B, p. 95.

139   *'Disappointment spread,' Cajus Bekker* . . . Bekker, p. 189 PB.

140   *'From the very beginning the English . . .'* Galland, pp. 20–1 PB.

140   *After Eagle Day, when Luftwaffe intelligence* . . . TIME/LIFE B.o.B., p. 95.

140   *'For us and for our Command . . .'* Galland, pp. 20–1 PB.

140   *'rumours about new detection . . .'* Steinhilper, p. 263.

140   *'however hard one tries . . .'* Galland, quoted by B. Johnson, p. 81.

141   *There were equally crucial* . . . TIME/LIFE, B.o.B., p. 95.

Chapter Twenty-Five – A Bonfire of Tactics

145   *'. . . the best flying club in the world . . .'* In May 1940, Pilot Officer Geoffrey Wellum, not yet 19, joined 92 Squadron in 11 Group. He had trained on Harvards but he had never even sat in a Spitfire, let alone flown one; in effect he taught himself to fly it. The squadron was on ops over Dunkirk; not surprisingly, other pilots had no time to train Wellum how to fight. Not unnaturally, he wanted to know. He recorded: 'In the Mess I ask questions and this is frowned upon. My fellow pilots, now

battle-experienced . . . do not talk shop when off duty in the Mess.' The best flying club could be very clubby. (Wellum, p. 107)

146   *Trial and error proved that* . . . Steinhilper, p. 143.
146   *'I had an opportunity to ascertain* . . .' Mason, B.O.B., p. 69.
146   *'This was noted . . . say its minutes* . . .' National Archives, AIR 5/1126.
147   *(The Luftwaffe had its share* . . .) Caidin, p. 75 PB.
147   *'The Spitfire hadn't got back* . . .' Gelb, p. 28 PB.
147   *. . . its pilots felt better for knowing* . . . Forrester, p. 110.
147   *. . . noticed that some had no* . . . Rolls, p. 84.
147   *'it was by no means axiomatic* . . .' National Archives, AIR 20/3604.
147   *'The average standard of shooting* . . .' J. Johnson, p. 140 PB.
147   *'it was usual for the machine guns* . . .' ibid., p. 298 PB.
148   *'the essence of leadership in* . . .' ibid., p. 119 PB.
148   *'I was mildly rebuked by* . . .' ibid., p. 119 PB.
148   *This was created in the Thirties* . . . ibid., pp. 117, 119 PB.
148   *'. . . composed at Northolt* . . .' Group Captain Myles Duke-Woolley, DSO, DFC and Bar: Letter to the author, 25 October 1987.
149   *'wallowing and bucking in the slipstream* . . .' Neil, p. 51.
149   *'These formation attacks were useless* . . .' J. Johnson, pp. 118–9 PB.
150   *'. . . eleven pairs of eyes were focused* . . .' H.R. Allen, p. 90 PB.
150   *'We made a fine sight* . . .' Bowyer, p. 50.
150   *'like guardsmen on parade* . . .' Neil, p. 60.
150   *'We're trying to fight a battle* . . .' Richard Collier, pp. 188–9.
150   *'I see that in 616 Squadron* . . .' Air Vice-Marshal Johnnie Johnson, CBE, DSO, DFC: letter to the author, 8 October 1987.

Chapter Twenty-Six – Throw Out These Radios!

151   *Schlipssoldaten.* Steinhilper, p. 57.
151   *'We have two New Zealand officers* . . .' Spurdle, p. 24.
151   *'74 had a tremendous élan* . . . ibid., p. 33.
151   *By contrast, the RAF Volunteer Reserve* . . . Terraine, TROTL, p. 43.
152   *'They talked real tactics* . . .' Steinhilper, p. 89.
152   *'They had decided that we hadn't* . . .' ibid., p. 90.
152   *'within the Luftwaffe there was* . . .' ibid., pp. 125–6.
152   *. . . it had avoided using radio* . . . ibid., p. 129.
153   *'. . . it would be best to throw out* . . .' ibid., p. 182.
153   *'were so entrenched in their views* . . .' ibid., pp. 129–30.
153   *'the frequency would be swamped* . . .' ibid., p. 264.
153   *'Operationally speaking,'* Heinz Knoke, p. 74.
153   *When Sergeant Pilot Ginger Lacey* . . . Bickers, pp. 15–17 PB.

154   *. . . only 16 of about 40 squadrons had VHF . . .* Denis Richards in *The Battle Re-Thought*, p. 58.

154   *'Unfavourable reports submitted by . . .'* Luftwaffe, p. 120.

154   *On all points he was exactly wrong . . .* Sebastian Cox in *The Battle Re-Thought*, p. 67, also Terraine, TROTL, p. 176.

154   *'their forces are tied to their respective . . .'* Deighton, *Fighter*, p. 196.

154–5   *On 16 August Schmid told Goering . . .* Terraine, TROTL, p. 190.

155   *'A situation almost unbelievable . . .'* Steinhilper, p. 129.

155   *'For the German Air Force, war had come . . .'* Cooper, p. 92.

Chapter Twenty-Seven – The Red Light Blinks

157   *. . . Germany invaded Russia and Stalin . . .* Toland, pp. 673–4.

157   *Tankers, especially, were easy . . .* Also: *Between January and July 1942 . . .* Chalmers, pp. 153–4.

158   *'will be at a disadvantage compared . . .'* Terraine, TROTL, p. 703, Appendix G.

158   *was convinced that 'an aircraft . . .'* Webster & Frankland, *The Strategic Air Offensive Against Germany*, quoted by Terraine in Appendix G.

159   *'With additional fuel tanks . . .'* Galland, p. 24 PB.

159   *. . . the Heinkel 51, carried an extra . . .* Mason, B.O.B., illustration, p. 68.

159   *. . . with a jettisonable belly tank . . .* Caidin, p. 94 and facing illustration.

159   *One is that the Luftwaffe did not . . .* Deighton, *Fighter*, pp. 282–3.

160   *The Luftwaffe was supplied . . .* Wood & Dempster, p. 59 PB.

160   *One aircraft maker was using . . .* ibid., p. 59 PB.

160   *'We had always demanded ejectable . . .'* Galland, p. 42 PB.

160   *There was a brief discussion . . .* Deighton, *Fighter*, p. 283.

160   *'a veritable storehouse of energy'* Luftwaffe, p. 54.

160   *Galland had face-to-face meetings . . .* Galland, pp. 26–9; 36–8 PB.

160   *'a piece of land on The Island'* Steinhilper, p. 303.

161   *'Hitler and Goering firmly believed . . .'* Luftwaffe, p. 100.

161   *'He thought it could be achieved . . .'* Dean, p. 139.

Chapter Twenty-Eight – Numbers

163   *. . . from start to finish, just over 3,000 men . . .* Mason, B.O.B., p. 488.

163   *Often the number of aircraft available . . .* Churchill, vol. 2, Appendix C., p. 568 PB.

163   *'The German fighter force at the start . . .'* Bekker, LWD, p. 234 PB.

164   *The Luftwaffe kept many aircraft in Norway . . .* Steinhilper's Me109 squadron moved back to Germany after the fall of France and 'spent

quite a lot of time on patrol over and around Berlin, waiting for the RAF to bomb Hitler in the Reichstag'; and on 23 July it assembled at Bayreuth, 'again flying fighter cover for the Fuhrer'. It returned to France but on 29 July it was recalled, briefly, to Germany 'to protect the Ruhr'. Transfers like this show how difficult it is to track the strength of the Luftwaffe at any one place and time. (Steinhilper, pp. 262 and 266)

164   *John Terraine has studied* . . . Terraine, TROTL, p. 181.

164   *'In the Battle of France we had fought* . . .' Churchill, vol. 2, p. 234 PB.

164   *'the entire operational strength of the Luftwaffe* . . .' Cooper, p. 134.

165   *The Germans are great book-keepers* . . . Luftwaffe, p. 202.

166   *'short of fully airworthy aircraft* . . .' Steinhilper, p. 291.

166   *'Because of the losses there were only* . . .' ibid., p.306.

166   . . . *at the time of* Adlertag . . . Telford Taylor, p. 99.

166   *In June 1940 they delivered* . . . Terraine, TROTL, p. 191.

166   *That was double the German rate* . . . Telford Taylor, p. 99.

166   *For 109s alone, the monthly rate* . . . Cooper, p. 148.

166   . . . *it was 160 pilots short* . . . *getting 50 trained replacements* . . . Telford Taylor, p. 99.

166   . . . *German flying schools turned out 10,000* . . .ibid., p. 99.

167   *(His* Gruppe *began the Battle with* . . .) Steinhilper, p. 324.

167   *'A combination of chronic stress* . . .' ibid., p. 285.

167   *Luftwaffe doctors could not advise* . . . ibid., p. 286.

167   *'So the doctors resorted to diagnosing* . . .' ibid., p. 286.

167   *'I glance at the clock* . . .' Gleed, p. 97.

168   *In September 1940 the Luftwaffe* . . . Steinhilper, p. 22.

168   *'Over the target, huge formations* . . .' Price, RAF Historical Society, Journal 29, p. 16.

Chapter Twenty-Nine – Hearsay Is Not Evidence

169   *Horchdienst.* Terraine, TROTL, p. 177. Steinhilper saw reports on the monitoring of the British radio frequencies 'which we could receive as clear as our own'. Fighter Command used codenames, but Luftwaffe pilots soon recognized British controllers and squadrons with names like 'Weapon' and 'Dogrose' , and it took little effort to work out who the 'Indians' were. (Steinhilper, p. 275)

169–71 For much of this chapter I am indebted to *The Intelligence Aspect*, an address by Mr Edward Thomas in *The Battle Re-Thought*, a Symposium on the Battle of Britain, 25 June 1990. These proceedings were published by the Royal Air Force Historical Society, for whose help I am equally grateful.

169   Edward Thomas rejects as 'fantasy' the idea that Dowding was on the very short list of those who knew the Enigma/Ultra secret. Thomas's view is strengthened by the fact that Arthur Harris, C-in-C Bomber Command from 1942 to 1945, was not on that list. When Harris gave a video-taped interview in 1982, he declared that 'he had never been informed of the Enigma intelligence source' during the war and 'had only learnt about it long afterwards.' (Air Commodore Henry Probert, Journal 31, p. 126, Royal Air Force Historical Society).

170   *There were three main reasons . . .* Alfred Price, Journal 29, p. 17, Royal Air Force Historical Society; and Edward Thomas, *The Battle Re-Thought*, pp. 44–5. Describing operations on 28 August 1940, when large numbers of fighters were scrambled to meet massed formations of raiders approaching Kent, Sussex and Hampshire, Francis Mason wrote: 'Although the first fighters to take off usually intercepted the raids successfully over the coast, the German tactics of splitting up their formations once over land so confused the Observer Corps . . . that it had proved almost impossible to guide subsequent fighters into the enemy formations with any accuracy.' Two-thirds of these fighters missed the enemy completely.

In 1940 there was no overland radar coverage. To help plug the gap, Park ordered his fighter leaders to give the 'Tally-ho', *not* as an order to attack but as a signal to the controller that enemy aircraft were in sight, adding their position, height, strength and course; fighters were then free to attack. (Mason, *Battle Over Britain*, p. 313.) This extra information certainly helped – but once a raider was inland, an interception was never guaranteed. Popular belief has it that the summer of 1940 was all sun and blue sky. In fact many days were overcast, cloudy or wet, and this poor visibility was frustrating both for the Observer Corps and for the fighter pilots. Even if the sky was cloudless, the smoke of London made a haze that might reach deep into Kent. Scrambled from Biggin Hill, Geoffrey Wellum broke through the haze at 2,000 feet. 'It blankets everything,' he noted, 'and from where we are it looks as solid as any cloud.' He thought the Observer Corps 'would have had quite a job on their hands to identify aircraft at height.' (Wellum, pp. 177–9)

The experience of 249 Squadron, flying Hurricanes in 11 Group, was typical. In September 1940 it was scrambled 41 times. 14 scrambles led to interceptions; six of these resulted in claims of aircraft destroyed. That leaves 27 scrambles which failed to lead to contact. On ten occasions, 249's pilots saw enemy aircraft that were too distant to be reached; on the remaining 17 they saw nothing. So 27 scrambles out of 41 were abortive. (George Barclay, pp. 43–75) 249 was by no means an unsuccessful squadron, but it faced the same problem as everyone in 11

Group: hunting an enemy formation which might have divided and then changed course and height and be hidden by a thicket of cloud.

Chapter Thirty – An Accidental Success

175   'confined to nuisance raids . . .' Cooper, p. 128.

175   Kanalkampfer Ansel, p. 90.

175   From 1 July to mid-August, in combats . . . Cooper, p. 129.

175–6 On 20 July, the highest Luftwaffe officers . . . Telford Taylor, p. 127.

176   No final decision was reached. Ibid., p. 128.

176   Hitler lost patience first . . . ibid., p. 129.

176   'The Fuhrer has commanded that . . .' Ansel, p. 194.

176   . . . a Fuhrer Conference made it clear . . . ibid., pp. 194–5.

176   Theo Osterkamp was there . . . Telford Taylor, pp. 130–1.

177   'The whole of England is trembling . . .' Bishop, p. 49.

177   'In England, men and women feel . . .' ibid., p. 62.

178   . . . took 'two new bets offered by . . .' Shirer, Berlin Diary, p. 363.

178   'Would we actually get the chance . . .' Steinhilper, p. 276.

178   . . . Steinhilper asked a girlfriend for . . . ibid., p. 282. Overconfidence was widespread. On 12 September 1940, German Army High Command issued a directive aimed at avoiding confusion when Sealion forces advanced by ordering that all English place-names must be pronounced in German phonetics. (Ansel, p. 291) No problem with Newhaven, but Duddleswell might have been a challenge, not to mention Boughton Monchelsea.

Chapter Thirty-One – A Perilous State

179   On 21 May 1940, Admiral Raeder . . . Telford Taylor, p. 204.

179   On 30 June 1940, a memorandum . . . ibid., p. 207.

179   Two days later, a Fuhrer Directive . . . Ansel, p. 118.

179   . . . a Wehrmacht High Command paper . . . ibid., p. 131.

179   On 21 July, at his Karinhall . . . ibid., p. 193.

179   on 1 August a new Fuhrer . . . Telford Taylor, p. 71.

179   . . . a previous Directive, of 16 July . . . ibid., p. 67.

180   'We therefore had to get used to . . .' Galland, pp. 31–2 PB.

182   'The enemy's bombing attacks by day . . .' Cooper, p. 148; also Mason, B.O.B., p. 107.

182   (on one airfield a Waaf planted . . .) Deighton, Fighter, p. 232; also Mason, B.O.B.; p. 337; Wood & Dempster, p. 311 PB.

182   'it was precisely at this stage . . .' Terraine, TROTL, pp. 190, 209.

182   'wasting away under Dowding's eyes' Wood & Dempster, p. 342 PB.

182   'Experienced pilots were like . . .' ibid., p. 340 PB.

183   *'In the fighting between August 24 and ...'* Churchill, vol. 2, p. 271 PB.

183   *In the first seven days of September* ... Mason, B.O.B, p. 335.

183   *Squadron establishments* ... Terraine, TROTL, p. 209.

183   *... in the month from 13 August to* ... Cooper, p. 162.

183   *Matthew Cooper has calculated* ... ibid., p. 162.

183   *'Statistically the Luftwaffe was winning the battle ...'* Mason, B.O.B, p. 351.

183   *TODAY'S SCORE* ... Richard Collier, p. 111, photograph.

183   *The 'numbers game' was played* ... Mason, B.O.B., p. 391.

183   *John Terraine's analysis* ... Terraine, TROTL, pp. 219–220.

184   *At the start of September, Dowding* ... Cooper, pp. 148–9.

184   *'massed in a single huge phalanx ...'* Mason, B.O.B., p. 359.

Chapter Thirty-Two – Nothing But German Aircraft

185   *Reichsmarschall Goering's armoured* ... Butler and Young, pp. 185–7 PB.

185   *A recording van was* ... TIME/LIFE, p. 119; ibid., p. 187 PB.

186   *'... the world's largest air force was now ...'* Fleming, p. 282, quoting Denis Richards.

186   *The capital covered about 800* ... ibid., p. 284.

186   *'September 7 amounted to a victory ...'* Terraine, TROTL, p. 208, quoting the Official History.

186   *'One German bomber formation ...'* Gelb, pp. 229–30 PB.

186   *'could hardly believe it. As far ...'* ibid., p. 230 PB.

186   *The Luftwaffe lost 41 aircraft* ... Mason, B.O.B pp. 365–369.
The Daily Loss Tables compiled by Mason are probably the most reliable indicators of Luftwaffe and Fighter Command losses day by day in the Battle. However, Mason points out (p. 128) that there are 'widely differing definitions of "losses" or, for that matter, what constituted a combat or operational sortie.' With that caveat in mind, I have studied his Daily Loss Tables more closely, and concluded that in many cases the totals should be reduced.

The Loss Tables for 7 September 1940 are a good example. Mason lists 42 aircraft under 'R.A.F. Fighter Command Losses'. But 11 of those fighters were only damaged, and they landed or force-landed. Some returned safely to their aerodromes. One pilot was 'wounded', one 'slightly wounded'; the other nine were 'unhurt'. I find it hard to write off aircraft which could soon be repaired and flown again, perhaps by the same pilots. In addition, one 'loss' was a non-combat training accident. If those 12 items are deducted, the Fighter Command loss total becomes 30.

Similarly, the Luftwaffe Loss Table totals 63 but nine of these are marked NCM: Non Combat Mission – mostly landings accidents, the crews unhurt. There were thirteen Combat Missions from which the aircraft returned to base with varying degrees of damage and injury. In four cases, crew members were wounded; in the other nine, crews were unhurt. One Luftwaffe aircraft landed undamaged; it seems that the reason for listing it as a 'loss' was the wound suffered by a crew member.

The Luftwaffe rated damage by percentages (Mason, p. 129). Four of the 13 aircraft had 10 per cent damage. Typically, this was minor gunfire damage, repairable locally. Three had 20 per cent damage, such as might be caused by shrapnel, needing minor replacements. Two had suffered 30 or 35 per cent damage; they might need major inspections on the base. The remaining three had severe damage; major components would have to be replaced. None came near 100%, the Luftwaffe's category of total loss.

Fighter Command would not have written off as 'lost' a Spitfire or Hurricane that landed with 10 or 20 per cent damage, and I can see no reason why a Luftwaffe aircraft with 10 per cent damage (or more) should be included in the Daily Loss Table when in fact the aircraft returned to base.

Deducting the nine Non Combat Mission losses, and the 13 instances where damaged aircraft returned safely, I make the Luftwaffe total of losses only 41. So on 7 September 1940, Fighter Command lost 30 aircraft in combat, not 42; and the Luftwaffe lost 41 in combat, not 63.

186   *One was shot down, by anti-aircraft* . . . T.C.G. James, p. 242.
187   *He has identified three essential* . . . Group Captain Tom Gleave, *The Battle Re-Thought*, pp. 47–8.
187   *The planned date to launch Sealion* . . . Cooper, p. 151.
187   *But when he postponed Sealion* again . . . Cooper, p. 157.

Chapter Thirty-Three – A Little Help From Upstairs

189   *'Attacks against the London area* . . .' Telford Taylor, p. 154.
189   *Part of Hitler admired the British* . . . One of Hitler's favourite movies was 'Lives of a Bengal Lancer', starring Gary Cooper, Franchot Tone and C. Aubrey Smith. Hitler thought the British Empire was a desirable force for order in the world.
189   *'He alternately wanted them* . . .' Fleming, p. 73.
189   *Hitler held out a faint hope* . . . Telford Taylor, p. 274; also Ansel, p. 226.

190   *In the week after 7 September* ... Wood & Dempster, pp. 348–358 PB.

190   *On two of those seven days* ... Mason, B.O.B., pp.371–385. I have adjusted his Daily Loss Tables according to the guidelines in my Note for the losses on 7 September 1940.

190   *They reported that Fighter Command was* ... Telford Taylor, pp. 152–3.

190   Quotes from Hitler on September 6; from Naval Staff Diary on September 10; from Hitler on September 14; and from General Jodl – see Cooper, pp. 155–6.

191   *Mason says that the German* ... Mason, pp. 387–8.

191   *'The stupidity of large formations* ...' Wood & Dempster, p. 360 PB.

191   *'Whether from carelessness* ...' Telford Taylor, p. 164.

191   *'. . . the success that the RAF squadrons* ...' T.C.G. James, p. 258.

191   *'Park was able to alert* ...' Terraine, TROTL, p. 211.

191   *'Both the height and the complexity* ...' Deighton, *Fighter*, p. 263.

192   *... Dr Alfred Price gave an address* ... In 2003 this was published by the Royal Air Force Historical Society in its Journal 29, with the title, 'Battle of Britain Day'.

192   *... his research has rewritten* ... Price, Journal 29, pp. 5–16.

192   *'That powerful wind* ...' *Alfred Price said* ... ibid., p. 6. Four years later, a high-altitude jet stream of 140 m.p.h. had an even more profound effect on B29 Superfortresses trying to bomb Tokyo. It blew them over the city so fast that their Norden bombsights were useless. The jet stream persisted and the USAF was forced to bomb from low altitude. (BBC-4, 29 November 2004)

193   *(each fighter-bomber carried only one, bomb).* According to Cooper, these fighter-bombers each carried one 110 lb bomb. A later model, the 109E-4, could carry a bomb weighing up to 500 lbs. (Cooper, p. 158)

193   *'fought an excellent covering* ...' Journal 29, p. 8.

193   *'tolerably accurate,' Price said* ... ibid., pp. 8–9.

194   *'Considering the overwhelming* ...' ibid., p. 10.

194   *'a large proportion of these made it* ...' ibid., p. 13.

195   *'most of the capital was blanketed* ...' ibid., p. 13.

195   *'In fact, the Dornier formation had* ...' ibid., p. 14.

Chapter Thirty-Four – Spectacular Entry

197   *'For Fighter Command, just about* ...' Terraine, TROTL, p. 211.

197   *The story of the Big Wing* ... ibid., pp. 194–205.

198   *'cumbersome and time-wasting* ...' The Battle Re-Thought, p. 40.

198   *Over the target huge formations* . . . Journal 29, p. 16.

199   *In my analysis, I could confirm* . . . Journal 29, p. 15.

199   *'using only a small proportion* . . .' Mason, B.O.B., p. 391.

199   *'in spite of tremendous numbers* . . .' Parkinson, p. 185. Churchill said that, in war, the truth was so precious that it must be protected by a bodyguard of lies. He was not slow to be one of that bodyguard. For the first eight months of the war, he was First Lord of the Admiralty – the Cabinet Minister in charge of the Royal Navy. Admiral Godfrey was Director of Naval Intelligence. On 18 January 1940, Godfrey circulated a report which said that, of the 66 U-boats which the German navy had when war broke out, only nine had definitely been sunk. Two days later, on 20 January, Churchill made a speech. He said that it was 'pretty certain' that half of all U-boats had been sunk. He sent Godfrey a personal minute, telling him that 35 sinkings represented 'the lowest figure that can be accepted'. Even by April 1940, Naval Intelligence believed that only 22 U-boats had been lost. (Paul Addison, *The Road to 1945*, p. 80.) Postwar research has shown that Germany began the war with 55, not 66, U-boats; otherwise, Naval Intelligence was fairly accurate: 15 U-boats were sunk by February 1940 and 24 by May 1940. Churchill's 'lowest acceptable figure' of 35 sinkings was not achieved in 1940. (von der Porten, *The German Navy in World War II*, Appendix I.) Churchill had been in the political wilderness for a decade. It would have been in character if he was determined to advertise his return to office with a notable success at sea. Perhaps, too, he felt that the British people needed a boost in the tedium of the Phoney War. But his speech did not impress the German navy – or British Naval Intelligence.

200   . . . *a bloody nose over Dunkirk* . . . Irving (pp. 90–91) writes of 'the local daylight air superiority achieved over the Me109 by the British Spitfire fighter, operating at short ranges over Dunkirk.'

Chapter Thirty-Five – Sawing the Baby in Half

203   . . . *'if it is so easy for the Germans* . . .' Churchill, vol. 2, pp. 204–5.

204   . . . *he summoned Raeder to a conference* . . . Ansel, p. 103.

204   *Raeder ran through a long agenda* . . . Telford Taylor, p. 206.

204   *Jodl was skilled at that* . . . ibid., p. 207.

205   *Hitler agreed. Two days later* . . . ibid., p. 208.

205   . . . *von Brauchitsch* . . . *presented Hitler* . . . ibid., p. 218.

205   *The army's term for the operation* . . . ibid., p. 216.

205   '. . . *a mighty river-crossing on a broad* . . .' Ansel, p. 131.

206   *Of course it was preposterous* . . . Telford Taylor, pp. 219–221.

206   *In the first wave, the army wanted* . . . ibid., p. 221.

206   *... it states that Navy needs ...* ibid., p. 221.

206   *The navy said it could put ashore ...* ibid., p. 227.

206   *'Sheer suicide,' Halder, called it ...* Ansel, pp. 210–211.

207   *For most of August he showed ...* Telford Taylor, p. 225.

207   *... now his front was only 80 miles ...* Ansel, p. 257.

207   *'Thus OKW sawed the baby ...'* Telford Taylor, p. 236.

207   *In this new, slimmer operation, the first ...* ibid., p. 244.

207   *125,000 horses eat a lot ...* Deighton, *Blitzkrieg*, p. 200.

Chapter Thirty-Six – Bold Arrows

209   *There were only six motorized ...* Keegan, WW2, p. 54.

210   *Motor vehicles were never ...* Deighton, *Blitzkrieg*, pp. 171–2.

210   *By the time the war ended ...* World War Two Almanac, p. 96.

210   *In theory, the standard German ...* Deighton, *Blitzkrieg*, p. 200.

210   *In declining order of size ...* Telford Taylor, p. 270; Ansel, p. 216.

211   *Those considered seaworthy went ...* Ansel, pp. 308 and 216.

212   *The assembly area stretched ...* Gilbert, p. 28 (quoting Ansel).

212   *The barges alone would need ...* Telford Taylor, p. 251.

212   *By the end of August the shipping ...* ibid., p. 263.

212   *Tugs were still scarce ...* ibid., p. 271.

212   *... Wilhelmshaven, now left with only ...* Ansel, p. 238.

212   *... the signs were that the navy ...* Telford Taylor, p. 263.

212   *'I walked for miles from prahm ...'* Ansel, p. 216.

Chapter Thirty-Seven – Schwerpunkt

213   *Operation Overlord ... began with an attack ...* Keegan, pp. 382–5.

213   *The German army has always prided itself ...* The German naval staff also worked night and day. After the war, Admiral Ansel saw their final plan, *Directive for Executive Sealion*, and was impressed: 'To anyone acquainted with the problems that had faced them – the tension of strife, the meagerness of resource in working staff, in experience and in material, and most of all, in the shortness of time – these men had performed veritable prodigies of amphibious warfare planning and preparations.' But he added that the middle-ranking naval officers worked alone: 'No one of rank at Navy ever took up the cudgels for Sealion. The truth was he belonged to the Army.' (Ansel, pp. 235–6)

213   *... amphibious operations inevitably result ...* Telford Taylor, pp. 259–60.

213   *Army High Command issued invasion ...* ibid., p. 238.

214   *All day the Port Commanders ... hustled ...* Ansel, p. 170, footnote.

214   *'The numerous proposed landing craft ...'* Bennett, p. 81.

214   *From right to left, they were labelled ...* Ansel, p. 245.

Chapter Thirty-Eight – Problems for Cross-Channel Traffic

217   'Dover Strait, and the sea areas on either . . .' Admiralty Sailing Directions: Dover Strait Pilot, p. 25: Sea and Swell: sea conditions (Section 1.176).

217   . . . a gap which at its smallest, is only 18 miles across . . . ibid., p. 23: Maritime Topography (Section 1.158)
The well-known fact that the shortest distance between England and France is 23 (or 22) miles turns out to be a myth.

218   Nobody sings of the White . . . ibid., pp. 110, 115 and 107. (Sections 5.37; 5.80; 5.8)

218   'The whole area is shallow . . .' ibid., Maritime Topography, (Section 1.158).

218   It adds that, because of these banks . . . ibid., p. 56, Off-lying banks. (Section 2.15)

218   The seabed is also littered with wrecks . . . ibid., p. 1, Navigational Dangers and Hazards. (Section 1.2)

218   . . . and in 1940 both sides laid minefields . . . ibid., p. 115, Danger Area, (Section 5.81) and p. 135, Danger Area (Section 6.60); also Appendix III, p.332, Former mined areas.

218   The Ridge . . . 'a dangerous steep-to shoal . . .' ibid., p. 59 (Section 2.40).

218   The Varne . . . 'with strong tide rips . . .' ibid., p. 62 (Section 2.62).

218   Bullock Bank . . . 'generally marked by strong tide rips . . .' ibid., p. 62 (Section 2.63).

218   Sandettié Bank . . . ibid., p. 58 (Section 2.40).

218   Royal Sovereign Shoals . . . ibid., p. 83 (Section 3.116).

219   . . . with time on their hands read Caesar's . . . Ansel, p. 158; also The Conquest of Gaul, Penguin Classics, 1951.

219   'It was now near the end of summer . . .' Caesar, p. 119 PB.

219   'such a violent storm suddenly arose . . .' ibid., p. 124 PB.

220   'feeling little anxiety about the ships . . .' ibid., p. 133 PB.

220   'of a great storm in the night . . .' ibid., p. 134 PB.

221   Either divine intervention or, the greatest of good luck . . . Matthew, The Norman Conquest.
William had another stroke of luck: the English fleet had been patrolling the south coast throughout the summer of 1066. Autumn came, with no sign of the Normans. The fleet disbanded. If William had got the wind he wanted a month earlier, he might have been forced to fight a sea battle *and* a land battle – which turned out to be a very close thing – and the outcome might have been different.

221   'a ditch that shall be leaped . . .' Longmate, Island Fortress, p. 258.

221   'Celerity is better than artillery.' Longmate, ditto, p. 200.

221   'had found that owing to the frequent . . .' Caesar, p. 128 PB.
221   'Only in the very nick of time . . .' Fleming, p. 249 footnote.
221   At the end of July, naval operations . . . Ansel, p. 170 footnote.
222   . . . the Beaufort Scale climbs through . . . Britannia Micropaedia.

Chapter Thirty-Nine – Long Shot

225   The force aiming to go ashore . . . Telford Taylor, p. 243.
225   There were 80 wrecks . . . Ansel, p. 312.
226   Each tug (Schlepper) . . . Telford Taylor, pp. 243–4.
226   The Sealion timetable required . . . Ansel, p. 280; also Telford Taylor, p. 244.
227   . . . transport fleet B would stretch over . . . ibid., p. 312.
227   From Calais, 100 tug units . . . ibid., p. 312.
227   Finally, Le Havre would send. . . ibid., pp. 226 and 263.
227   The motorboats would do well . . . ibid., p. 263.
228   These mine barriers were codenamed . . . ibid., p. 261.
228   As early as 30 May, when the . . . ibid., p. 130.
228   . . . evidence that the German army kept . . . In 1944, German scientists at Mimoyecques in the Pas de Calais were still trying to make a gun that could hit London. The 6-inch shells had collapsible fins, and the muzzle velocity was about 5,000 feet per second. But the project was a total failure, and the site was abandoned in May 1944, shortly before Allied aircraft bombed it as part of the raids on V1 and V2 sites. (Olsen, Aphrodite: Desperate Mission, p. 255, and Basil Collier, The Battle of the V-Weapons, p. 35)
228   The army kept two batteries . . . Ansel, p. 133.
228   Next day the chief of naval ordnance . . . Telford Taylor, p. 220 footnote.
228   . . . gave the Calais area the firepower . . . Grinnell-Milne, p. 102.
229   'No British or foreign merchant ship . . .' ibid., p. 103 footnote.
229   'Many long-range duels were fought . . .' Roskill, p. 256.

Chapter Forty – Bullets Versus Barges

231   . . . by September 1940 the Luftwaffe was stronger than the RAF . . . Cooper, pp. 146 and 148.
232   In all, his fighters flew 1,000 . . . ibid., pp. 153 and 156.

Chapter Forty-One – The Great Shield

235   'it was definitely Bomber Command's . . .' Fleming, p. 295.
235   'RAF bombing crippled about 12 per cent' Terraine, p. 210.
235   'less than 10 per cent of the assembled . . .' Grinnell-Milne, p. 154.
235   Walter Ansel's estimate was smaller. Ansel, p. 307 footnote.

235   *'Every port from Antwerp to Dieppe ...'* Gibson, p. 107 PB.

235   *Bomber Command raided them on* ... Middlebrook, pp. 79–87.

236   *(Gibson believed he sank ...)* Gibson, p. 108 PB.

236   *'many small bombs, even hand grenades ...'* Gibson, p. 107 PB.

236   *'The RAF disturbed rather than ...'* Fleming, p. 294.

236   *... Bomber Command had called a halt ...* Terraine, pp. 111–2.

236   *Dunkirk provides good evidence* ... Richards, *The Fight At Odds*, pp. 140–1 PB.

Chapter Forty-Two – Dawn or Nothing

241   *The German navy wanted to ship Sealion* ... Ansel, pp. 168–9 and p. 170 footnote; also p. 310, quoting Captain Kleikamp; also Telford Taylor, p. 271.

Chapter Forty-Three – Hit the Beach

243   *The official term was* ... Vorausabteilung ... Telford Taylor, p. 243 footnote and p. 244.

243   *... it was known as* Himmelfahrtskommando ... Ansel, p. 263. The Third Reich attempted to eliminate English expressions from the language by replacing them with German alternatives. Thus 'bus' became *Offentliches Personenverkehrsfahrzeug*, or Public Persons Traffic Vehicle. (Letter, TIME, 14 December 1998)

243   *... arrive at speed on 16 minecraft* ... Ansel, p. 279.

244   *... the 16th Army laid on a big* ... ibid., p. 229.

244   *In the end the navy had 27* ... von der Porten, p. 89.

244–5 *Richthofen ... believed he had too few* ... Telford Taylor, p. 269.

245   *... no pre-arranged fire* ... Ansel, p. 277 footnote.

245   *General Reinhardt had had* ... Telford Taylor, p. 247.

245   *By 22 August he had 210* ... ibid., p. 261.

246   *... urged the Luftwaffe not to bomb* ... ibid., p. 250 and Ansel, p. 209 footnote.

246   *Each underwater tank weighed* ... Ansel, p. 261.

246   *... no underwater tank ever reached him* ... Ansel, p. 278.

246   *Captain Puttkamer ... reported* ... Toland, p. 628.

246   *... he orders every tug unit to turn* ... Ansel, p. 262.

247   *'Imagine turning one hundred ...'* ibid., p. 263.

247   *... the unpowered barge accepted* ... Telford Taylor, pp. 243–4.

247   *'There were few good ports ...'* Ansel, p. 259 footnote.

247   *'guns and torpedo tubes to defend ...'* Roskill, p. 256.

247–8 *The reality is that Sealion* ... Ansel, pp. 235–7.

248   *... it wasn't until mid-September* ... Telford Taylor, p. 269.

248   *The final decision seems to have been* ... Ansel, p. 274 footnote.

248   *To save the Ju52s from massacre* . . . Mrazek, pp. 34–5. Gliders, being largely of wood, make a poor radar-echo; even so, it is hard to believe that a fleet of 150 gliders would not be detected while it was still over the Channel.

248   *'airborne troops can influence neither* . . .' Telford Taylor, p. 230.

Chapter Forty-Four – Salt Horse

249   List of warships building and list of true fleet in 1939: see Roskill, Appendix E.

249   *There were separate Commands* . . . ibid., Appendix E.

249   *. . . a Home Fleet in July 1940* . . . Basil Collier, Appendix V.

250   *. . . not to risk his few big warships* . . . von den Porten, p. 44. Hitler worried about losing a big ship, especially the battle-cruiser *Deutschland*, whose name had great propaganda value. In 1940 he had her renamed the *Lützow*, which solved that problem. She survived the war and was scuttled in 1945.

250   *. . . and eight destroyers* . . . Grinnell-Milne, p. 51. Ansel and Telford Taylor each give a figure of ten German destroyers. All agree that half the destroyer fleet was sunk in the Norwegian campaign.

250   *. . . the navy planned to keep its U-boats* . . . Ansel, p. 261.

250   *U-39 found the carrier* Ark Royal . . . Porten, p. 39.

250   *. . . it had to fire seven torpedoes* . . . ibid., p. 40.

250   *And so it continued* . . . Roskill, p. 74.

250   *. . . Herbert Schultze, a veteran* . . . Porten, p. 73.

250   *In U-47, Günther Prien* . . . ibid., p. 73.

251   *In 28 U-boat attacks* . . . ibid., p. 74.

251   *Raeder ordered an inquiry* . . . *German Naval History 1939–1945*, Section 47 (Ministry of Defence, HMSO, 1989).

251   *British destroyers were small* . . . Roskill, Appendix D.

251   *(German destroyers performed even worse* . . .) Bekker, *The German Navy*, p. 24.

251   'There never was a class of ship . . .' Haines and Coward, p. 265.

251   *. . . known as the 'Salt Horse'* . . . ibid., p. 270.

252   *'The thrill of handling* . . .' ibid., p. 270.

Chapter Forty-Five – Clean Sweep

253   *The German navy kept six* . . . Grinnell-Milne, map facing p. 206.

253   *. . . a door had been slammed* . . . Roskill, p. 267.

254   *. . . have about four hours of daylight* . . . Ansel, p. 311.

254   *. . . a deception, meant to distract* . . . ibid., p. 263.

255   *... they made up the Nore Command ...* Grinnell-Milne, p. 138 and map facing p. 206.

255   *'Between February and September 1940 ...'* Roskill, p. 329.

255   German minecraft worked ... Bekker, *The German Navy*, p. 54.

255   *'The preparations for a landing ...'* Grinnell-Milne, p. 159.

255–6   *'completely inaccessible' to enemy ...'* ibid., p. 112.

256   *'over a thousand armed patrolling ...'* Churchill, vol. 2, p. 237 PB.

256   *In the ten days of the Evacuation* ... ibid., vol. 2, Table on p. 97, PB.

256   *These steamers were merchant ships* ... Grinnell-Milne, p. 101.

257   *Each had six 6-inch guns* ... Roskill, Appendix D.

257   *'Think too of the lowliest amphibian ...'* Ansel, p. 280.

258   *'To wreck invasion at sea must ...'* Ansel, p. 315.

258   *'There is evidence of the havoc ...'* Alan Clark, pp. 111–112 PB.

259   *Of the two Alpine Battalions* ... Lucus, p. 58.

259   *'Early next morning ...'* W.M. James, pp. 100–102.

259   *Somewhere behind it came* ... Ansel, map, p. 314.

Chapter Forty-Six – Trapped on a Far Shore

262   *... there were nightly patrols* ... Grinnell-Milne, pp. 135–139.

263   *... weather conditions were 'completely abnormal ...'* ibid., p. 141.

263   *Next night, British destroyers* ... Longmate, *Island Fortress*, pp. 516–7.

263   *The battleship* Revenge, *with an escort* ... Basil Collier, p. 226.

Chapter Forty-Seven – The Chameleon of Truth

265   *'the stamina and valour of our fighter pilots ...'* Churchill, vol. 2, p. 279 PB.

265   *'Our little Navy,' Hitler sighed* ... Ansel, p. 187.

265   *'accomplishments are beyond all praise ...'* Telford Taylor, p. 273.

266   *Hitler blamed the only non-military element* ... Ansel; p. 299. Also Telford Taylor, p. 273: 'Largely due to the hindrance of bad weather, according to Hitler, the British fighter forces had not yet been eliminated, and therefore "the prerequisites for Sealion have not yet been completely realized."' Also Denis Richards, *The Fight At Odds*, p. 188, quoting from the German War Diary: 'RAF undefeated and weather situation unsatisfactory: Fuhrer therefore decides to postpone Sealion ...'

266   *'The surface forces are so inferior ...'* Telford Taylor, p. 22.

267   *'At the time the heroism of young ...'* Peter Clarke, p. 197.

268   *'On this I said that I was not ...'* Churchill, vol. 2, p. 137 PB.

Bibliography

Addison, Paul and Craig, Jeremy, editors, *The Burning Blue*, Pimlico, 2000

Admiralty Sailing Directions: *Dover Strait Pilot*, Sixth Edition, United Kingdom Hydrographic Office, Taunton

Alanbrooke, Field Marshal Lord, *War Diaries 1939–1945*, Weidenfeld & Nicolson, 2001

Allen, H.R., *Who Won The Battle of Britain*, Arthur Barker Ltd., 1974 and Panther, 1976

Ansel, Walter, *Hitler Confronts England*, Duke University Press, 1960

Barclay, George, *Fighter Pilot*, William Kimber, 1976

Barclay, Glen St J., *Their Finest Hour*, Weidenfeld & Nicolson, 1977

Barker, A. J., *Dunkirk: The Great Escape*, J.M. Dent & Sons, 1977

Bekker, Cajus, *The Luftwaffe War Diaries*, Macdonald, 1967 and Corgi, 1969

——, *The German Navy 1939–1945*, Chancellor Press, 1997

Bennett, G.H. and Bennett, R., *Hitler's Admirals*, Naval Institute Press, 2004

Bickers, Richard Townshend, *Ginger Lacey – Fighter Pilot*, Robert Hale, 1962 and Corgi, 1978

Bishop, Edward, *The Battle of Britain*, Allen & Unwin, 1960

Bowyer, Chaz, *Fighter Command*, J.M. Dent & Sons, 1980

Bullock, Alan, *Hitler: A Study in Tyranny*, Odhams, 1952 and Penguin, 1962

Butler, Ewan & Young, Gordon, *Marshal Without Glory*, Hodder & Stoughton, 1951, and Tandem, 1973

Caesar, Julius, *The Conquest of Gaul*, Translated by S.A. Handford, Penguin Classics, 1951

Caidin, Martin, *Me109*, Purnell's History of the Second World War, 1968

Chalmers, Rear-Admiral W.S., *Max Horton and the Western Approaches*, Hodder & Stoughton, 1954

Churchill, Winston S., *The Second World War*, Cassell, 1949

Clark, Alan, *The Fall of Crete*, Anthony Blond, 1962 and NEL Mentor, 1969

Clarke, Peter, *Hope and Glory*, Penguin History of Britain, 2003

Collier, Basil, *The Battle of the V-Weapons, 1944–45*, Hodder & Stoughton, 1964 and Elmfield Press, 1976

——, *The Defence of the United Kingdom*, H.M.S.O., 1957

Collier, Richard, *Eagle Day*, J.M. Dent, 1980
Cooper, Matthew, *The German Air Force 1939–1945*, Jane's, 1981
Cowles, Virginia, *Looking For Trouble*, Hamish Hamilton, 1941
Dean, Sir Maurice, *The Royal Air Force and Two World Wars*, Cassell, 1979
Deere, Alan C, *Nine Lives*, Hodder & Stoughton, 1959
Deighton, Len, *Blitzkrieg*, Jonathan Cape, 1979
——, *Fighter*, Jonathan Cape, 1977
Encyclopaedia of World War II, Edited by Thomas Parrish. Secker & Warburg, 1978
Fest, Joachim C., *Speer – The Final Verdict*, Weidenfeld & Nicolson, 2001
——, *The Face of the Third Reich*, Weidenfeld & Nicolson, 1970
Fleming, Peter, *Operation Sea Lion*, Simon & Schuster, 1957
Flood, C.E., *Hitler: The Path to Power*, Houghton Mifflin, 1989
Forrester, Larry, *Fly For Your Life*, The Companion Book Club, 1958
Galland, Adolf, *The First and the Last*, Ballantine Books, 1954
Gelb, Norman, *Scramble: A Narrative History of the Battle of Britain*, Michael Joseph, 1986 and Pan, 1986
Gibson, Guy, *Enemy Coast Ahead*, Michael Joseph, 1946 and Pan, 1955
Gilbert, Adrian, *Britain Invaded*, Century, 1990
Gilbert, Martin, *A History of the Twentieth Century*, HarperCollins, 1998
——, *Churchill: A Life*, Heinemann, 1991 and Minerva, 1992
Gleed, Ian, *Arise to Conquer*, Severn House, 1975
Goldsmith-Carter, George, *The Battle of Britain*, Mason & Lipscomb, 1974
Grinnell-Milne, Duncan, *The Silent Victory*, The Bodley Head, 1958 and White Lion Publishers, 1976
Haines, Gregory & Coward, Cdr. B.R. R.N., *Battleship, Cruiser, Destroyer*, Ian Allan, 1982–87 and The Promotional Reprint Co. Ltd., 1994
Hamilton, Nigel, *JFK: Reckless Youth*, Century, 1992 and Arrow, 1992
Harman, Nicholas, *Dunkirk: The Necessary Myth*, Hodder & Stoughton, 1980
Hitler, Adolf, *Mein Kampf*
Hohne, Heinz, *Canaris*, Secker & Warburg, 1979
Hooker, Sir Stanley, *Not Much of an Engineer*, Airlife, 1984
Humble, Richard, *Hitler's Generals*, Granada, 1976
Irving, David, *The Rise and Fall of the Luftwaffe*, Weidenfeld & Nicolson, 1974 and Futura, 1976
James, T.C.G., *The Battle of Britain*, Frank Cass, 2000
James, Admiral W.M., *The British Navies in the Second World War*, Longmans, Green, 1946
Jane's Fighting Aircraft of World War II, Jane's, 1946/7 and Bracken Books, 1989
Johnson, Brian, *The Secret War*, BBC, 1978
Johnson, J.E. 'Johnnie', *Full Circle*, Chatto & Windus, 1964 and Pan, 1968
Keegan, John , *The Face of Battle*, Jonathan Cape, 1976, and Penguin, 1978

——, *The Second World War*, Random House, 1989

Knoke, Heinz, *I Flew For The Fuhrer*, Evans Brothers Ltd., 1953

Longmate, Norman, *Island Fortress*, Grafton, 1993

——, *The Bombers*, Hutchinson, 1983 and Arrow, 1988

Lucas, James, *Storming Eagles: German Airborne Forces of World War Two*, Guild Publishing, 1988

Luftwaffe, ed. Harold Faber, Sidgwick & Jackson, 1979 and Arms & Armour Press, 1988

Macleod, Iain, *Neville Chamberlain*, Frederick Muller, 1961

Macksey, Kenneth, *Invasion: The German Invasion of England, July 1940*, Arms & Armour Press, 1980

——, *Kesselring*, Batsford, 1978

Mason, Francis K., *Battle Over Britain*, McWhirter Twins, 1969

——, *The Hawker Hurricane*, Aston Publications, 1987

Masterman, J.C., *The Double-Cross System 1939–1945*, Yale University Press, 1972 and Sphere, 1973

Masters, David, *'So Few'*, Eyre & Spottiswoode, 1943

Matthew, D.J.A., *The Norman Conquest*, Batsford, 1966

Middlebrook, Martin and Everitt, Chris, *The Bomber Command War Diaries*, Viking, 1985

Mrazek, James E., *The Glider War*, Robert Hale & Co., 1975

Neil, Tom., *Gun Button to 'Fire'*, William Kimber, 1987

Olson, Jack, *Aphrodite: Desperate Mission*, Putnam, 1970

Overy, Richard, *The Battle*, Penguin, 2000

Parkinson, Roger, *Dawn On Our Darkness*, Granada/Hart-Davis, MacGibbon, 1977

Porten, Edward P. von der, *The German Navy in World War II*, Thomas Y. Crowell Co, 1969

Price, Alfred, *Pictorial History of the Luftwaffe*, Ian Allan, 1969

——, *Blitz On Britain*, Ian Allan, 1977

——, *'Battle of Britain Day'*, published in Journal 29 by the Royal Air Force Historical Society, 2003

——, *Instruments of Darkness*, Macdonald & Jane's, 1977 and Panther, 1979

——, *The Hardest Day*, Macdonald & Jane's, 1979 and Granada, 1980

Reynolds, Quentin, *They Fought For The Sky*, Holt, Rinehart & Winston, 1957 and Bantam, 1972

Richards, Denis, *Royal Air Force, 1939–1945. Vol. 1: The Fight At Odds*, HMSO, 1974

Richards, Denis and Saunders, Hilary StG., *Vol. 2: The Fight Avails*, HMSO, 1975

Rolls, Bill, *Spitfire Attack*, William Kimber, 1987

Rolls-Royce Heritage Trust: *'The Merlin In Perspective'*, 1987

Roskill, Captain S.W., *The War At Sea. Vol. 1,: The Defensive*, History of the Second World War: United Kingdom Military Series. HMSO, 1954

Schellenberg, Walter, *The Nazi Invasion Plan for Britain – Invasion 1940*, St Ermin's Press, 2000

Scott, Desmond, *Typhoon Pilot*, Leo Cooper, 1982

Shirer, William, *Berlin Diary*, Hamish Hamilton. Probably 1941

——, *Nightmare Years*, Little, Brown, 1984 and Bantam, 1985

Speer, Albert, *Inside The Third Reich*, Macmillan (NY), 1970 and Avon Books, 1971

Spurdle, Bob, *The Blue Arena*, William Kimber, 1986

Steinhilper, Ulrich, *Spitfire On My Tail*, Independent Books, Bromley, Kent, 1989

Taylor, A.J.P., *The Second World War*, Hamish Hamilton, 1975

——, *The Origins of the Second World War*, Hamish Hamilton, 1961

——, *English History 1914–1945*, Oxford University Press, 1965 and Penguin, 1970

Taylor, Telford, *The Breaking Wave*, Weidenfeld & Nicolson, 1967

Terraine, John, *The Right of the Line*, Hodder & Stoughton, 1985

——, *The Smoke and the Fire*, Sidgwick & Jackson, 1980

Thomas, Edward, 'The Intelligence Aspect', published in *The Battle Re-Thought*, by Airlife for the Royal Air Force Historical Society, 1990

Thompson, Laurence, *1940*, William Morrow, NY, 1966

TIME/LIFE Book, *World War II: Prelude To War*, 1977

——, *Battle of Britain*, 1977

Toland, John, *Adolf Hitler*, Doubleday & Co, 1976

Vader, John, *Spitfire*, Pan/Ballantine, 1972

Vassiltchikov, Marie, *The Berlin Diaries 1940–1945*, Chatto & Windus, 1985 and Mandarin, 1991

Webster, C. and Frankland, N., *The Strategic Air Offensive Against Germany, 1939–45*, HMSO, 1961

Weinberg, Gerhard L., *A World At Arms*, Cambridge University Press, 1994 and TSC, 1994

Wellum, Geoffrey, *First Light*, Viking, 2002 and Penguin, 2003

Westphal, Siegfried, *The German Army in the West*, Cassell, 1951

Wood, Derek, *Target England*, Jane's, 1980

Wood, Derek and Dempster, Derek, *The Narrow Margin*, Hutchinson, 1961 and Arrow, 1967

Wood, Tony and Gunston, Bill, *Hitler's Luftwaffe*, Salamander Books, 1977

Wright, Robert, *Dowding and the Battle of Britain*, MacDonald, 1969

Zimmerman, David, *Top Secret Exchange*, Alan Sutton Publishing, 1996

Acknowledgements

In 1940 I was eight, and living in Bristol, which got blitzed pretty fiercely. I remember watching a German bomber coned by searchlights, hearing the pounding of anti-aircraft guns, seeing the skyline red with the burning city, going next day to look at a house just like ours that had been demolished by a bomb.

But the greater meaning of 1940 passed me by. Clearly, I could not have written this book without access to the work of men and women who were much closer to the action and who saw the bigger picture and the telling detail. History depends on them. Tolstoy, born 16 years after Napoleon's retreat from Moscow, could never have written *War and Peace* without drawing on the experience of others. I do not put myself in Tolstoy's league, but our tasks were similar. As an English judge remarked in 1980: knowledge is built on knowledge.

I am especially indebted to certain authors. Duncan Grinnell-Milne's *The Silent Victory, 1940* first sparked my interest, and Peter Fleming's *Operation Sea Lion* brightened the spark. Winston Churchill's *The Second World War* was, of course, an invaluable guide to events on both sides of the Channel, and of the Atlantic. For air operations on 15 September 1940 I drew heavily on Dr Alfred Price's excellent research, which has opened up a completely fresh perspective on that supposed 'turning point'. I made similar use of Mr Edward Thomas's brisk analysis of the place of Ultra intelligence in the Battle. I am grateful for their permission to use material that appeared first in the Journals of the Royal Air Force Historical Society. These Journals form a uniquely valuable research tool. Of the many histories I consulted, John Terraine's account of the RAF in World War Two, *The Right of the Line*, is outstanding for its intelligence, insight and (not least) sheer readability. For the same reasons, I read and reread A.J.P. Taylor's *English History 1914–1945* and *The Second World War*.

Two books by American authors were of enormous value. Walter Ansel's *Hitler Confronts England* is a detailed journey through the invasion plan. It carries especial conviction because Ansel was an admiral with personal experience of the preparation of the Normandy invasion; later he interviewed many German officers involved in Sealion. The permission of Duke University Press to quote from his book is gratefully acknowledged; as is the permission of Weidenfeld and Nicolson to use material from Telford Taylor's *The Breaking Wave*, which also traces the life and death of Sealion. Taylor studied the German military machine when he served in Army Intelligence during the war; afterwards, he was chief counsel for the prosecution at the Nuremberg trials of the Nazi war criminals. As chroniclers of Sealion, Ansel and Taylor make a formidable team. As the leading authority on sea conditions around Britain, the Admiralty Pilot publications are, of course, unsurpassed; and my thanks go to the United Kingdom Hydrographic Office for permission to quote from their *Dover Sea Pilot*.

On the German side, Joachim Fest's *The Face of the Third Reich* sets the scene, and his *Speer – The Final Verdict* is a useful corrective to Speer's *Inside The Third Reich*. John Toland's *Adolf Hitler* provides a huge amount of very relevant information. So does Frederic Spotts's *Hitler and the Power of Aesthetics*, which reached me after I had completed this book; it digs deep into Hitler's convictions about not only architecture but also painting, sculpture and opera.

For coverage of the air war, Matthew Cooper's *The German Air Force 1939–1945* is comprehensive and fair-minded. Ulrich Steinhilper's memoirs *Spitfire On My Tail* offer a rare view of life (and death) on a Luftwaffe fighter base in 1940; I am grateful to his publisher, Peter Osborne of Independent Books, who made it possible for me to quote extensively from this work.

As for the performance of aircraft: Martin Caidin's *Me109*, John Vader's *Spitfire*, and Francis K. Mason's *The Hawker Hurricane* complement each other very well, while Johnnie Johnson's *Full Circle* tells the chequered story of combat tactics. Authors have found little to say about German warships' planned involvement in Sealion; however, Edward P. von der Porten's *The German Navy in World War II* is particularly valuable for his cover of the Norwegian campaign and the unhappy experience of German destroyers and submarines.

The rest of the bibliography, I hope, speaks for itself. My thanks go to all those authors.

Page numbers

Hardback and paperback editions of the same book often have very different page numbers for items in the text. In my Notes, you can assume that a page number refers to the hardback edition unless it is followed by the letters PB, in which case the reference is to a paperback edition. This edition can be identified from the Bibliography.

Index